Charles Soule
Writer-In-Chief

Alberto J. Alburquerque
Executive Artist

Dan Jackson
Executive Colorist

Crank!
Chief of Letters

THE WHITE HOUSE

1600 PENNSYLVANIA AVE NW, WASHINGTON, DC 20500

FROM THE DESK OF THE 44TH PRESIDENT, STEPHEN HENRY BLADES

TO THE MEN AND WOMEN OF THE CLARKE:

It is possible that this message will never reach you. As of the moment I compose this letter, we have been unable to contact any of you, or raise any signals from your vessel, for a length of time that my advisors tell me is... extremely unpromising. No. That is not the word they used.

They said it is hopeless.

But I do not believe in hopelessness. I don't think you can, if you choose to run for President. The odds are astronomically stacked against anyone ever succeeding at that particular goal... but someone pulls it off, once every four years. I did it, for instance.

And so I do not believe in giving up hope—ever.

Brave explorers—I do not know your location in the cosmos. I do not know what dangers and miracles you might be experiencing. And yes, I do not know whether you are alive or dead. But I will send you this message regardless, because I have not forgotten you, despite the trials that convulse this planet. Nor have the rest of your people—your sacrifice is no longer secret. I told the planet about our visitors in the asteroid belt, and your mission to greet them on behalf of humanity.

The reaction has been... complex. As I'm sure you all recall from when you first learned the truth, it is a heavy burden to bear. But know this: every one of you is hailed as a hero to your species. You are all beloved, and honored in every way we know how. Scant comfort, perhaps, as you float in the darkness so far from home—but as I have said to you before, and now more than ever—you are not alone.

Be safe, and discover wonders.

Stephen Henry Blades
44th President of the United States of America

LETTER 44 VOLUME III:
DARK MATTER

WRITTEN BY
CHARLES SOULE

ILLUSTRATED BY
ALBERTO JIMÉNEZ ALBURQUERQUE

COLORED BY
DAN JACKSON

LETTERED BY
CRANK!

DESIGNED BY
HILARY THOMPSON

EDITED BY
ROBIN HERRERA

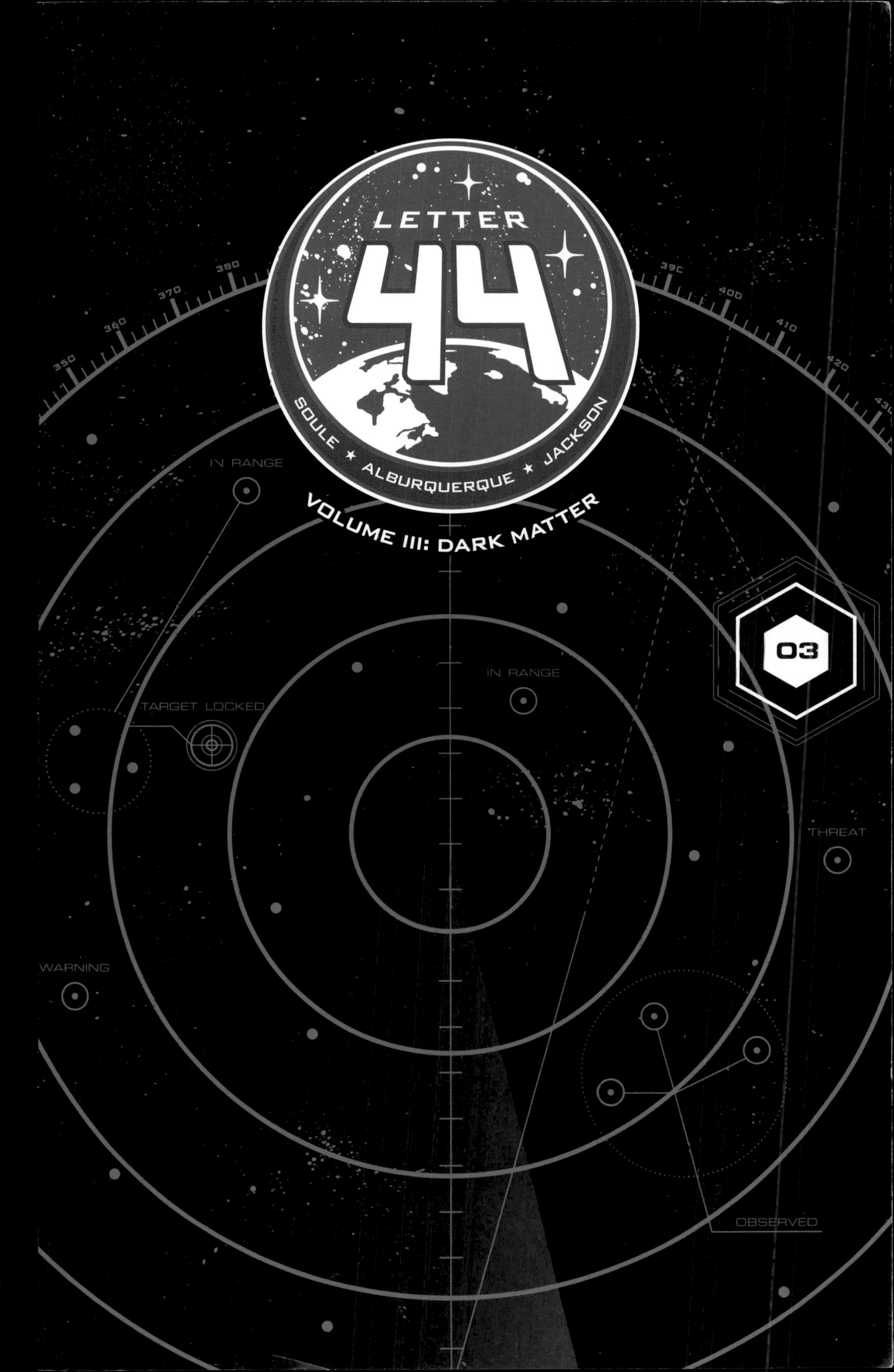

LETTER
44
SOULE ★ ALBURQUERQUE ★ JACKSON
VOLUME III: DARK MATTER
03
IN RANGE
TARGET LOCKED
IN RANGE
THREAT
WARNING
OBSERVED

LETTER 44

THIS VOLUME COLLECTS ISSUES 15-20 OF THE ONI PRESS SERIES *LETTER 44*

Oni Press, Inc.

Publisher /// **Joe Nozemack**
Editor In Chief /// **James Lucas Jones**
Director of Sales /// **Cheyenne Allott**
Director of Publicity /// **Fred Reckling**
Production Manager /// **Troy Look**
Senior Editor /// **Charlie Chu**
Editor /// **Robin Herrera**
Associate Editor /// **Ari Yarwood**
Graphic Designer /// **Hilary Thompson**
Production Assistant /// **Jared Jones**
Inventory Coordinator /// **Brad Rooks**
Office Assistant /// **Jung Lee**

1305 SE Martin Luther King Jr. Blvd.
Suite A
Portland, OR 97214

onipress.com
facebook.com/onipress | twitter.com/onipress | onipress.tumblr.com

charlessoule.com | @charlessoule
ajaalbertojimenezalburquerque.blogspot.com

FIRST EDITION: JANUARY 2016

Letter 44 Volume 3. January 2016. Published by Oni Press, Inc. 1305 SE
Martin Luther King Jr. Blvd., Suite A, Portland, OR 97214. Letter 44 is ™ & ©
2016 Charles Soule. All rights reserved. Oni Press logo and icon ™ & © 2016
Oni Press, Inc. Oni Press logo and icon artwork created by Keith A. Wood.
The events, institutions, and characters presented in this book are fictional.
Any resemblance to actual persons, living or dead, is purely coincidental.
No portion of this publication may be reproduced, by any means, without the
express written permission of the copyright holders.

ISBN: 978-1-62010-272-5 | eISBN: 978-1-62010-277-0

Library of Congress Control Number: 2015947512

10 8 6 4 2 1 3 5 7 9

Printed in China

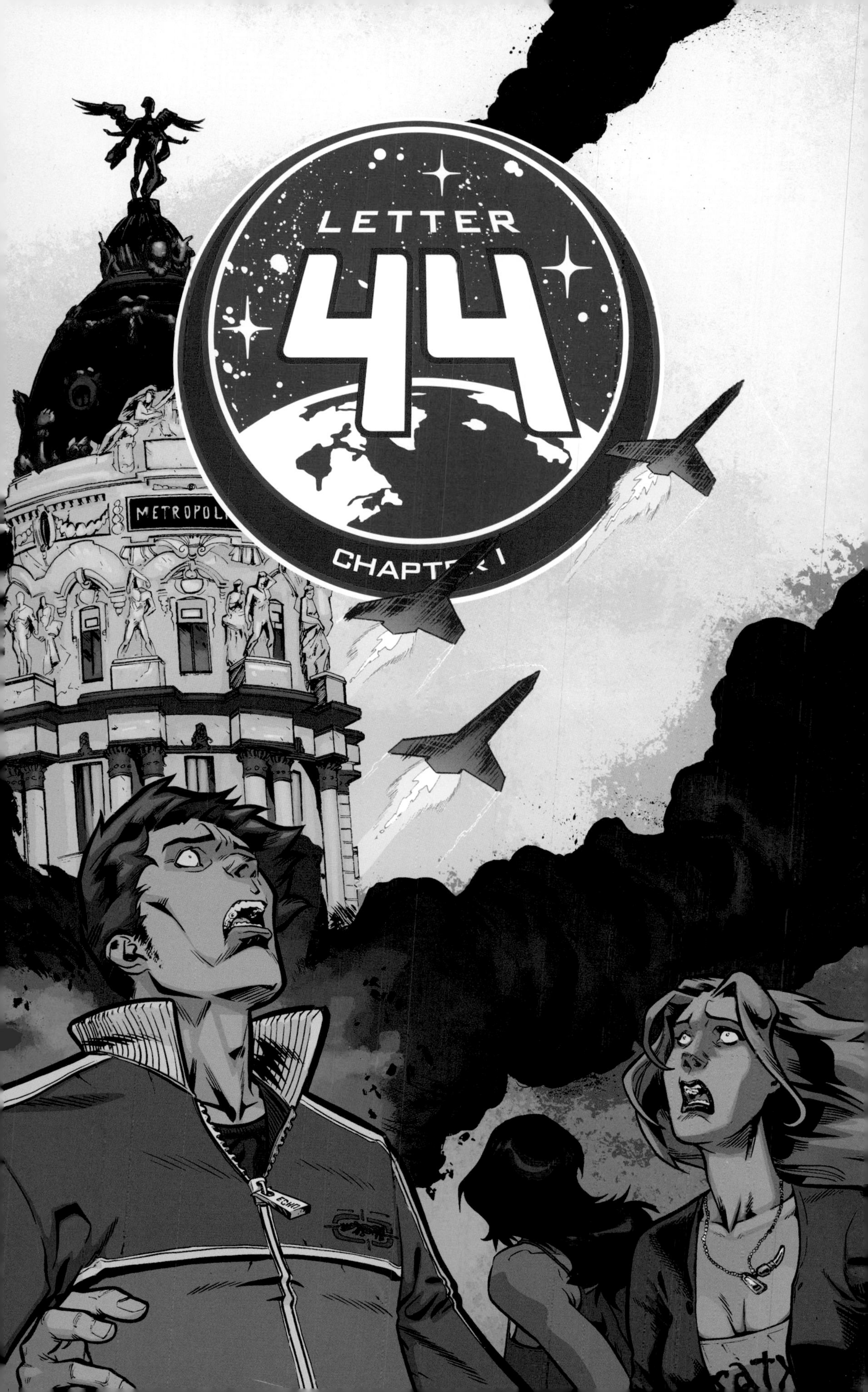
LETTER
44
METROPOL

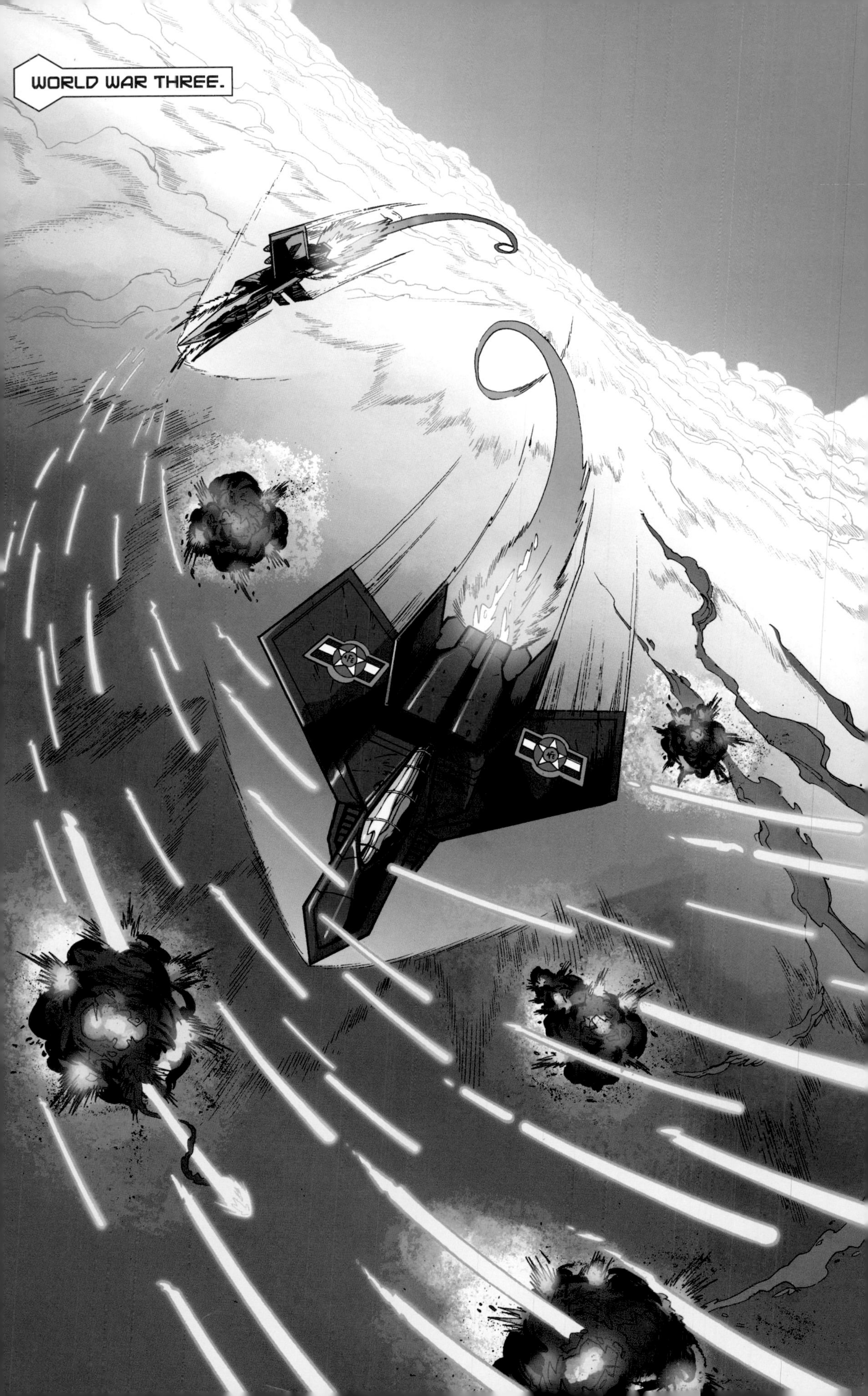
WORLD WAR THREE.

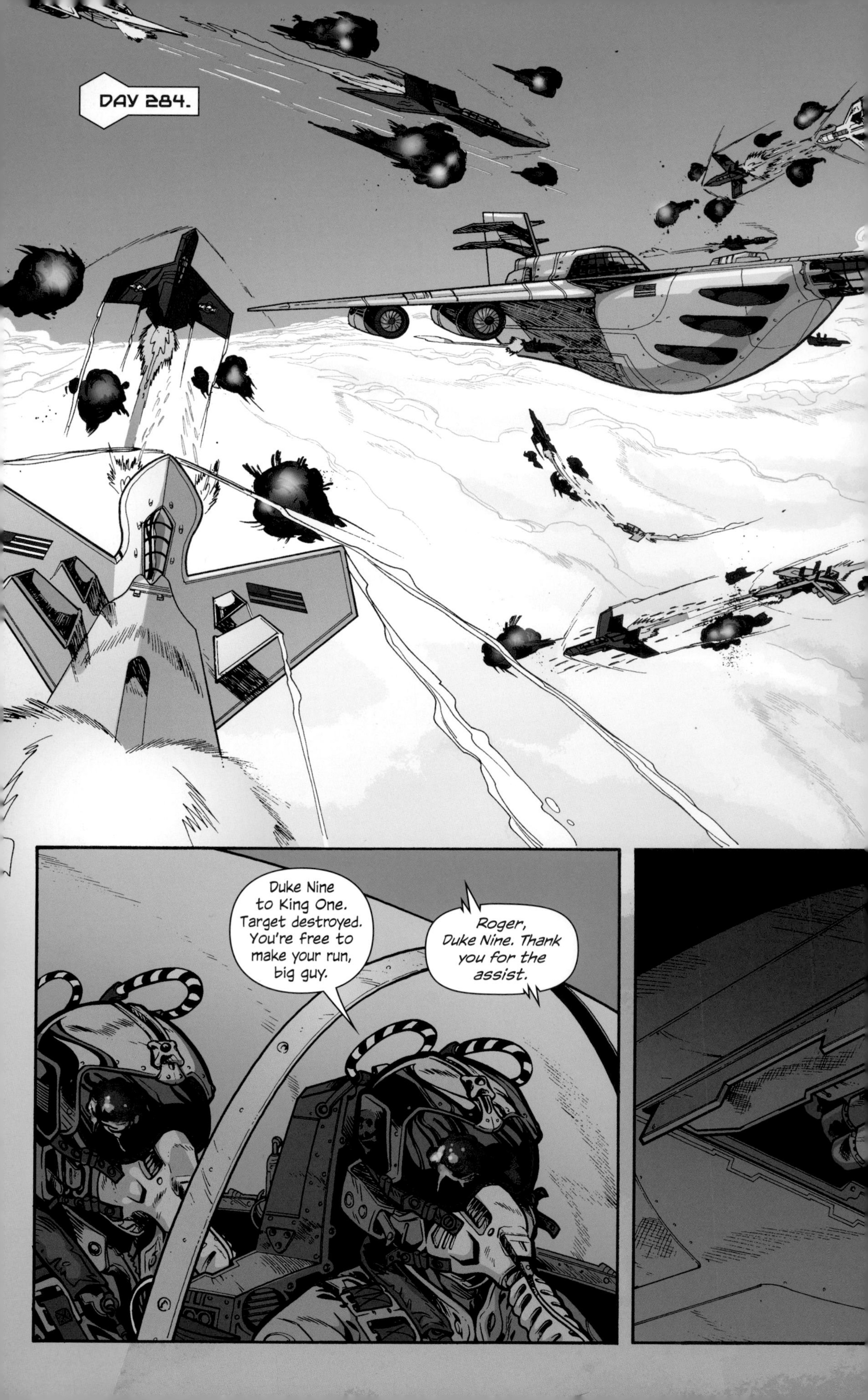
DAY 284.
Duke Nine to King One. Target destroyed. You're free to make your run, big guy.
Roger, Duke Nine. Thank you for the assist.

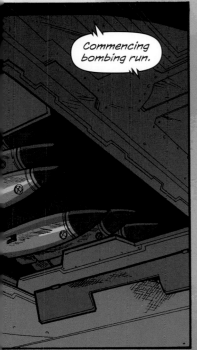

Commencing bombing run.

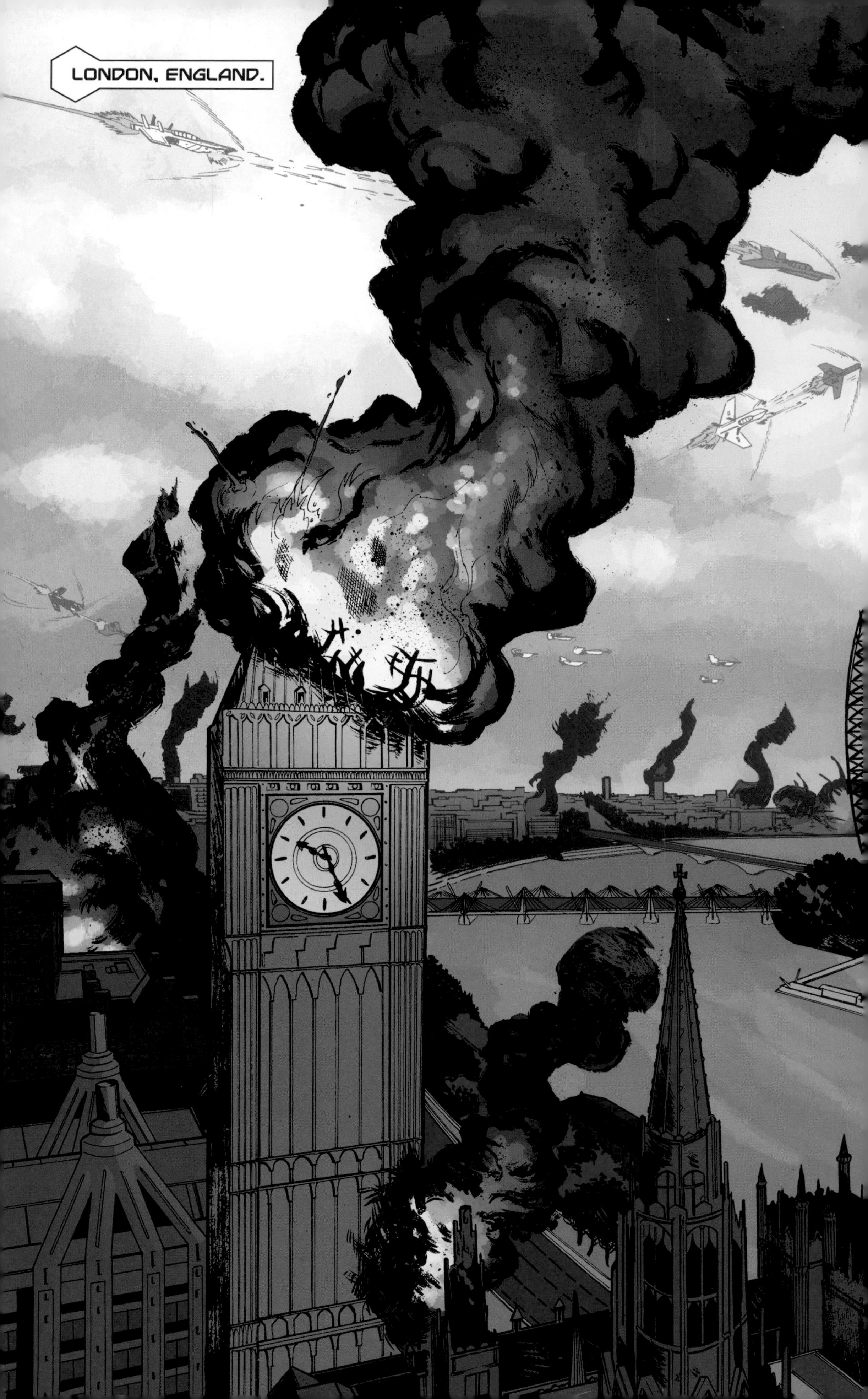
LONDON, ENGLAND.

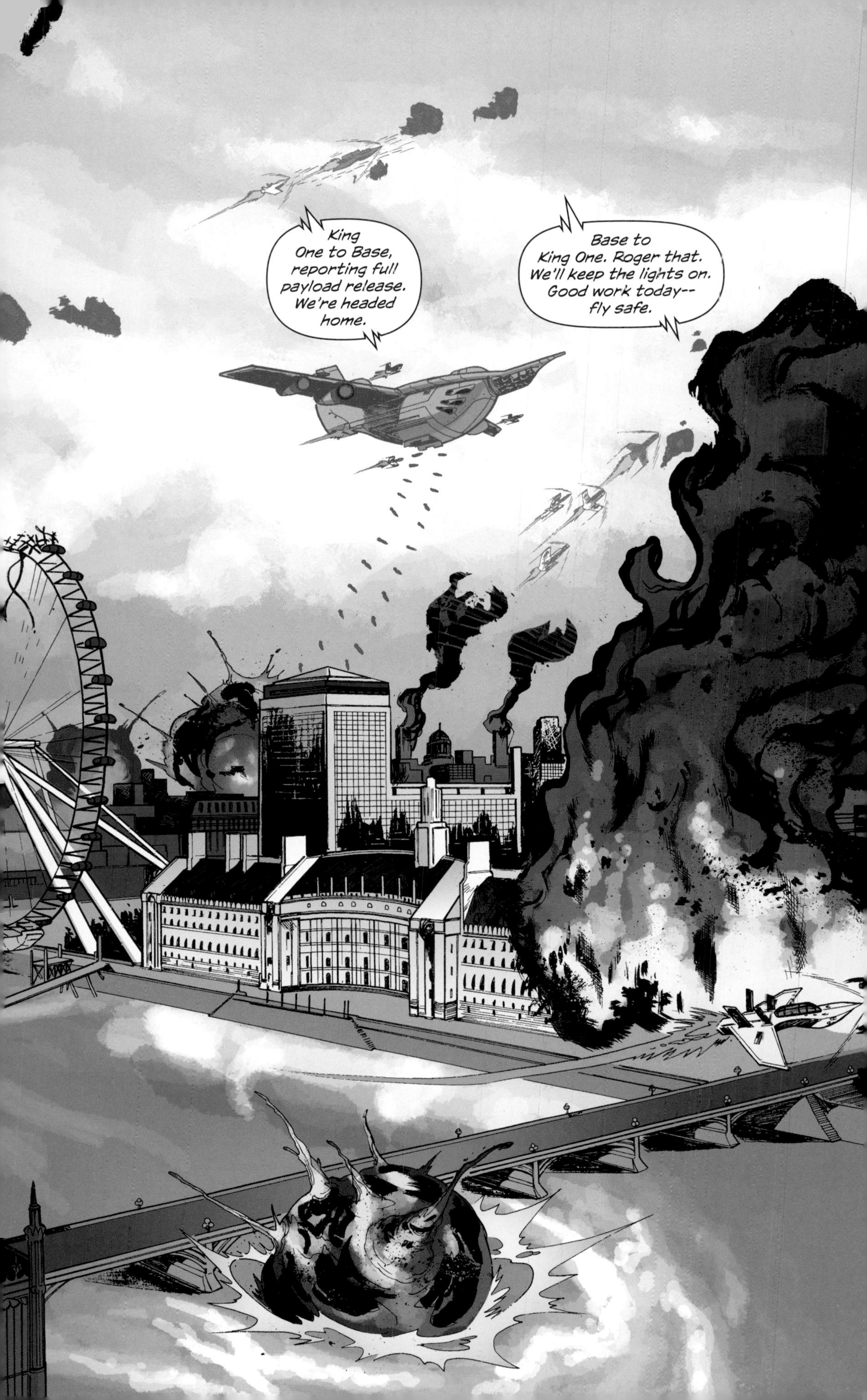
King One to Base, reporting full payload release. We're headed home.
Base to King One. Roger that. We'll keep the lights on. Good work today--fly safe.

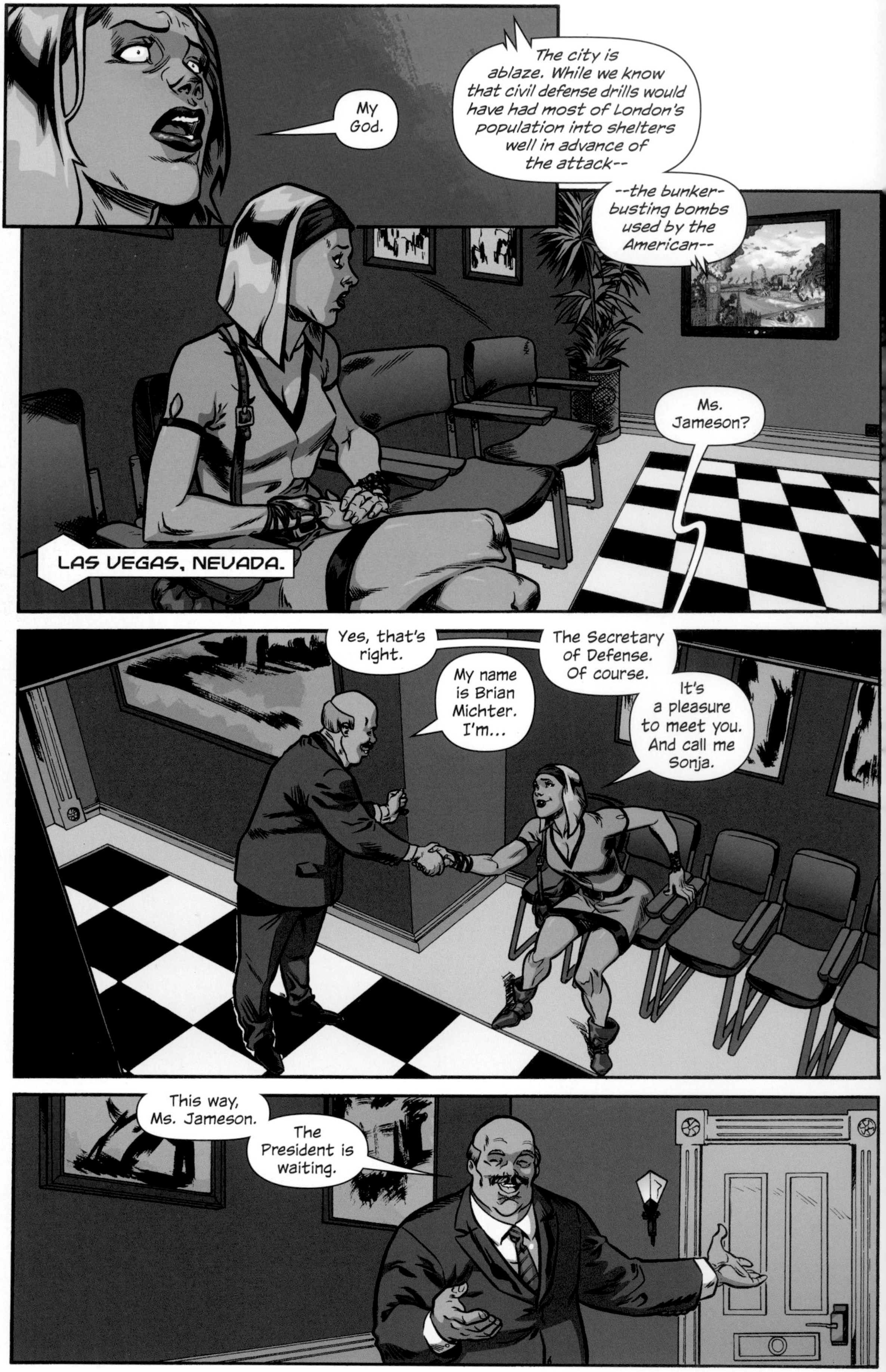
My God.
The city is ablaze. While we know that civil defense drills would have had most of London's population into shelters well in advance of the attack--
--the bunker-busting bombs used by the American--
LAS VEGAS, NEVADA.
Ms. Jameson?
Yes, that's right.
The Secretary of Defense. Of course.
My name is Brian Michter. I'm...
It's a pleasure to meet you. And call me Sonja.
This way, Ms. Jameson.
The President is waiting.

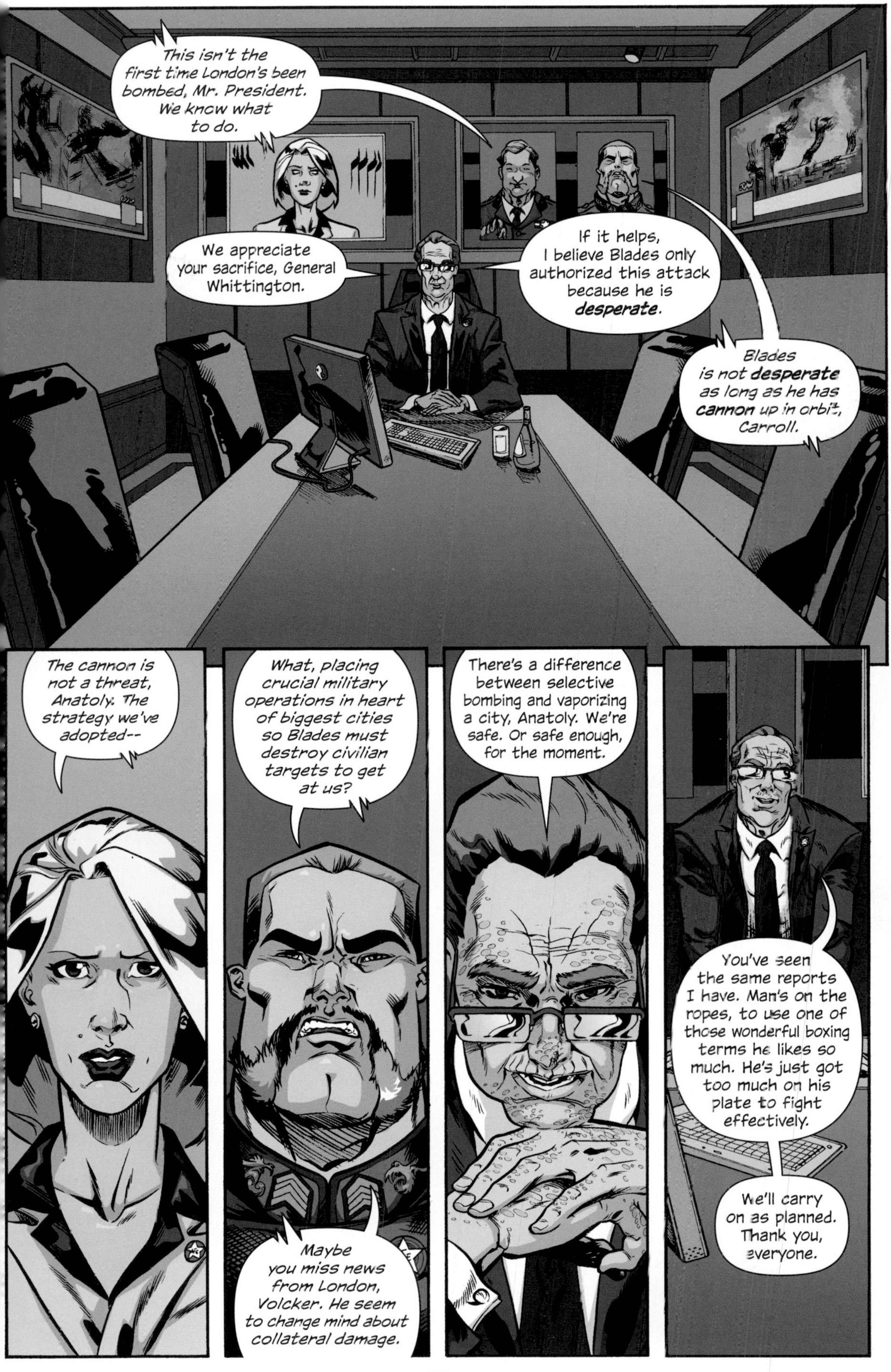
This isn't the first time London's been bombed, Mr. President. We know what to do.
We appreciate your sacrifice, General Whittington.
If it helps, I believe Blades only authorized this attack because he is **desperate**.
Blades is not **desperate** as long as he has **cannon** up in orbit, Carroll.
The cannon is not a threat, Anatoly. The strategy we've adopted--
What, placing crucial military operations in heart of biggest cities so Blades must destroy civilian targets to get at us?
Maybe you miss news from London, Volcker. He seem to change mind about collateral damage.
There's a difference between selective bombing and vaporizing a city, Anatoly. We're safe. Or safe enough, for the moment.
You've seen the same reports I have. Man's on the ropes, to use one of those wonderful boxing terms he likes so much. He's just got too much on his plate to fight effectively.
We'll carry on as planned. Thank you, everyone.

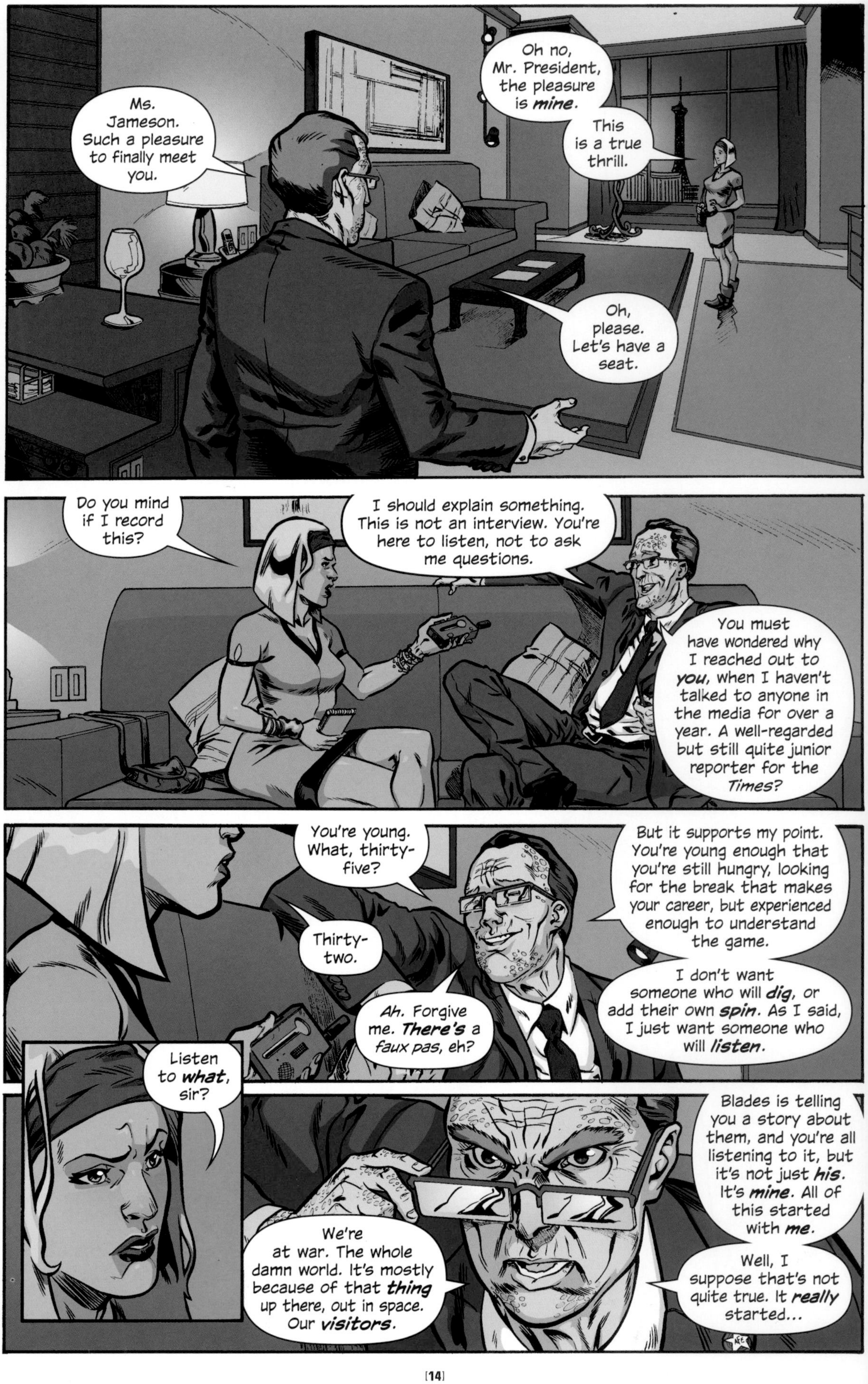
Ms. Jameson. Such a pleasure to finally meet you.
Oh no, Mr. President, the pleasure is ***mine***.
This is a true thrill.
Oh, please. Let's have a seat.
Do you mind if I record this?
I should explain something. This is not an interview. You're here to listen, not to ask me questions.
You must have wondered why I reached out to ***you***, when I haven't talked to anyone in the media for over a year. A well-regarded but still quite junior reporter for the *Times*?
You're young. What, thirty-five?
Thirty-two.
Ah. Forgive me. ***There's*** a *faux pas*, eh?
But it supports my point. You're young enough that you're still hungry, looking for the break that makes your career, but experienced enough to understand the game.
I don't want someone who will ***dig***, or add their own ***spin***. As I said, I just want someone who will ***listen***.
Listen to ***what***, sir?
We're at war. The whole damn world. It's mostly because of that ***thing*** up there, out in space. Our ***visitors***.
Blades is telling you a story about them, and you're all listening to it, but it's not just ***his***. It's ***mine***. All of this started with ***me***.
Well, I suppose that's not quite true. It ***really*** started...

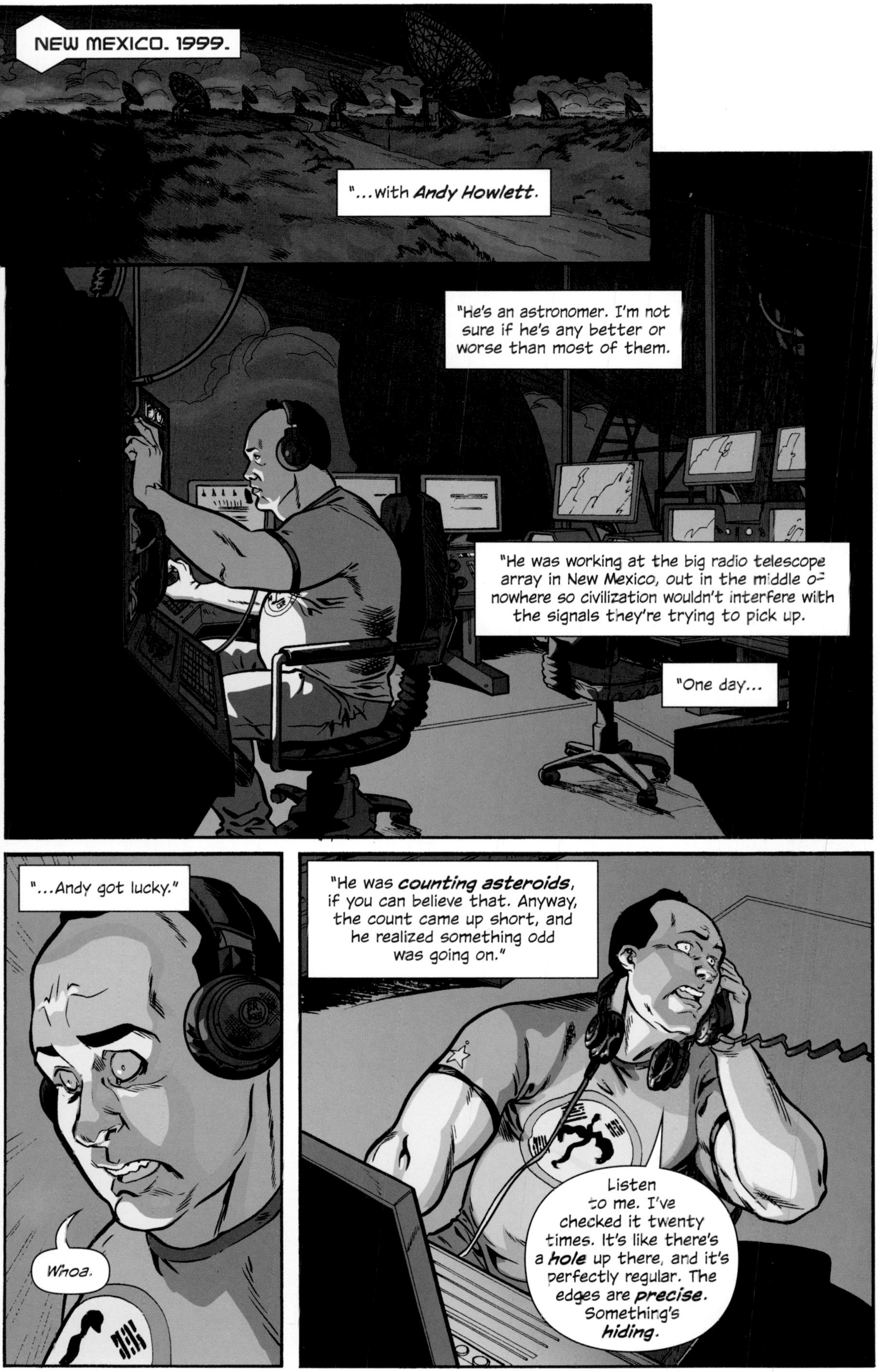
NEW MEXICO. 1999.
"...with Andy Howlett.
"He's an astronomer. I'm not sure if he's any better or worse than most of them.
"He was working at the big radio telescope array in New Mexico, out in the middle of nowhere so civilization wouldn't interfere with the signals they're trying to pick up.
"One day...
"...Andy got lucky."
Whoa.
"He was counting asteroids, if you can believe that. Anyway, the count came up short, and he realized something odd was going on."
Listen to me. I've checked it twenty times. It's like there's a hole up there, and it's perfectly regular. The edges are precise. Something's hiding.

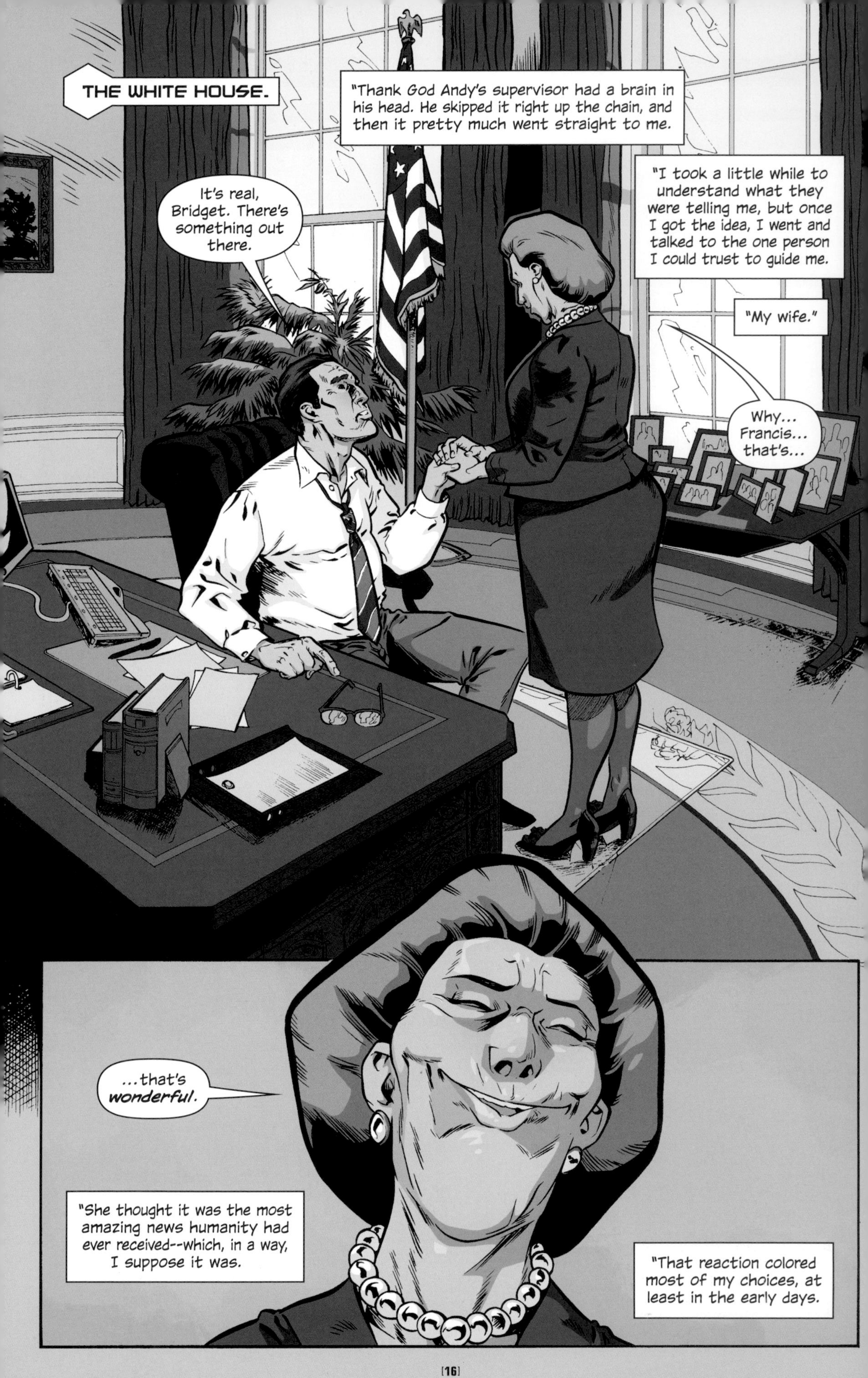
THE WHITE HOUSE.
"Thank God Andy's supervisor had a brain in his head. He skipped it right up the chain, and then it pretty much went straight to me.
It's real, Bridget. There's something out there.
"I took a little while to understand what they were telling me, but once I got the idea, I went and talked to the one person I could trust to guide me.
"My wife."
Why... Francis... that's...
...that's *wonderful*.
"She thought it was the most amazing news humanity had ever received--which, in a way, I suppose it was.
"That reaction colored most of my choices, at least in the early days.

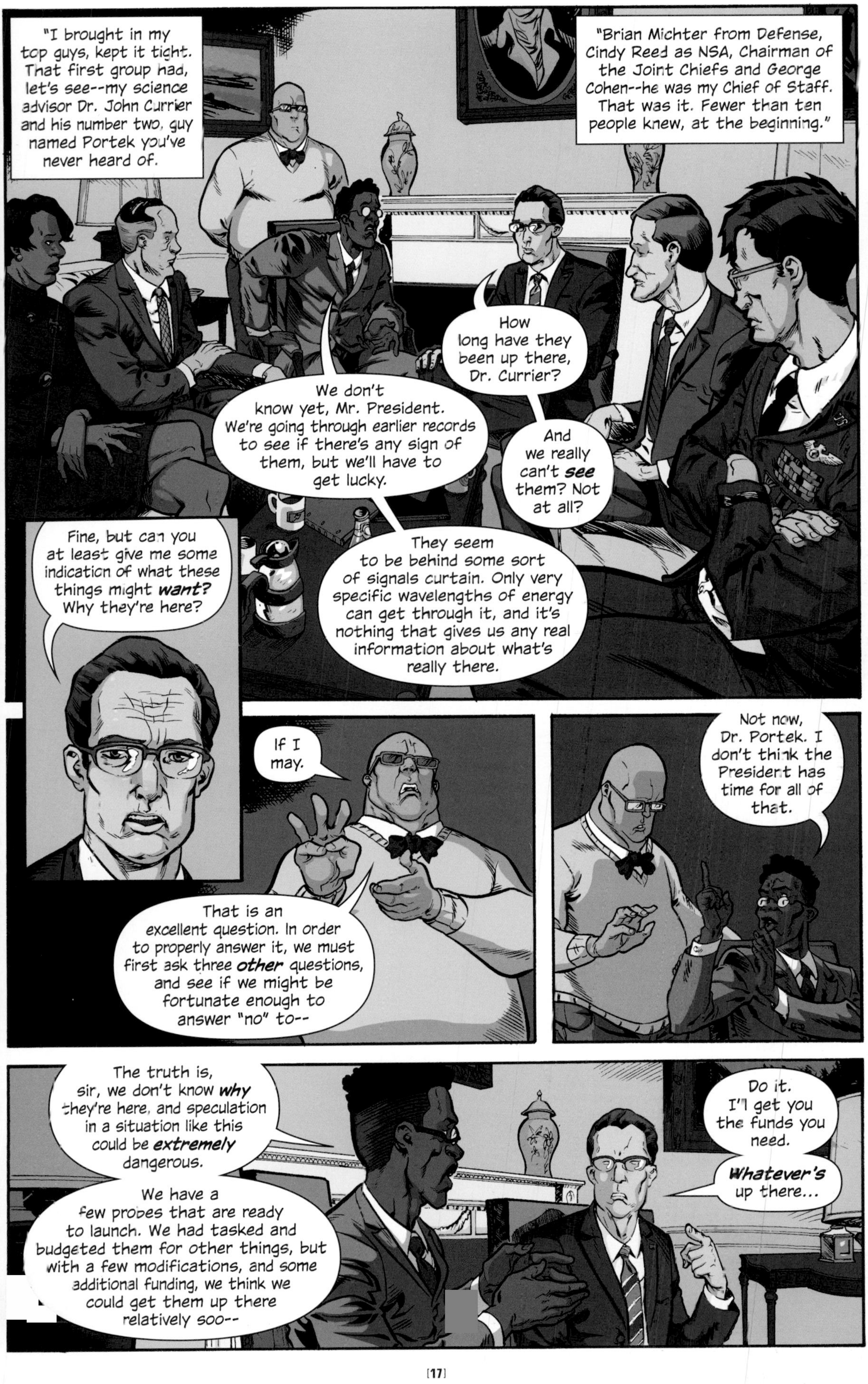

"I brought in my top guys, kept it tight. That first group had, let's see--my science advisor Dr. John Currier and his number two, guy named Portek you've never heard of.
"Brian Michter from Defense, Cindy Reed as NSA, Chairman of the Joint Chiefs and George Cohen--he was my Chief of Staff. That was it. Fewer than ten people knew, at the beginning."
How long have they been up there, Dr. Currier?
We don't know yet, Mr. President. We're going through earlier records to see if there's any sign of them, but we'll have to get lucky.
And we really can't ***see*** them? Not at all?
They seem to be behind some sort of signals curtain. Only very specific wavelengths of energy can get through it, and it's nothing that gives us any real information about what's really there.
Fine, but can you at least give me some indication of what these things might ***want?*** Why they're here?
If I may.
That is an excellent question. In order to properly answer it, we must first ask three ***other*** questions, and see if we might be fortunate enough to answer "no" to--
Not now, Dr. Portek. I don't think the President has time for all of that.
The truth is, sir, we don't know ***why*** they're here, and speculation in a situation like this could be ***extremely*** dangerous.
We have a few probes that are ready to launch. We had tasked and budgeted them for other things, but with a few modifications, and some additional funding, we think we could get them up there relatively soo--
Do it. I'll get you the funds you need.
Whatever's up there...

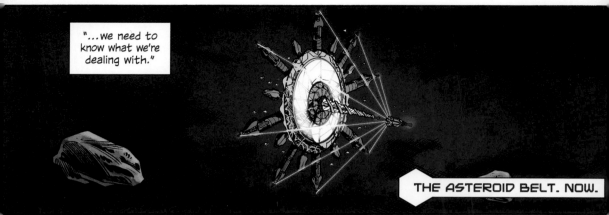

"...we need to know what we're dealing with."

THE ASTEROID BELT. NOW.

CLARKE MISSION.

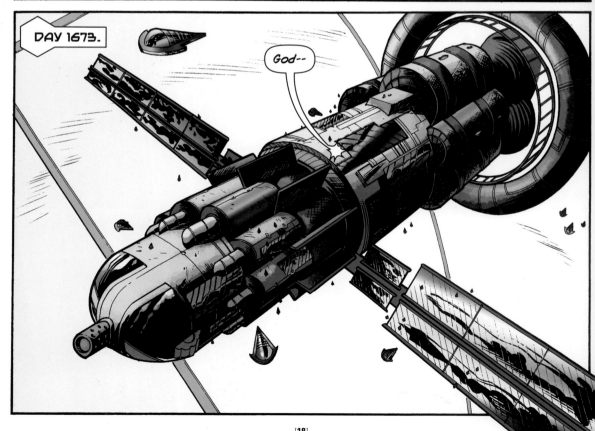

DAY 1673.

God--

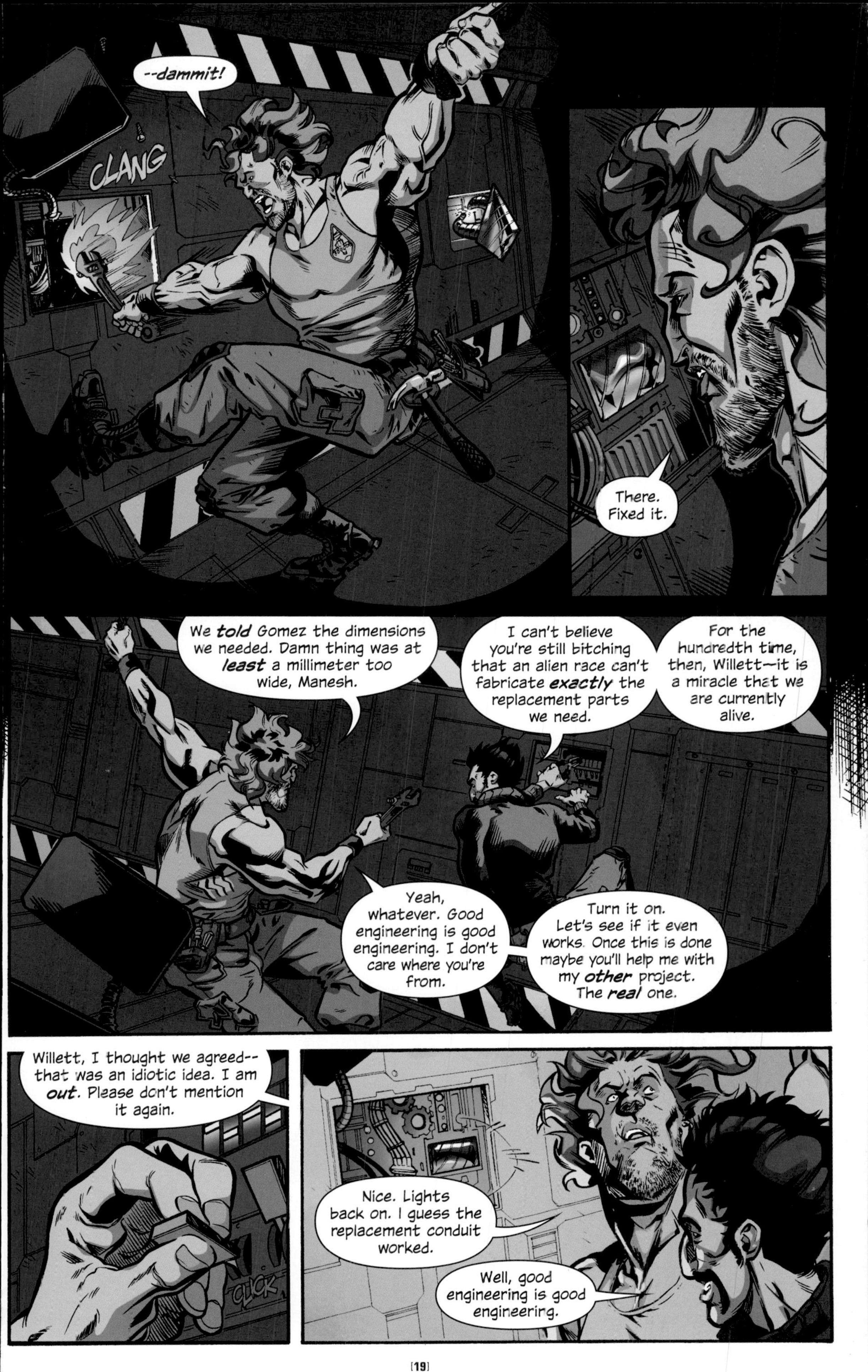
--dammit!
CLANG
There. Fixed it.
We *told* Gomez the dimensions we needed. Damn thing was at *least* a millimeter too wide, Manesh.
I can't believe you're still bitching that an alien race can't fabricate *exactly* the replacement parts we need.
For the hundredth time, then, Willett—it is a miracle that we are currently alive.
Yeah, whatever. Good engineering is good engineering. I don't care where you're from.
Turn it on. Let's see if it even works. Once this is done maybe you'll help me with my *other* project. The *real* one.
Willett, I thought we agreed--that was an idiotic idea. I am *out*. Please don't mention it again.
CLICK
Nice. Lights back on. I guess the replacement conduit worked.
Well, good engineering is good engineering.

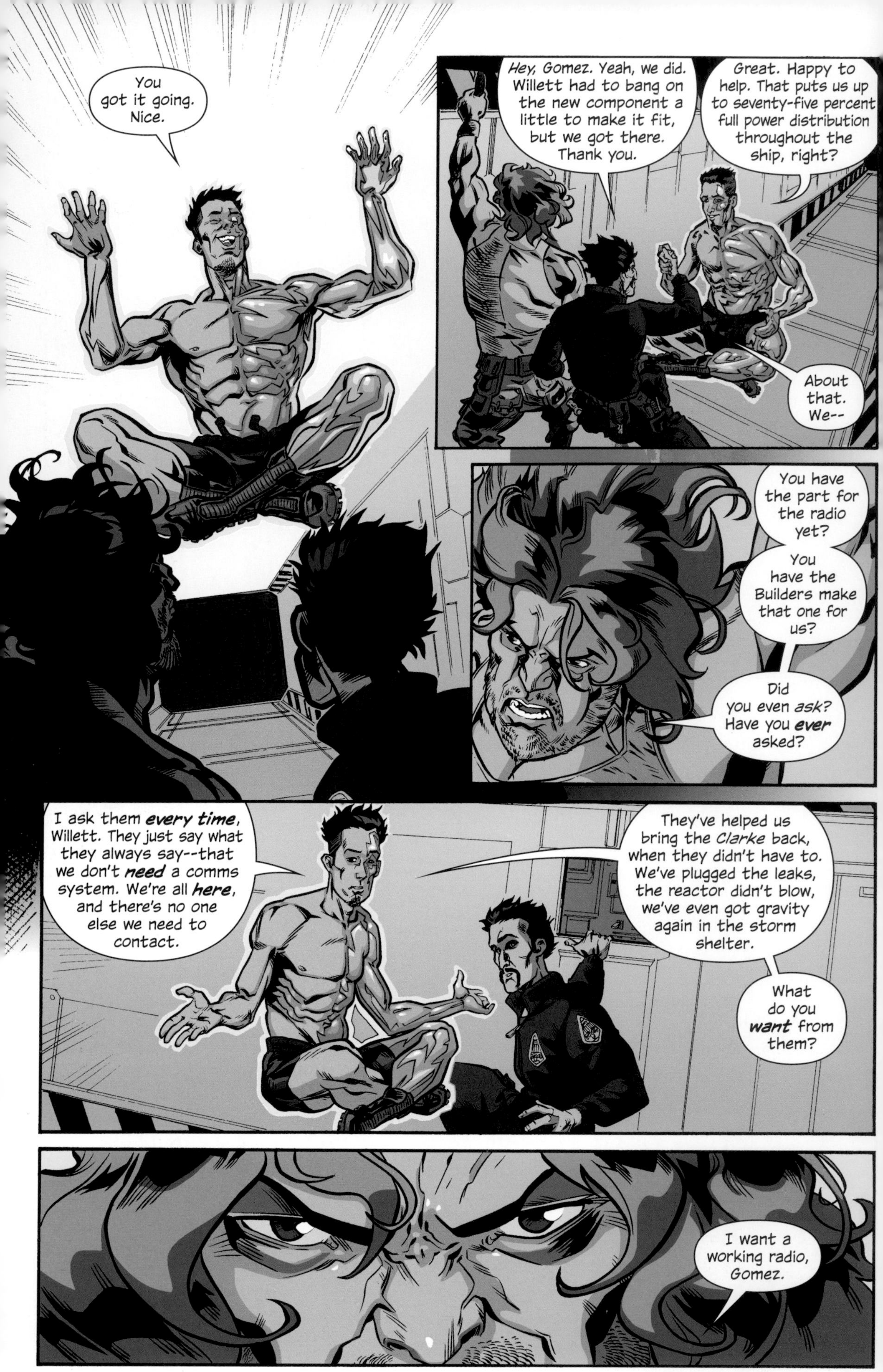
You got it going. Nice.
Hey, Gomez. Yeah, we did. Willett had to bang on the new component a little to make it fit, but we got there. Thank you.
Great. Happy to help. That puts us up to seventy-five percent full power distribution throughout the ship, right?
About that. We--
You have the part for the radio yet?
You have the Builders make that one for us?
Did you even *ask*? Have you ***ever*** asked?
I ask them ***every time***, Willett. They just say what they always say--that we don't ***need*** a comms system. We're all ***here***, and there's no one else we need to contact.
They've helped us bring the *Clarke* back, when they didn't have to. We've plugged the leaks, the reactor didn't blow, we've even got gravity again in the storm shelter.
What do you ***want*** from them?
I want a working radio, Gomez.

I think that's about enough for today. I'm headed back to the *Chandelier*.

Hot date, Manesh?

I *never* should have told you about that.

Heh.

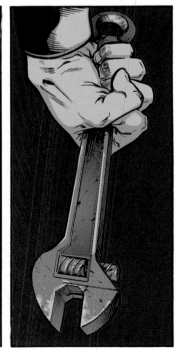

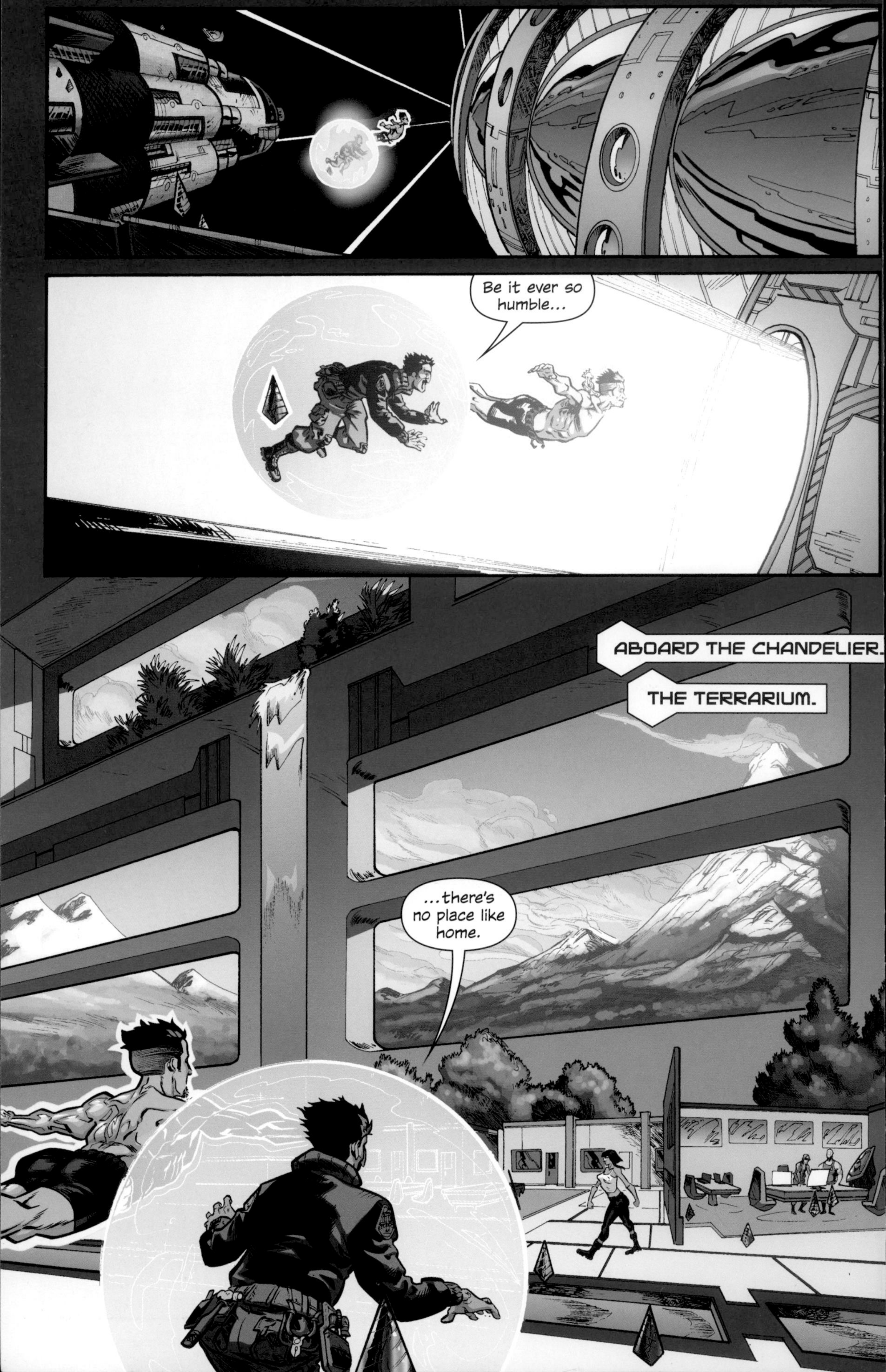
Be it ever so humble...
ABOARD THE CHANDELIER.
THE TERRARIUM.
...there's no place like home.

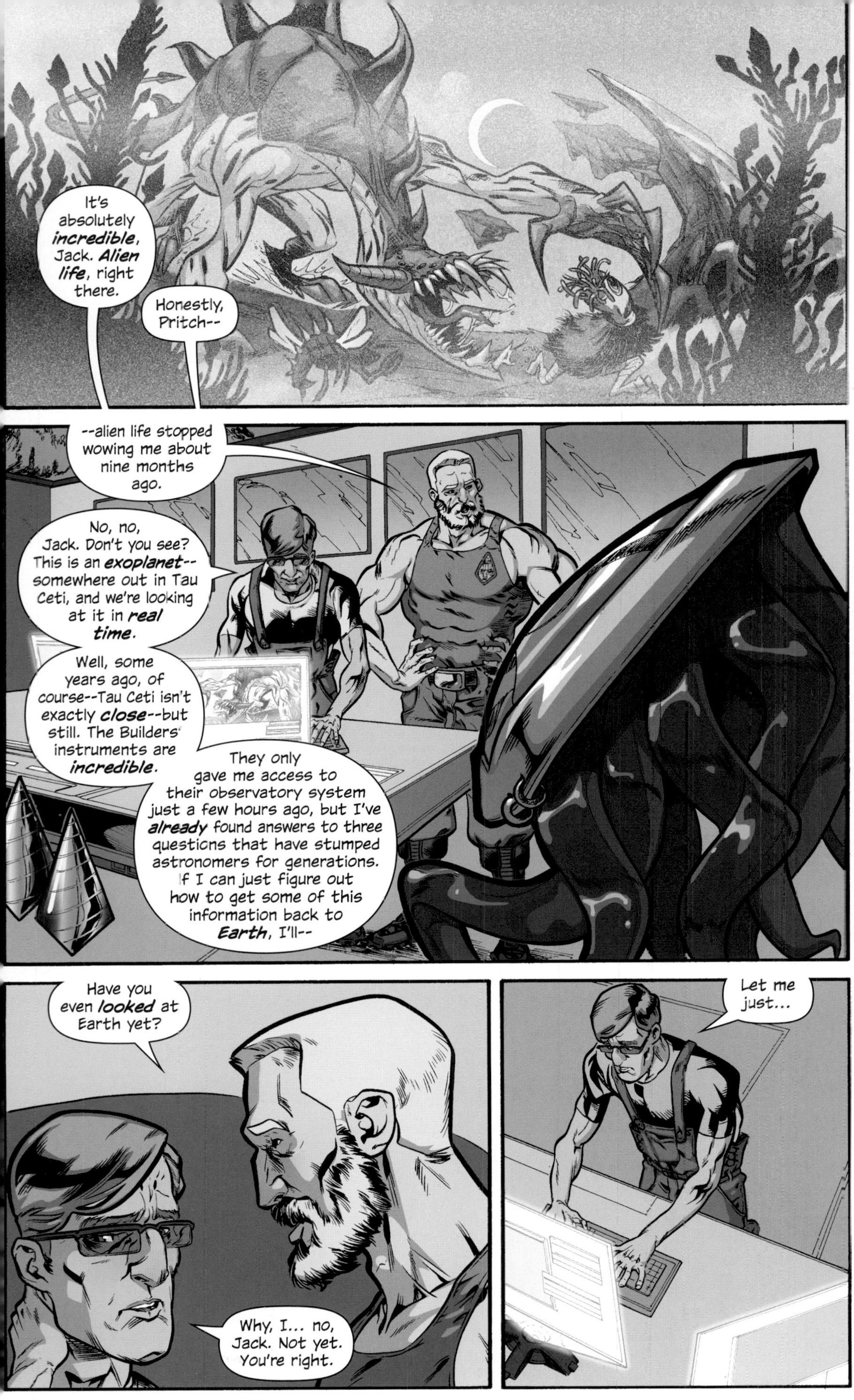

It's absolutely *incredible*, Jack. *Alien life*, right there.
Honestly, Pritch--
--alien life stopped wowing me about nine months ago.
No, no, Jack. Don't you see? This is an *exoplanet*--somewhere out in Tau Ceti, and we're looking at it in *real time*.
Well, some years ago, of course--Tau Ceti isn't exactly *close*--but still. The Builders' instruments are *incredible*.
They only gave me access to their observatory system just a few hours ago, but I've *already* found answers to three questions that have stumped astronomers for generations. If I can just figure out how to get some of this information back to *Earth*, I'll--
Have you even *looked* at Earth yet?
Why, I... no, Jack. Not yet. You're right.
Let me just...

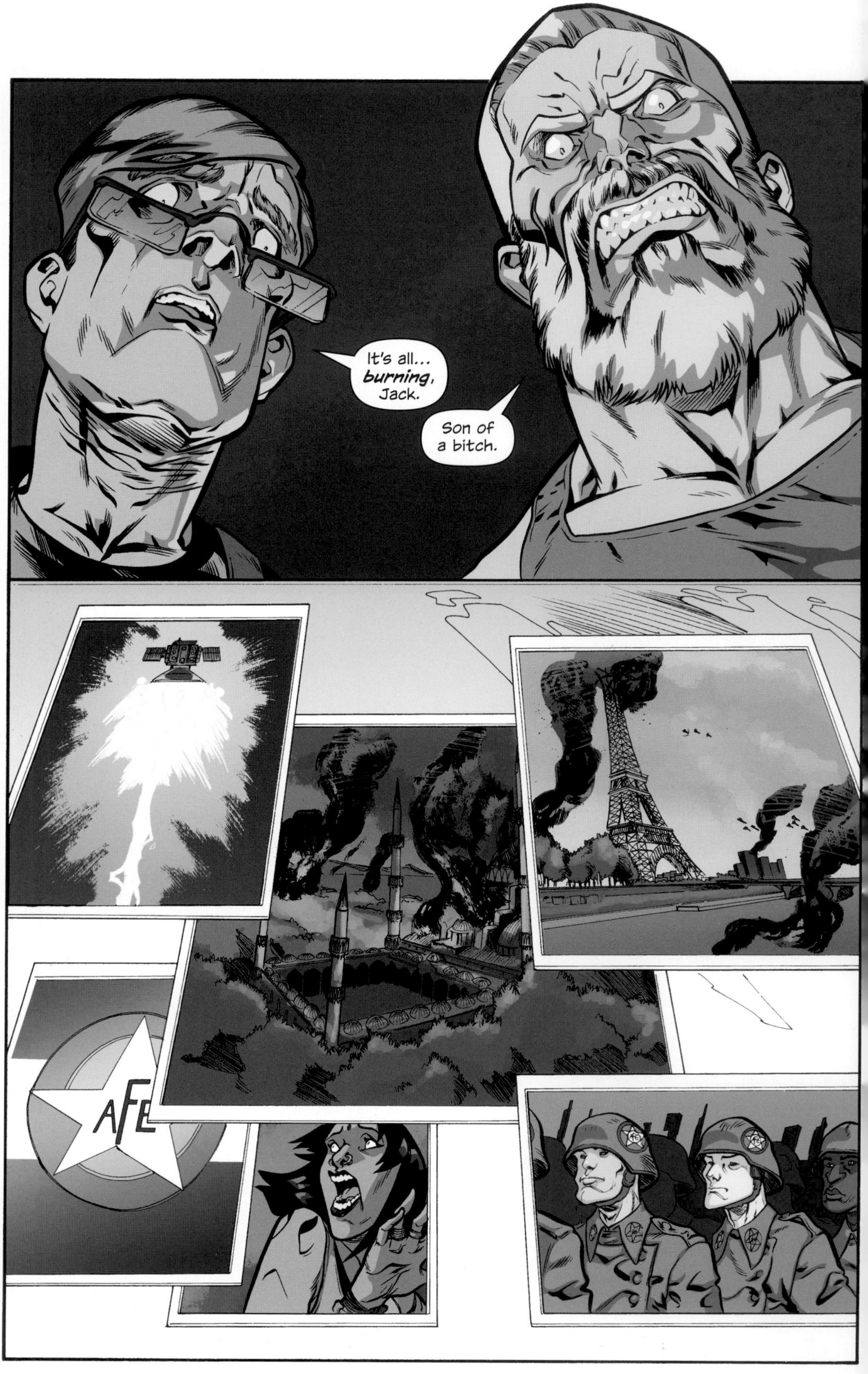
It's all... **burning**, Jack.
Son of a bitch.
AFE

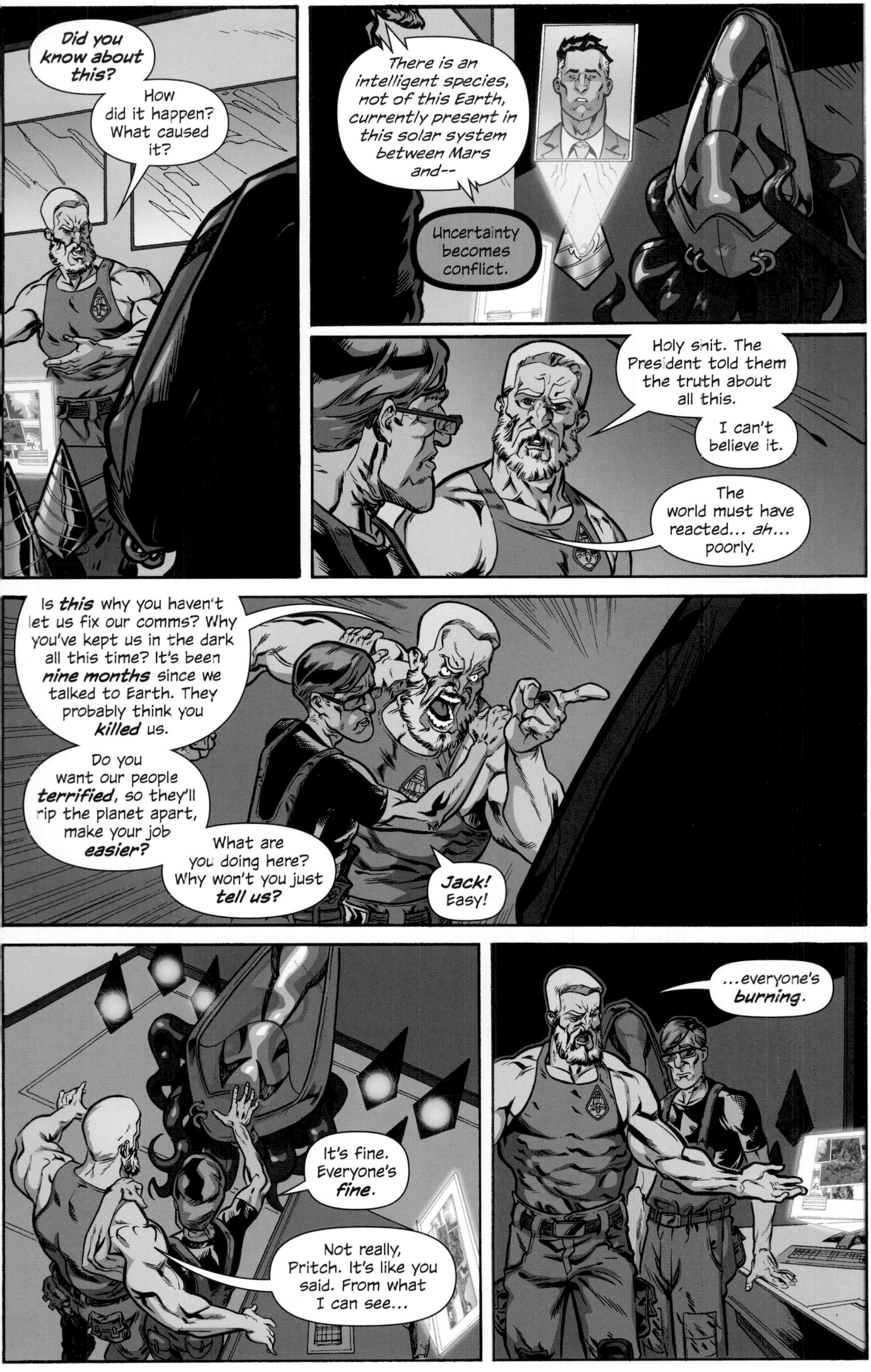

Did you know about this?
How did it happen? What caused it?
There is an intelligent species, not of this Earth, currently present in this solar system between Mars and--
Uncertainty becomes conflict.
Holy shit. The President told them the truth about all this.
I can't believe it.
The world must have reacted... ah... poorly.
Is this why you haven't let us fix our comms? Why you've kept us in the dark all this time? It's been nine months since we talked to Earth. They probably think you killed us.
Do you want our people terrified, so they'll rip the planet apart, make your job easier?
What are you doing here? Why won't you just tell us?
Jack! Easy!
It's fine. Everyone's fine.
Not really, Pritch. It's like you said. From what I can see...
...everyone's burning.

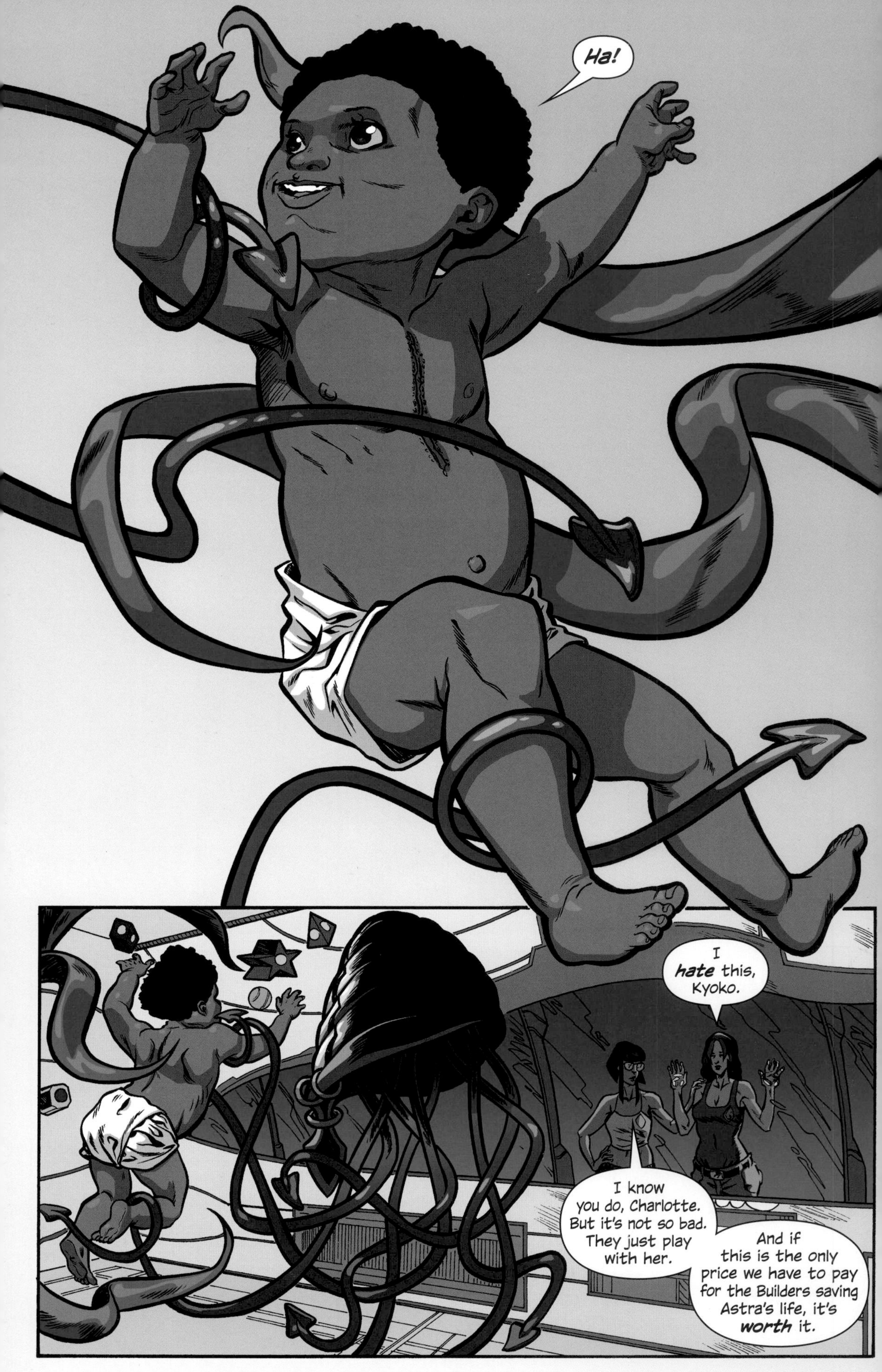
Ha!
I hate this, Kyoko.
I know you do, Charlotte. But it's not so bad. They just play with her.
And if this is the only price we have to pay for the Builders saving Astra's life, it's worth it.

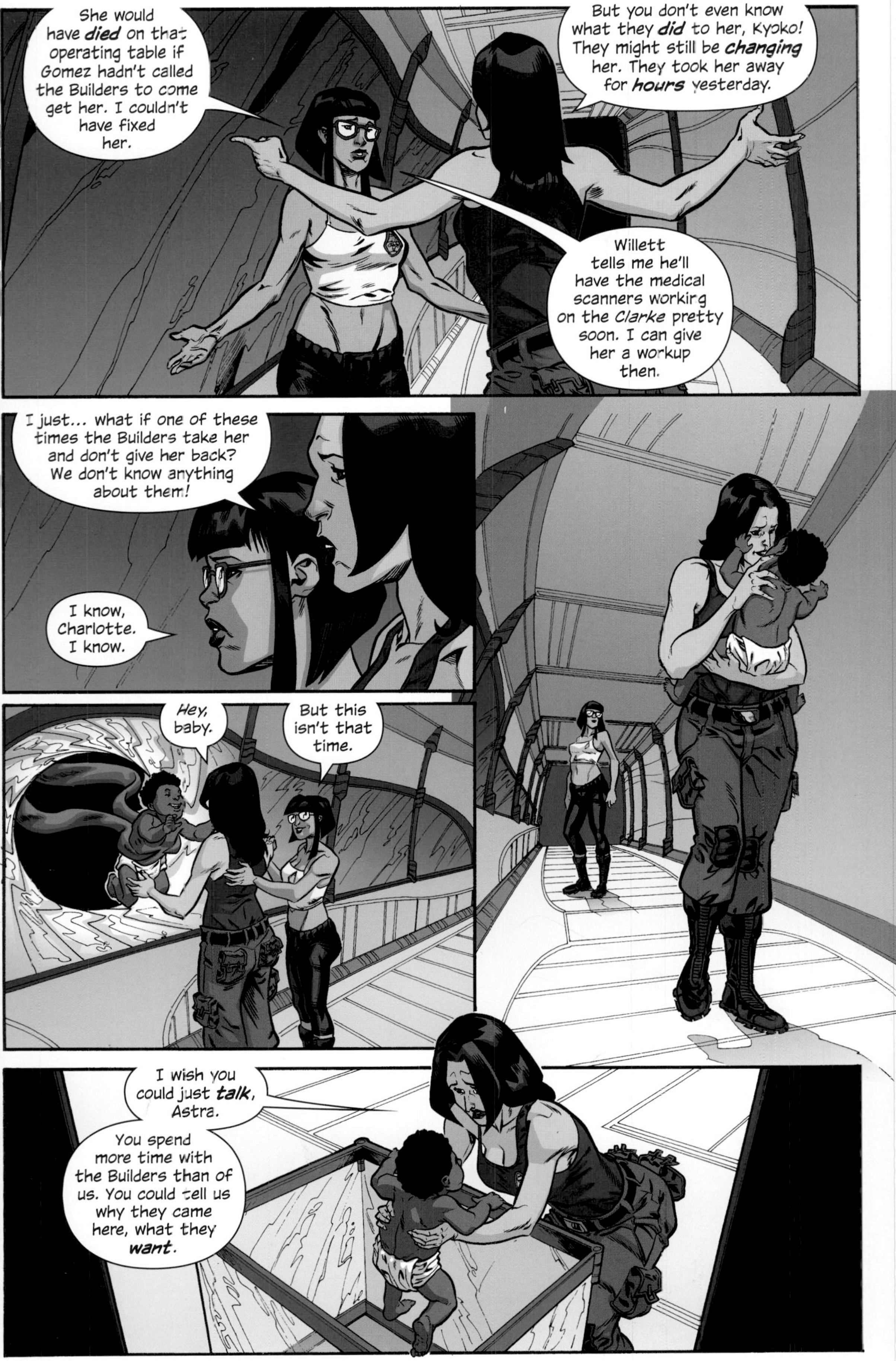
She would have *died* on that operating table if Gomez hadn't called the Builders to come get her. I couldn't have fixed her.
But you don't even know what they *did* to her, Kyoko! They might still be *changing* her. They took her away for *hours* yesterday.
Willett tells me he'll have the medical scanners working on the *Clarke* pretty soon. I can give her a workup then.
I just... what if one of these times the Builders take her and don't give her back? We don't know anything about them!
I know, Charlotte. I know.
Hey, baby.
But this isn't that time.
I wish you could just *talk*, Astra.
You spend more time with the Builders than of us. You could tell us why they came here, what they *want*.

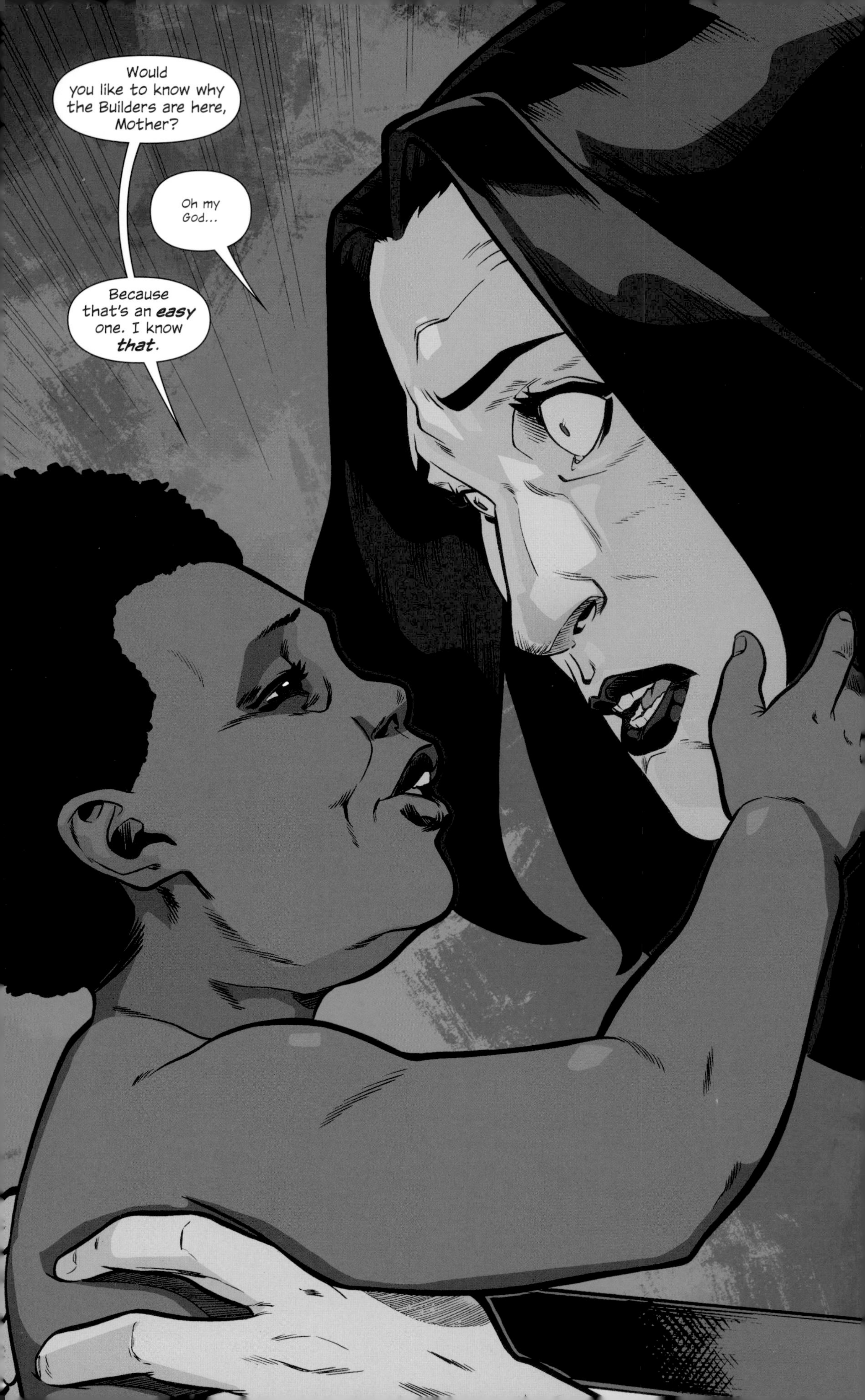
Would you like to know why the Builders are here, Mother?
Oh my God...
Because that's an *easy* one. I know ***that***.

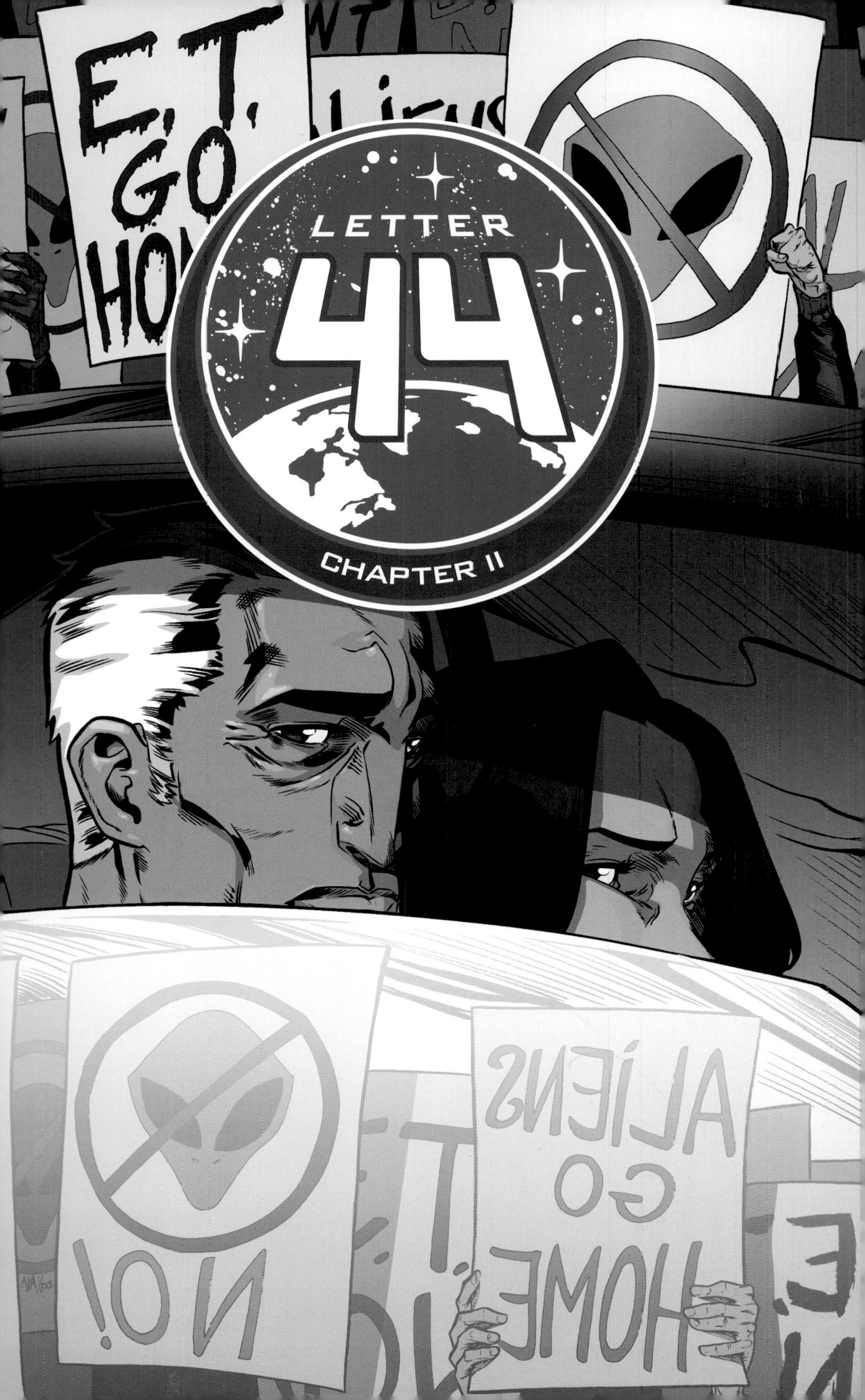
E.T.
GO
LETTER
44
CHAPTER II

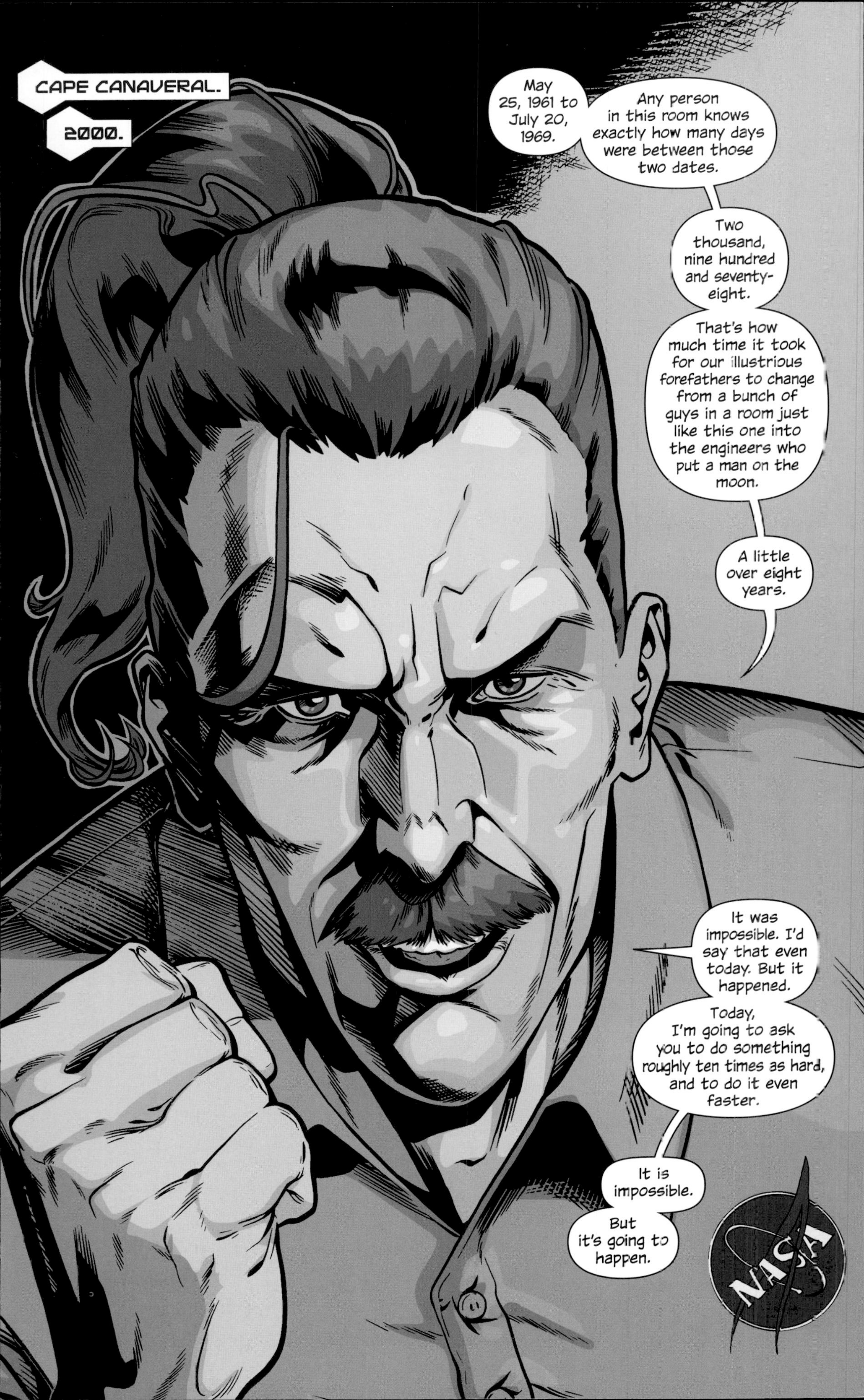
CAPE CANAVERAL.
2000.
May 25, 1961 to July 20, 1969.
Any person in this room knows exactly how many days were between those two dates.
Two thousand, nine hundred and seventy-eight.
That's how much time it took for our illustrious forefathers to change from a bunch of guys in a room just like this one into the engineers who put a man on the moon.
A little over eight years.
It was impossible. I'd say that even today. But it happened.
Today, I'm going to ask you to do something roughly ten times as hard, and to do it even faster.
It is impossible.
But it's going to happen.
NASA

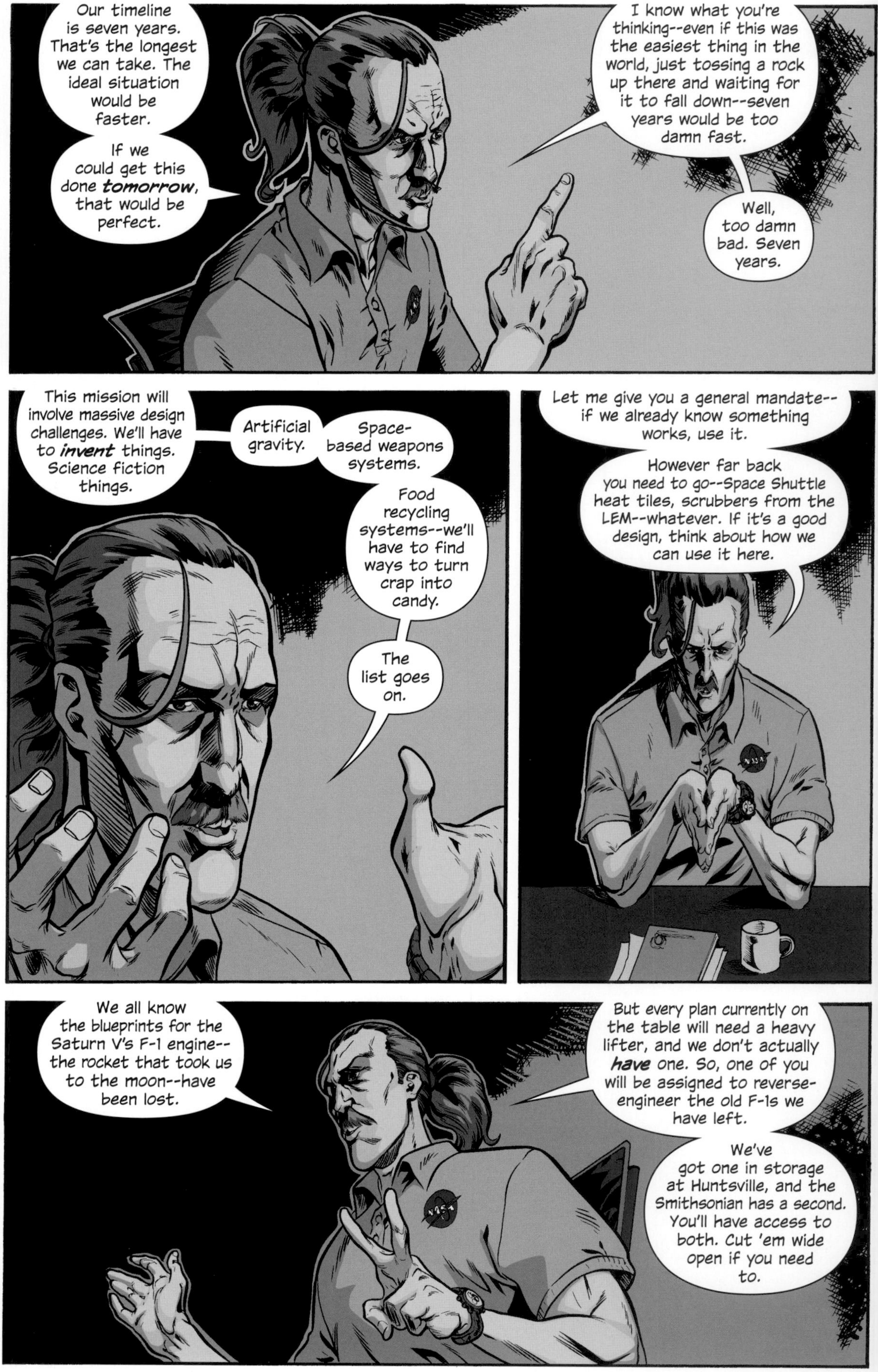

Our timeline is seven years. That's the longest we can take. The ideal situation would be faster.
If we could get this done ***tomorrow***, that would be perfect.
I know what you're thinking--even if this was the easiest thing in the world, just tossing a rock up there and waiting for it to fall down--seven years would be too damn fast.
Well, too damn bad. Seven years.
This mission will involve massive design challenges. We'll have to ***invent*** things. Science fiction things.
Artificial gravity.
Space-based weapons systems.
Food recycling systems--we'll have to find ways to turn crap into candy.
The list goes on.
Let me give you a general mandate--if we already know something works, use it.
However far back you need to go--Space Shuttle heat tiles, scrubbers from the LEM--whatever. If it's a good design, think about how we can use it here.
We all know the blueprints for the Saturn V's F-1 engine--the rocket that took us to the moon--have been lost.
But every plan currently on the table will need a heavy lifter, and we don't actually ***have*** one. So, one of you will be assigned to reverse-engineer the old F-1s we have left.
We've got one in storage at Huntsville, and the Smithsonian has a second. You'll have access to both. Cut 'em wide open if you need to.

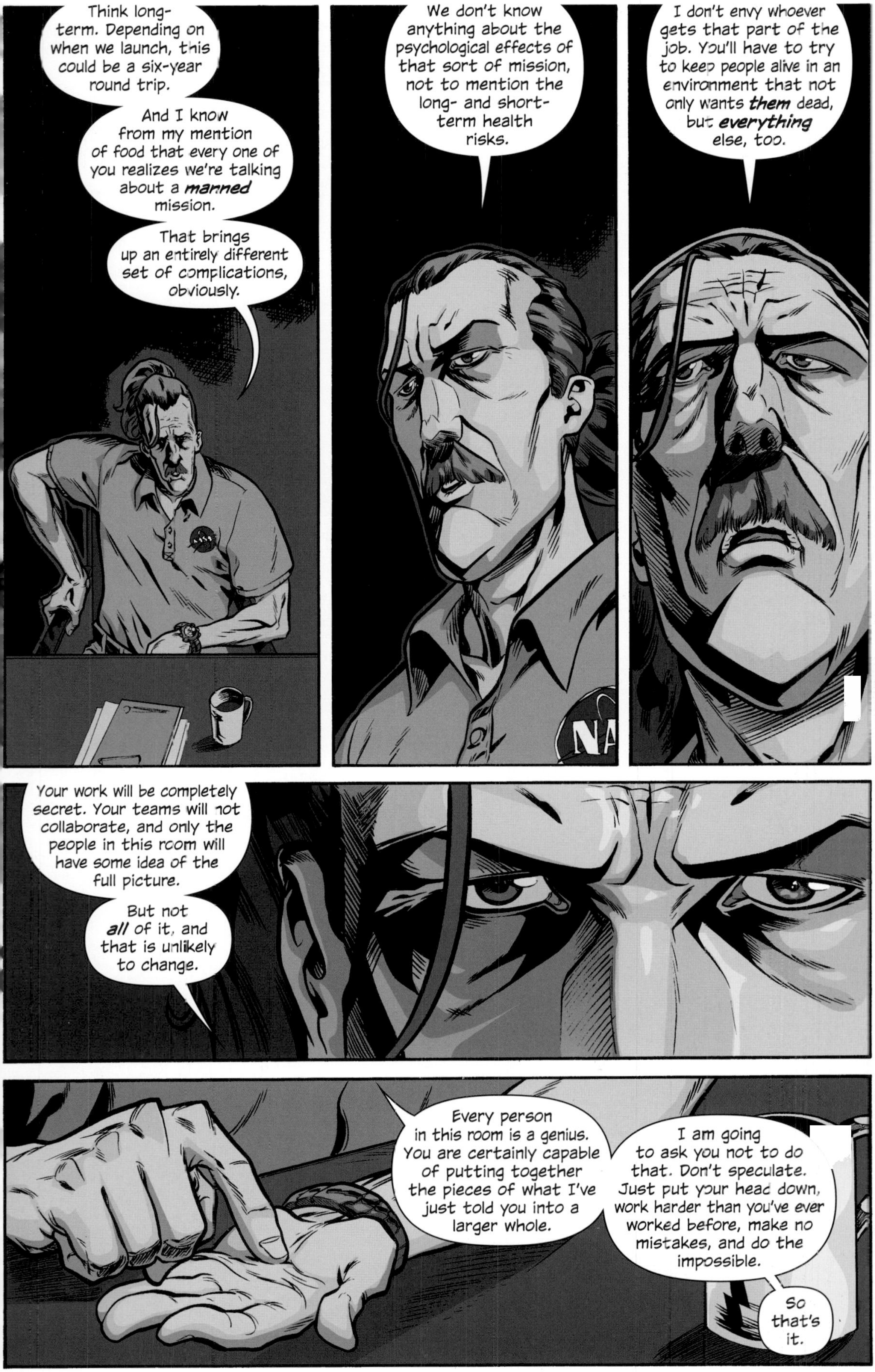
Think long-term. Depending on when we launch, this could be a six-year round trip.
And I know from my mention of food that every one of you realizes we're talking about a *manned* mission.
That brings up an entirely different set of complications, obviously.
We don't know anything about the psychological effects of that sort of mission, not to mention the long- and short-term health risks.
I don't envy whoever gets that part of the job. You'll have to try to keep people alive in an environment that not only wants *them* dead, but *everything* else, too.
Your work will be completely secret. Your teams will not collaborate, and only the people in this room will have some idea of the full picture.
But not *all* of it, and that is unlikely to change.
Every person in this room is a genius. You are certainly capable of putting together the pieces of what I've just told you into a larger whole.
I am going to ask you not to do that. Don't speculate. Just put your head down, work harder than you've ever worked before, make no mistakes, and do the impossible.
So that's it.

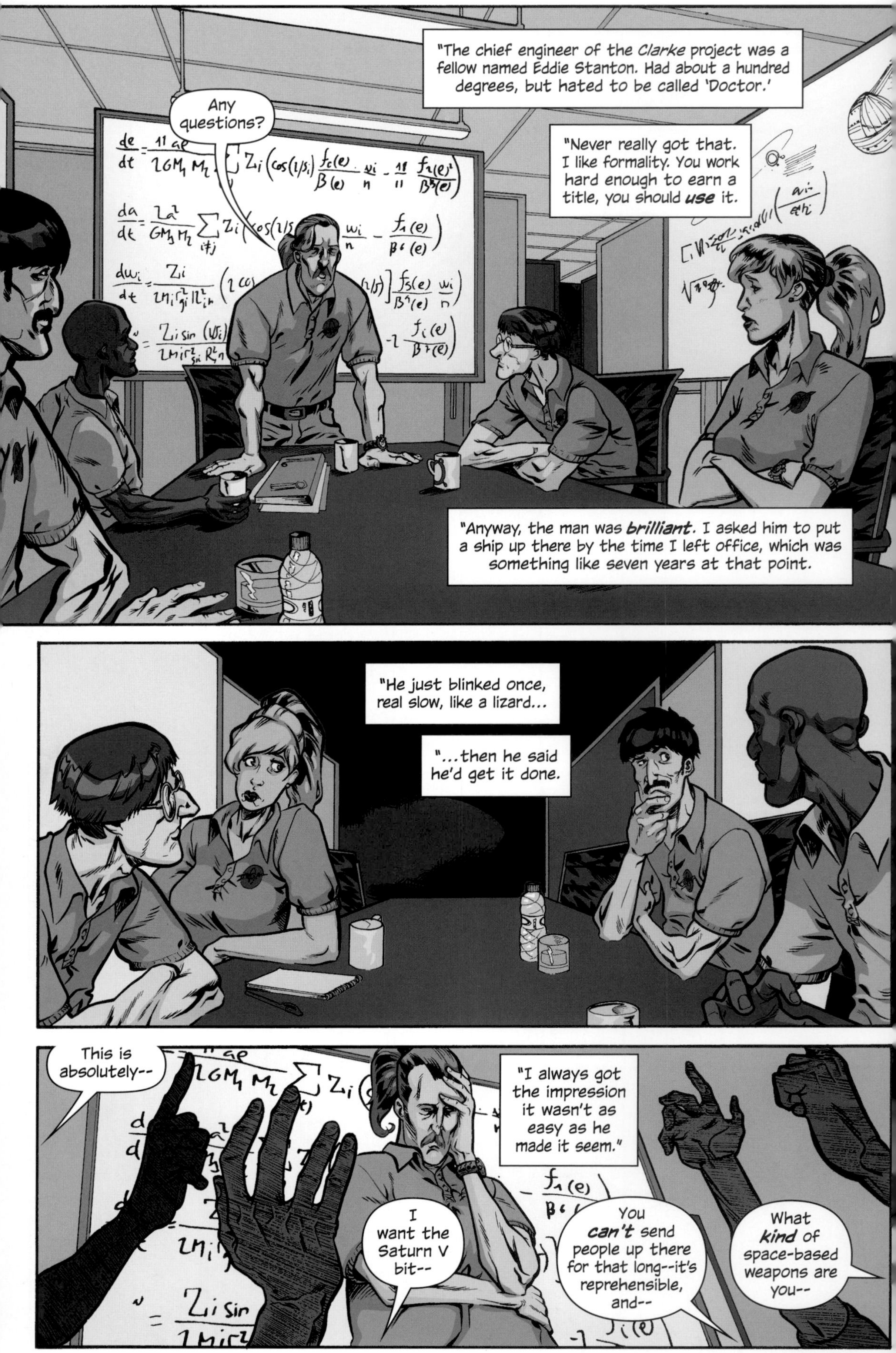
"The chief engineer of the *Clarke* project was a fellow named Eddie Stanton. Had about a hundred degrees, but hated to be called 'Doctor.'
Any questions?
"Never really got that. I like formality. You work hard enough to earn a title, you should ***use*** it.
"Anyway, the man was ***brilliant***. I asked him to put a ship up there by the time I left office, which was something like seven years at that point.
"He just blinked once, real slow, like a lizard...
"...then he said he'd get it done.
This is absolutely--
"I always got the impression it wasn't as easy as he made it seem."
I want the Saturn V bit--
You ***can't*** send people up there for that long--it's reprehensible, and--
What ***kind*** of space-based weapons are you--

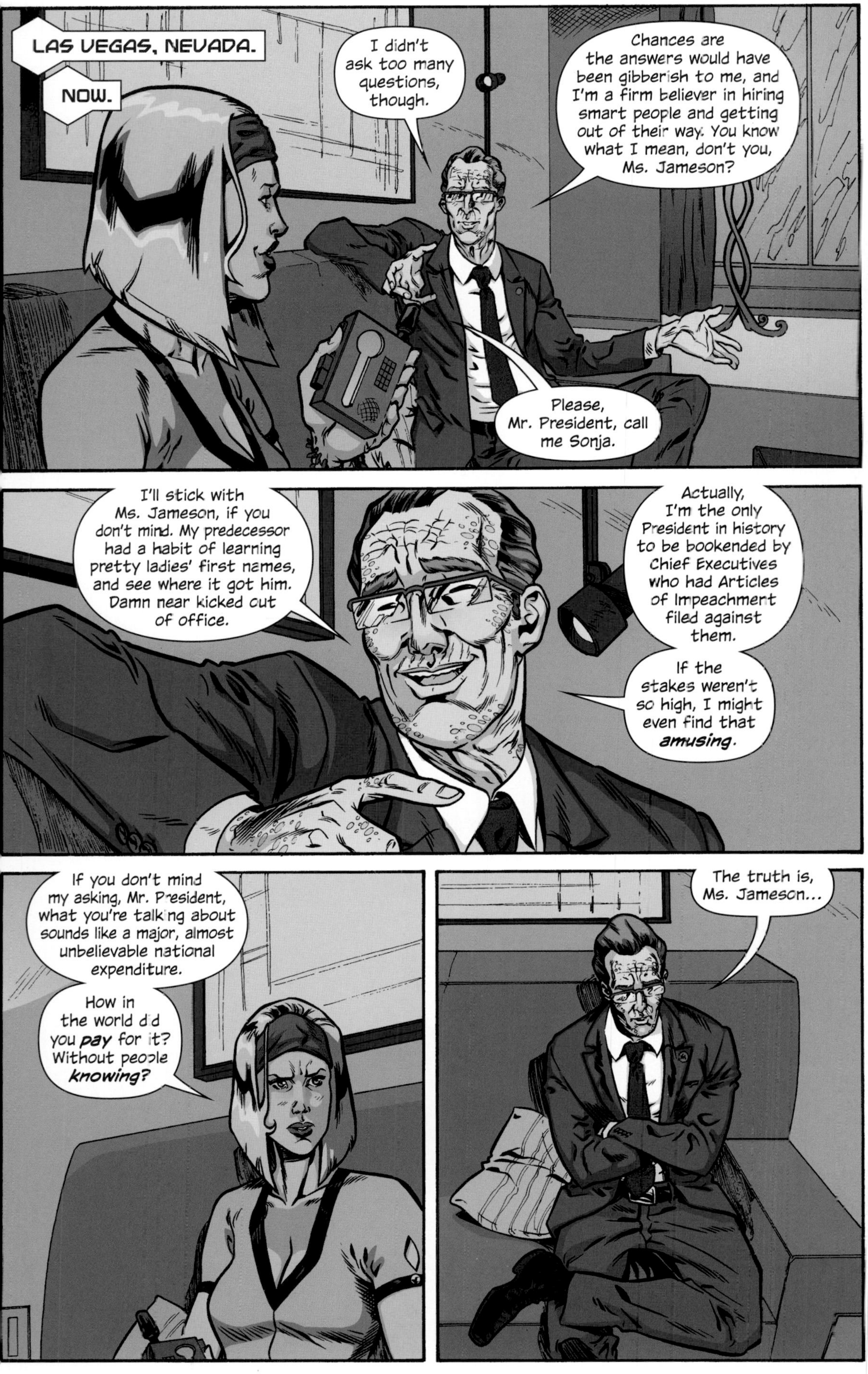
LAS VEGAS, NEVADA.
NOW.
I didn't ask too many questions, though.
Chances are the answers would have been gibberish to me, and I'm a firm believer in hiring smart people and getting out of their way. You know what I mean, don't you, Ms. Jameson?
Please, Mr. President, call me Sonja.
I'll stick with Ms. Jameson, if you don't mind. My predecessor had a habit of learning pretty ladies' first names, and see where it got him. Damn near kicked out of office.
Actually, I'm the only President in history to be bookended by Chief Executives who had Articles of Impeachment filed against them.
If the stakes weren't so high, I might even find that *amusing*.
If you don't mind my asking, Mr. President, what you're talking about sounds like a major, almost unbelievable national expenditure.
How in the world did you *pay* for it? Without people *knowing*?
The truth is, Ms. Jameson...

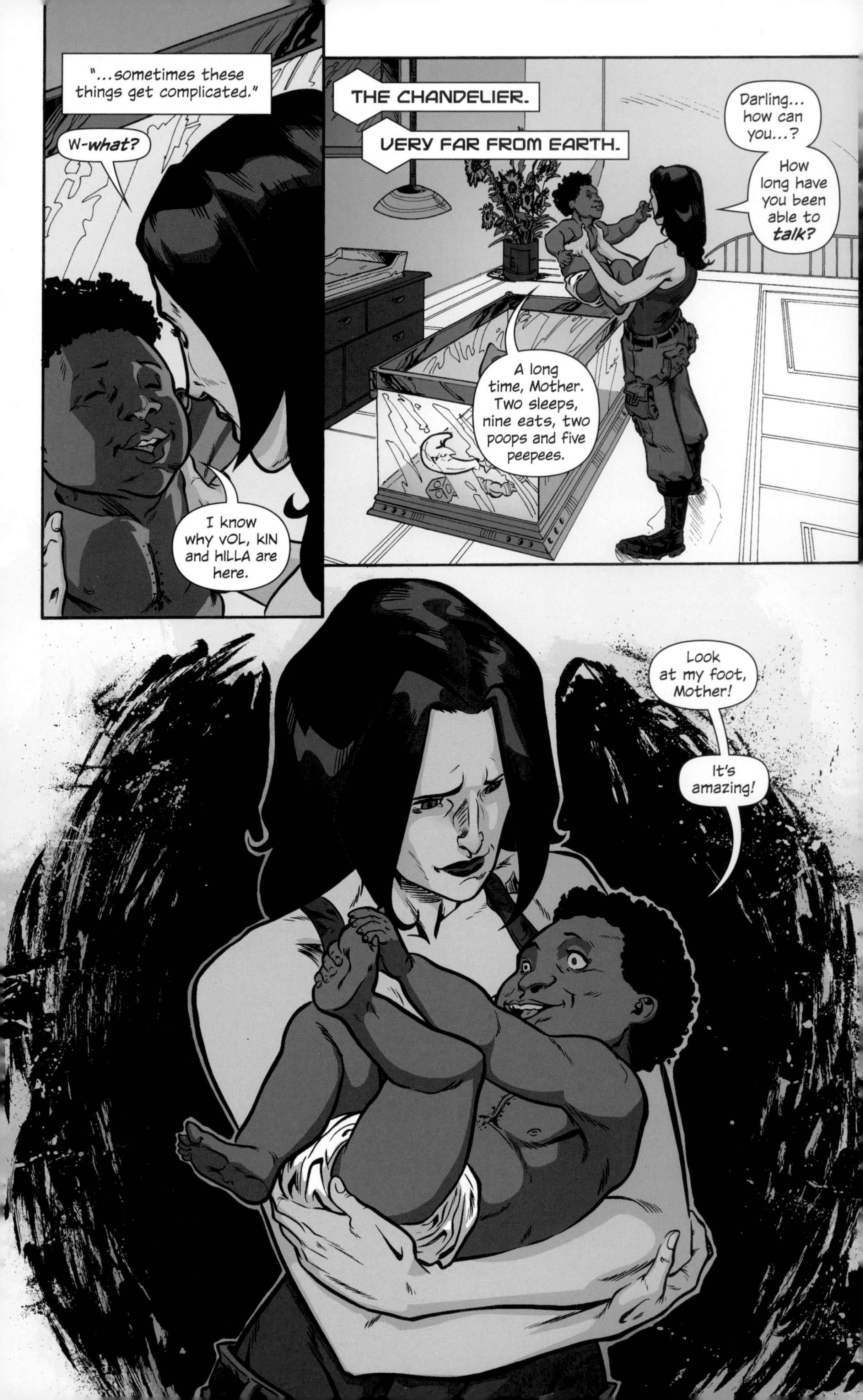
"...sometimes these things get complicated."
W-*what?*
I know why VOL, KIN and HILLA are here.
THE CHANDELIER.
VERY FAR FROM EARTH.
Darling... how can you...?
How long have you been able to *talk?*
A long time, Mother. Two sleeps, nine eats, two poops and five peepees.
Look at my foot, Mother!
It's amazing!

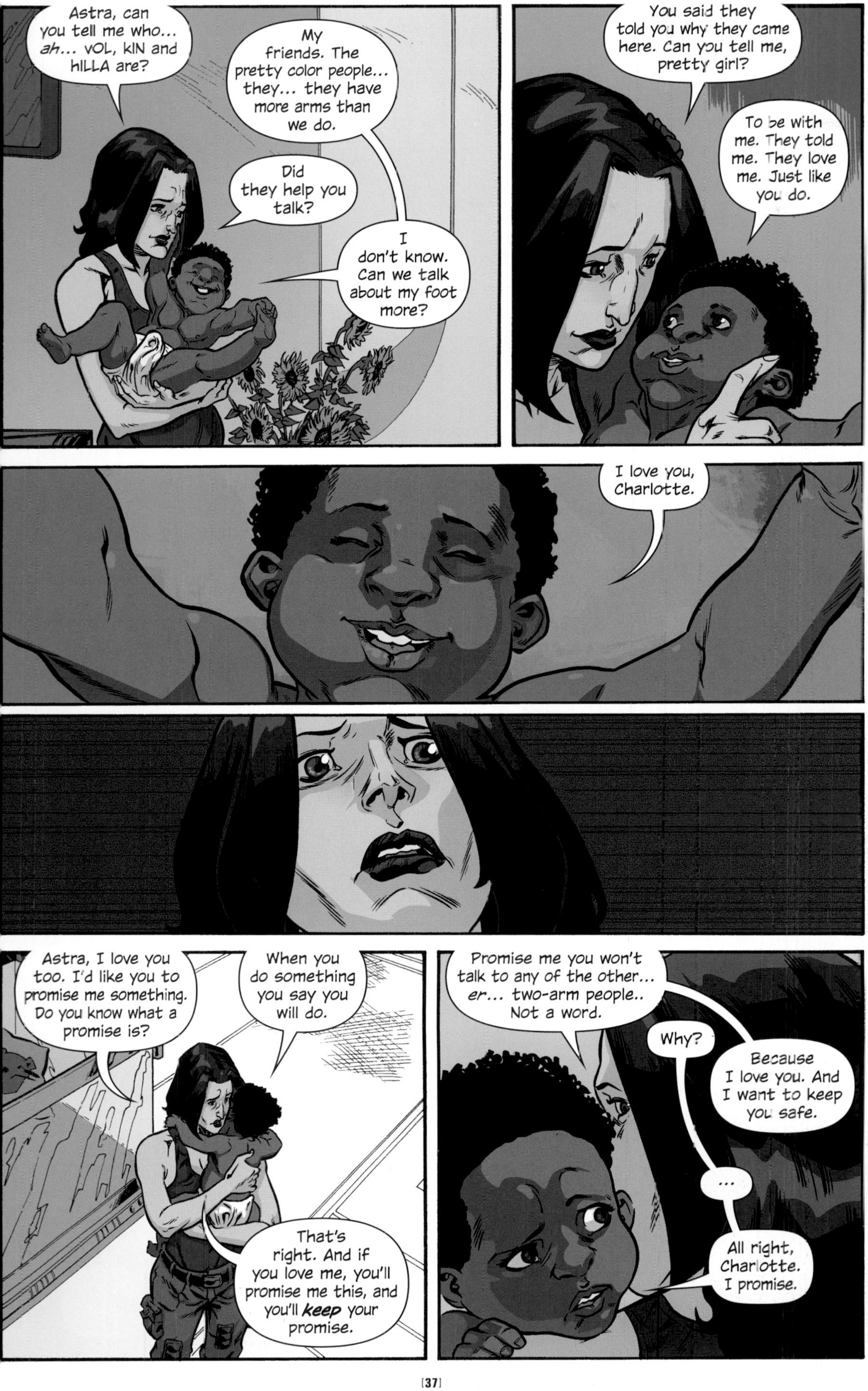
Astra, can you tell me who... *ah*... VOL, KIN and HILLA are?
My friends. The pretty color people... they... they have more arms than we do.
Did they help you talk?
I don't know. Can we talk about my foot more?
You said they told you why they came here. Can you tell me, pretty girl?
To be with me. They told me. They love me. Just like you do.
I love you, Charlotte.
Astra, I love you too. I'd like you to promise me something. Do you know what a promise is?
When you do something you say you will do.
That's right. And if you love me, you'll promise me this, and you'll ***keep*** your promise.
Promise me you won't talk to any of the other... *er*... two-arm people.. Not a word.
Why?
Because I love you. And I want to keep you safe.
...
All right, Charlotte. I promise.

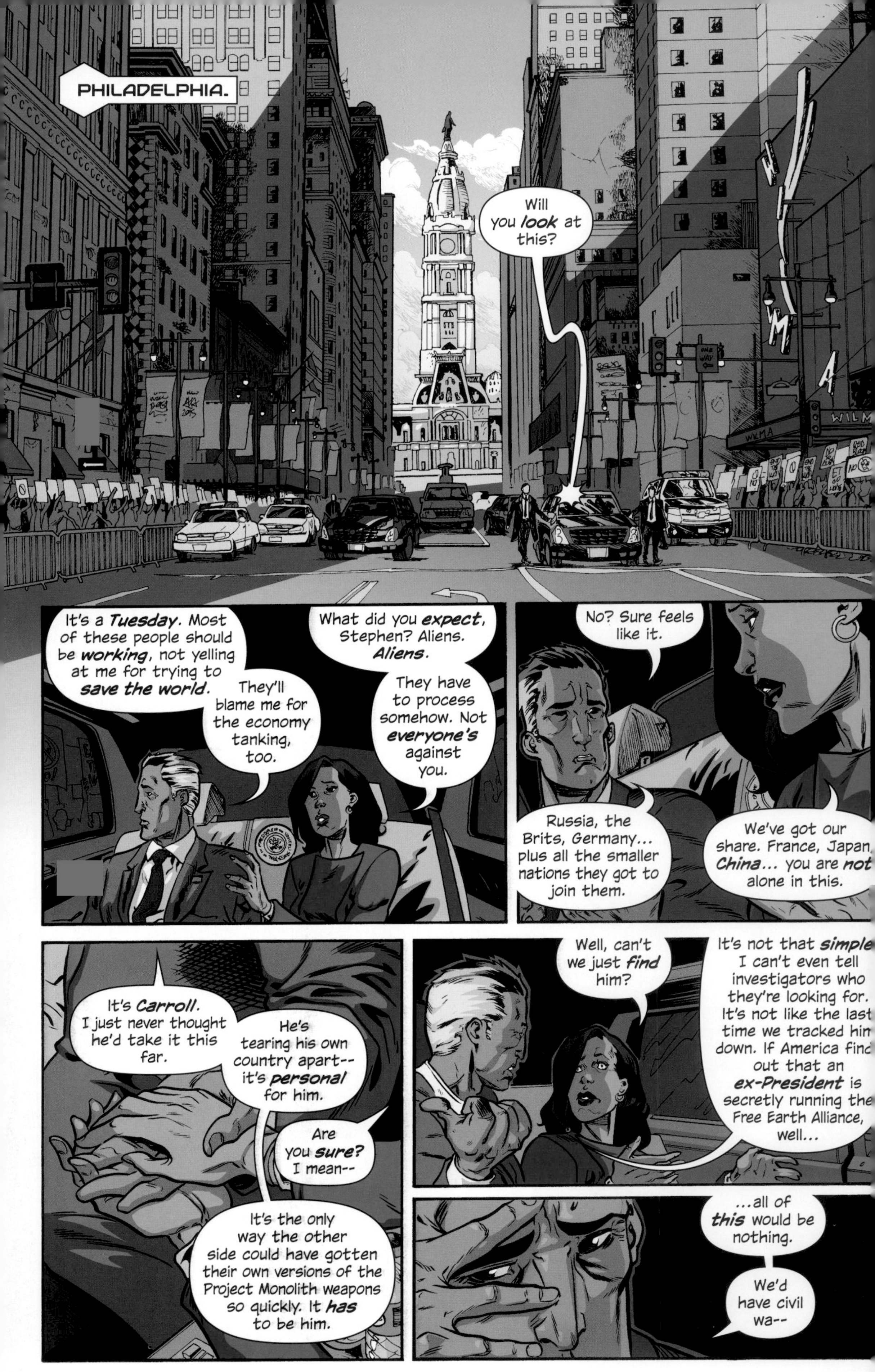
PHILADELPHIA.
Will you look at this?
It's a Tuesday. Most of these people should be working, not yelling at me for trying to save the world.
They'll blame me for the economy tanking, too.
What did you expect, Stephen? Aliens. Aliens.
They have to process somehow. Not everyone's against you.
No? Sure feels like it.
Russia, the Brits, Germany... plus all the smaller nations they got to join them.
We've got our share. France, Japan, China... you are not alone in this.
It's Carroll. I just never thought he'd take it this far.
He's tearing his own country apart--it's personal for him.
Are you sure? I mean--
It's the only way the other side could have gotten their own versions of the Project Monolith weapons so quickly. It has to be him.
Well, can't we just find him?
It's not that simple. I can't even tell investigators who they're looking for. It's not like the last time we tracked him down. If America finds out that an ex-President is secretly running the Free Earth Alliance, well...
...all of this would be nothing.
We'd have civil wa--

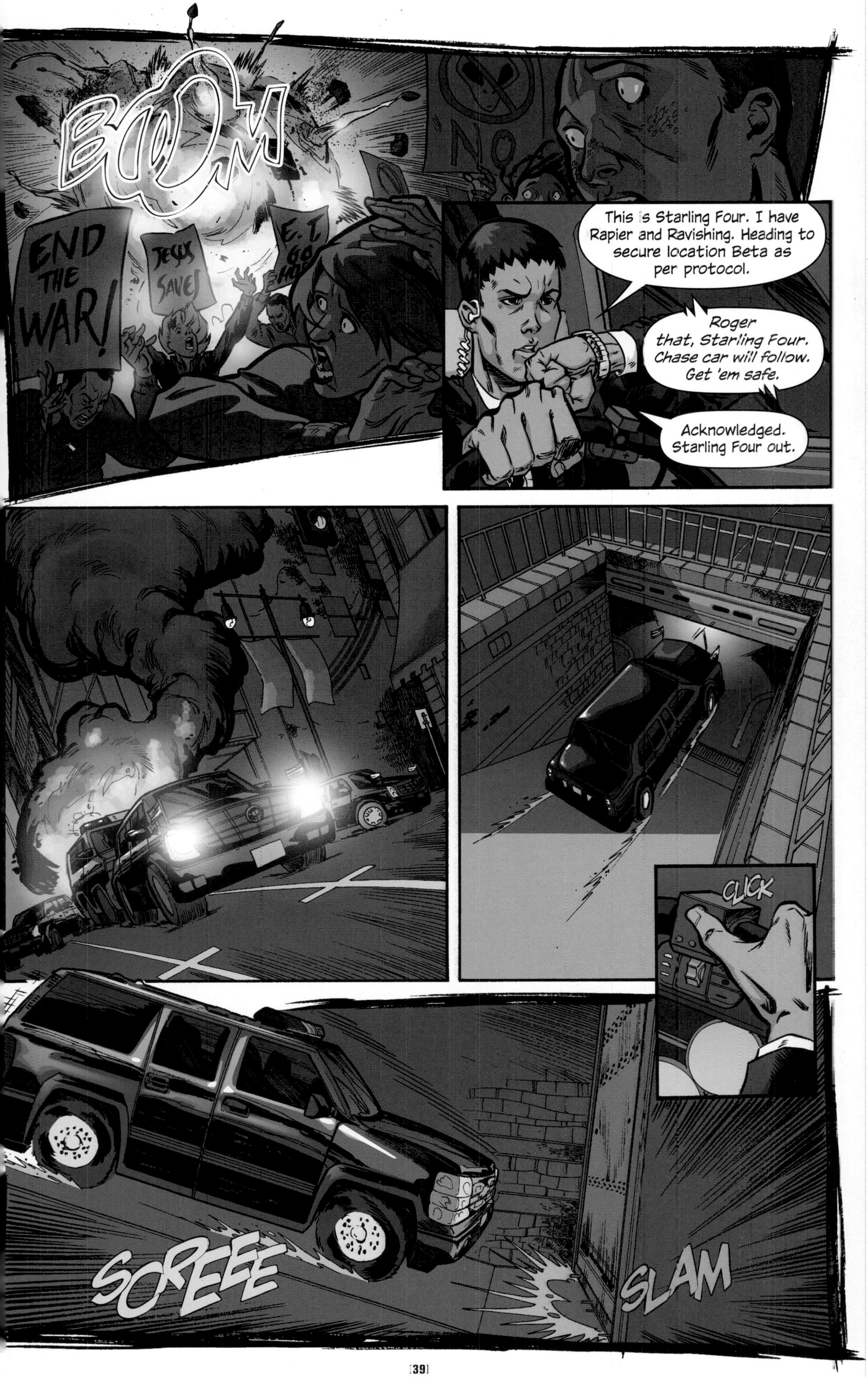
BOOM
END THE WAR!
JESUS SAVES
This is Starling Four. I have Rapier and Ravishing. Heading to secure location Beta as per protocol.
Roger that, Starling Four. Chase car will follow. Get 'em safe.
Acknowledged. Starling Four out.
CLICK
SCREEE
SLAM

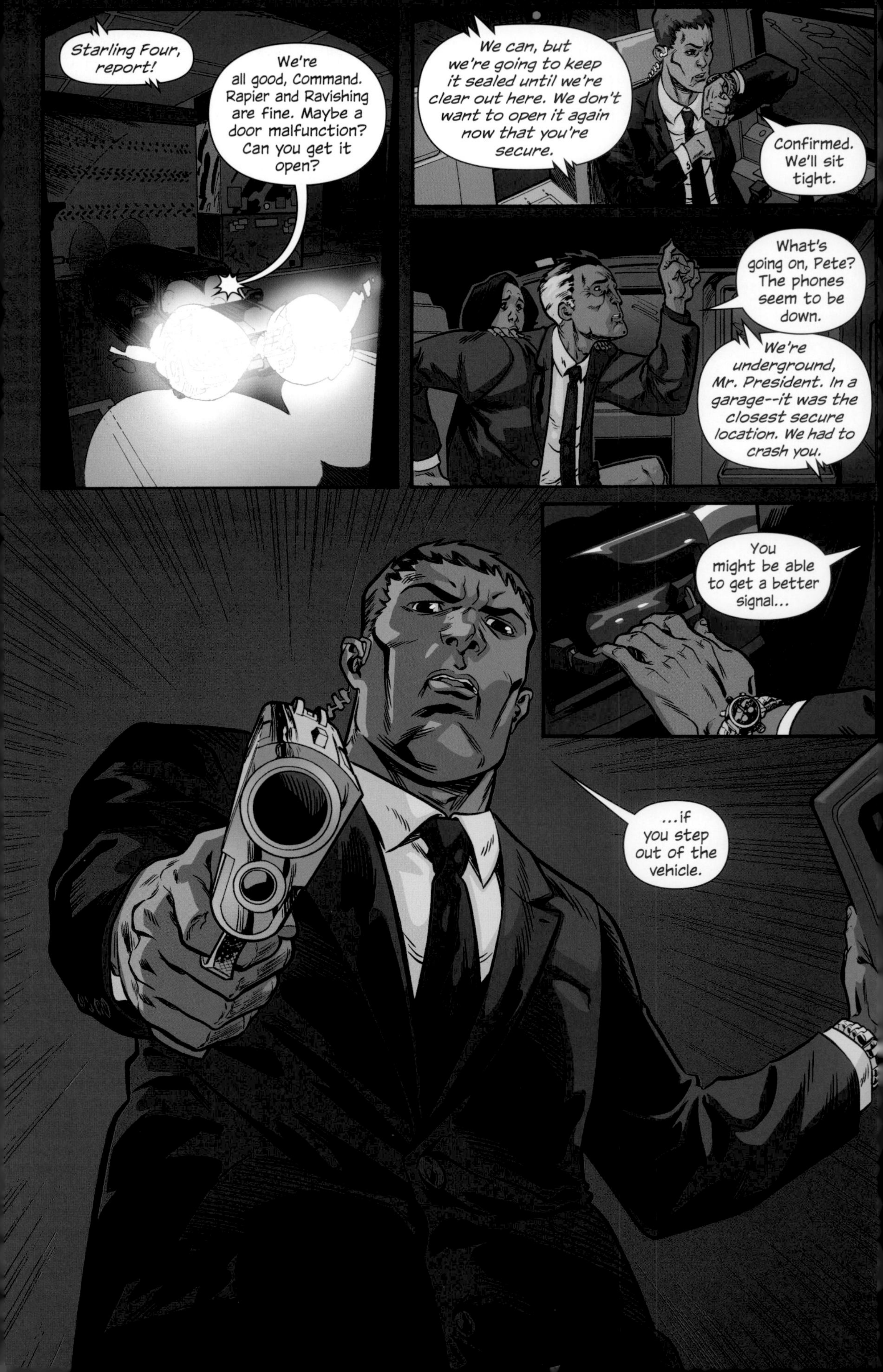
Starling Four, report!
We're all good, Command. Rapier and Ravishing are fine. Maybe a door malfunction? Can you get it open?
We can, but we're going to keep it sealed until we're clear out here. We don't want to open it again now that you're secure.
Confirmed. We'll sit tight.
What's going on, Pete? The phones seem to be down.
We're underground, Mr. President. In a garage--it was the closest secure location. We had to crash you.
You might be able to get a better signal...
...if you step out of the vehicle.

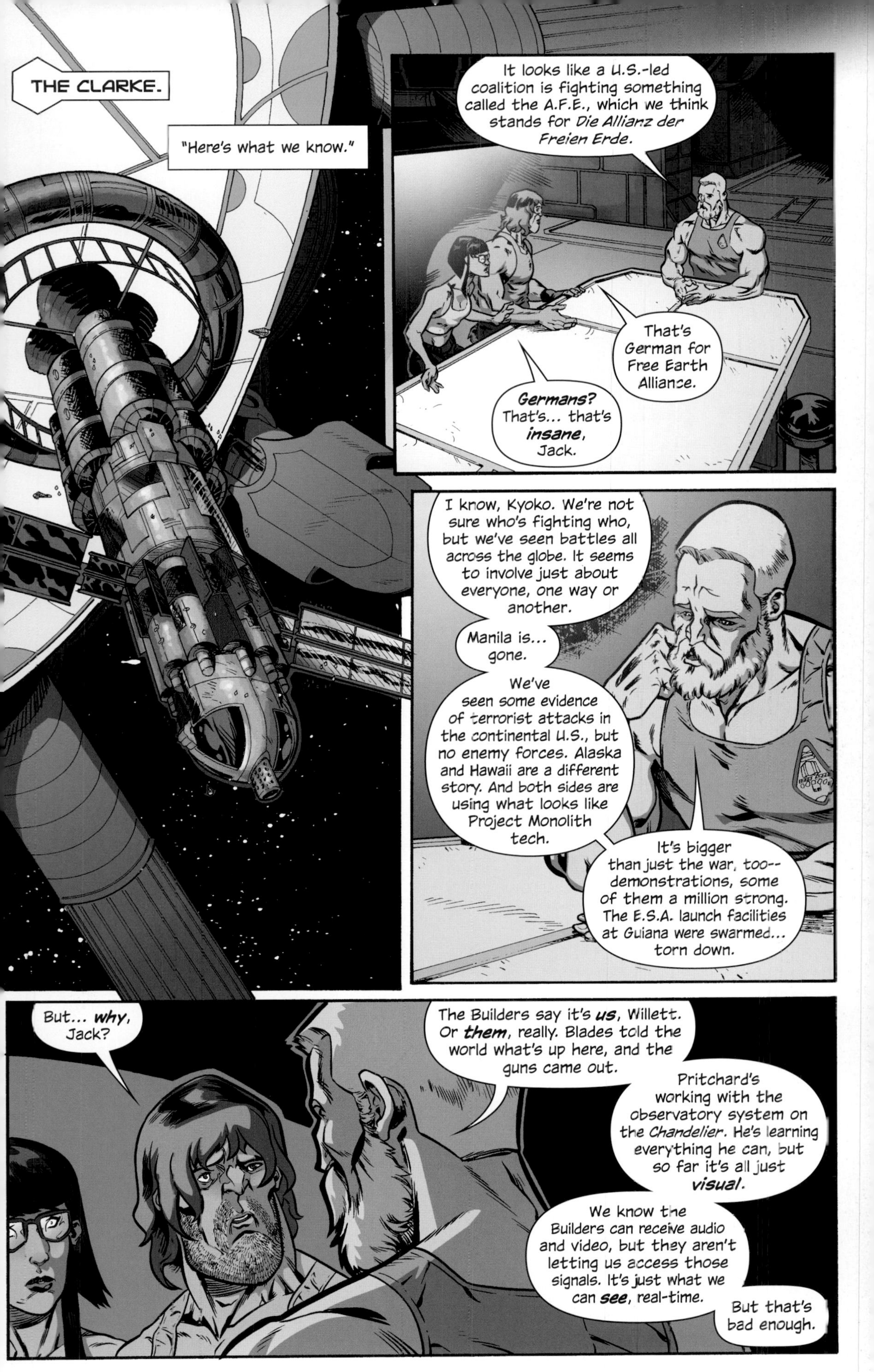
THE CLARKE.
"Here's what we know."
It looks like a U.S.-led coalition is fighting something called the A.F.E., which we think stands for *Die Allianz der Freien Erde*.
That's German for Free Earth Alliance.
Germans? That's... that's ***insane***, Jack.
I know, Kyoko. We're not sure who's fighting who, but we've seen battles all across the globe. It seems to involve just about everyone, one way or another.
Manila is... gone.
We've seen some evidence of terrorist attacks in the continental U.S., but no enemy forces. Alaska and Hawaii are a different story. And both sides are using what looks like Project Monolith tech.
It's bigger than just the war, too-- demonstrations, some of them a million strong. The E.S.A. launch facilities at Guiana were swarmed... torn down.
But... ***why***, Jack?
The Builders say it's ***us***, Willett. Or ***them***, really. Blades told the world what's up here, and the guns came out.
Pritchard's working with the observatory system on the *Chandelier*. He's learning everything he can, but so far it's all just ***visual***.
We know the Builders can receive audio and video, but they aren't letting us access those signals. It's just what we can ***see***, real-time.
But that's bad enough.

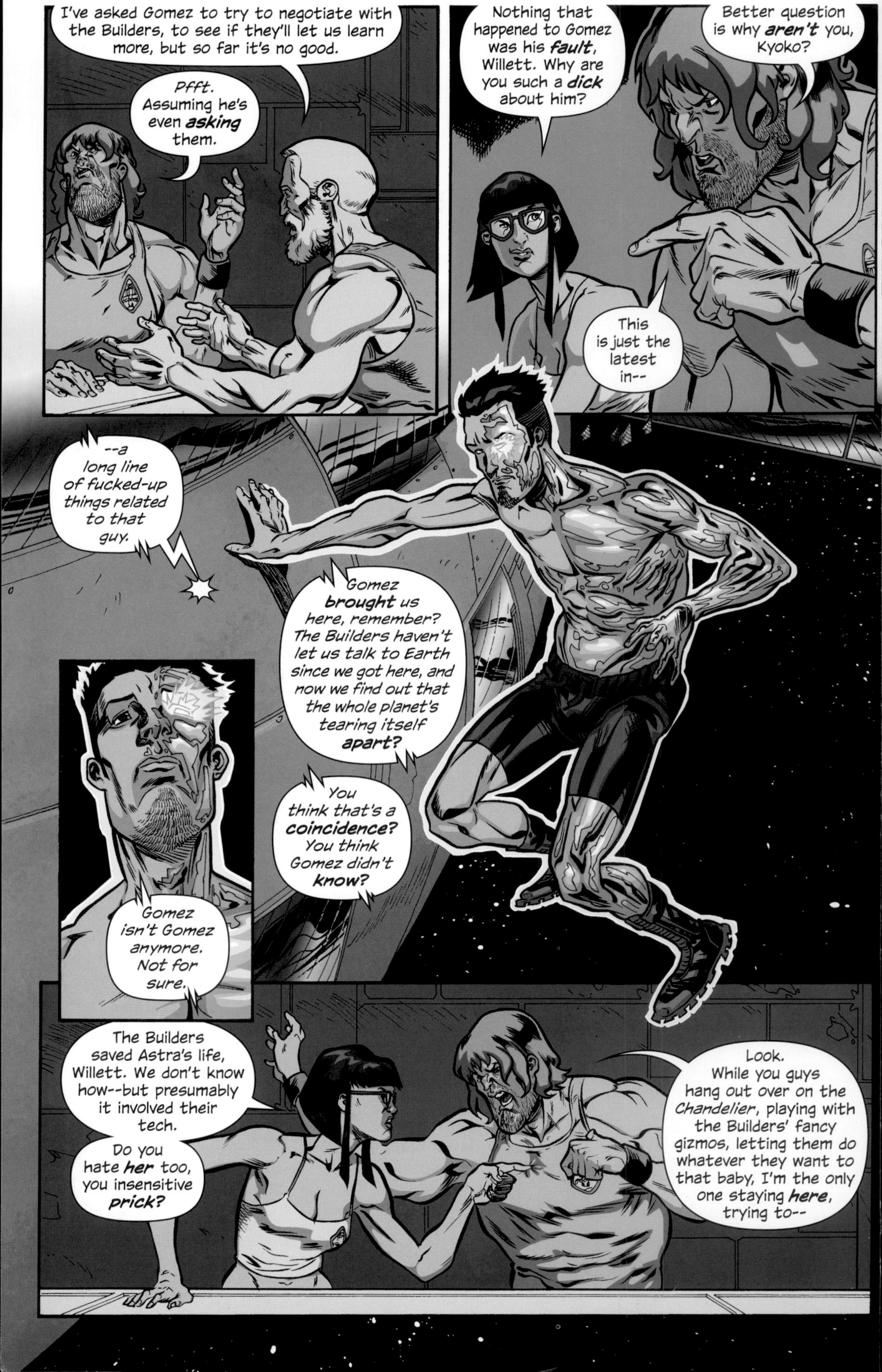
I've asked Gomez to try to negotiate with the Builders, to see if they'll let us learn more, but so far it's no good.
Pfft. Assuming he's even asking them.
Nothing that happened to Gomez was his fault, Willett. Why are you such a dick about him?
Better question is why aren't you, Kyoko?
This is just the latest in--
--a long line of fucked-up things related to that guy.
Gomez brought us here, remember? The Builders haven't let us talk to Earth since we got here, and now we find out that the whole planet's tearing itself apart?
You think that's a coincidence? You think Gomez didn't know?
Gomez isn't Gomez anymore. Not for sure.
The Builders saved Astra's life, Willett. We don't know how--but presumably it involved their tech.
Do you hate her too, you insensitive prick?
Look. While you guys hang out over on the Chandelier, playing with the Builders' fancy gizmos, letting them do whatever they want to that baby, I'm the only one staying here, trying to--

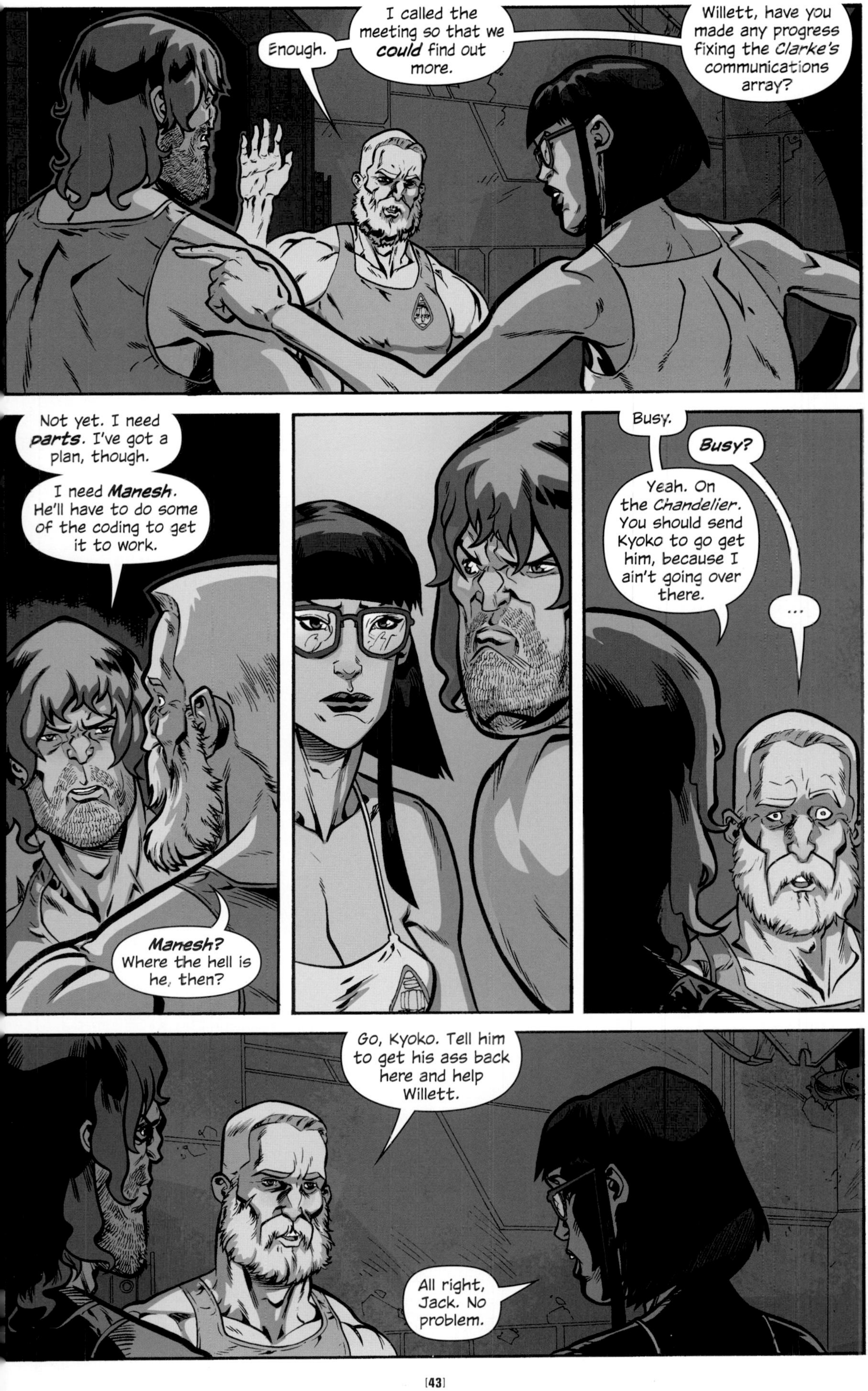
Enough.
I called the meeting so that we *could* find out more.
Willett, have you made any progress fixing the *Clarke's* communications array?
Not yet. I need *parts*. I've got a plan, though.
I need *Manesh*. He'll have to do some of the coding to get it to work.
Manesh? Where the hell is he, then?
Busy.
Busy?
Yeah. On the *Chandelier*. You should send Kyoko to go get him, because I ain't going over there.
...
Go, Kyoko. Tell him to get his ass back here and help Willett.
All right, Jack. No problem.

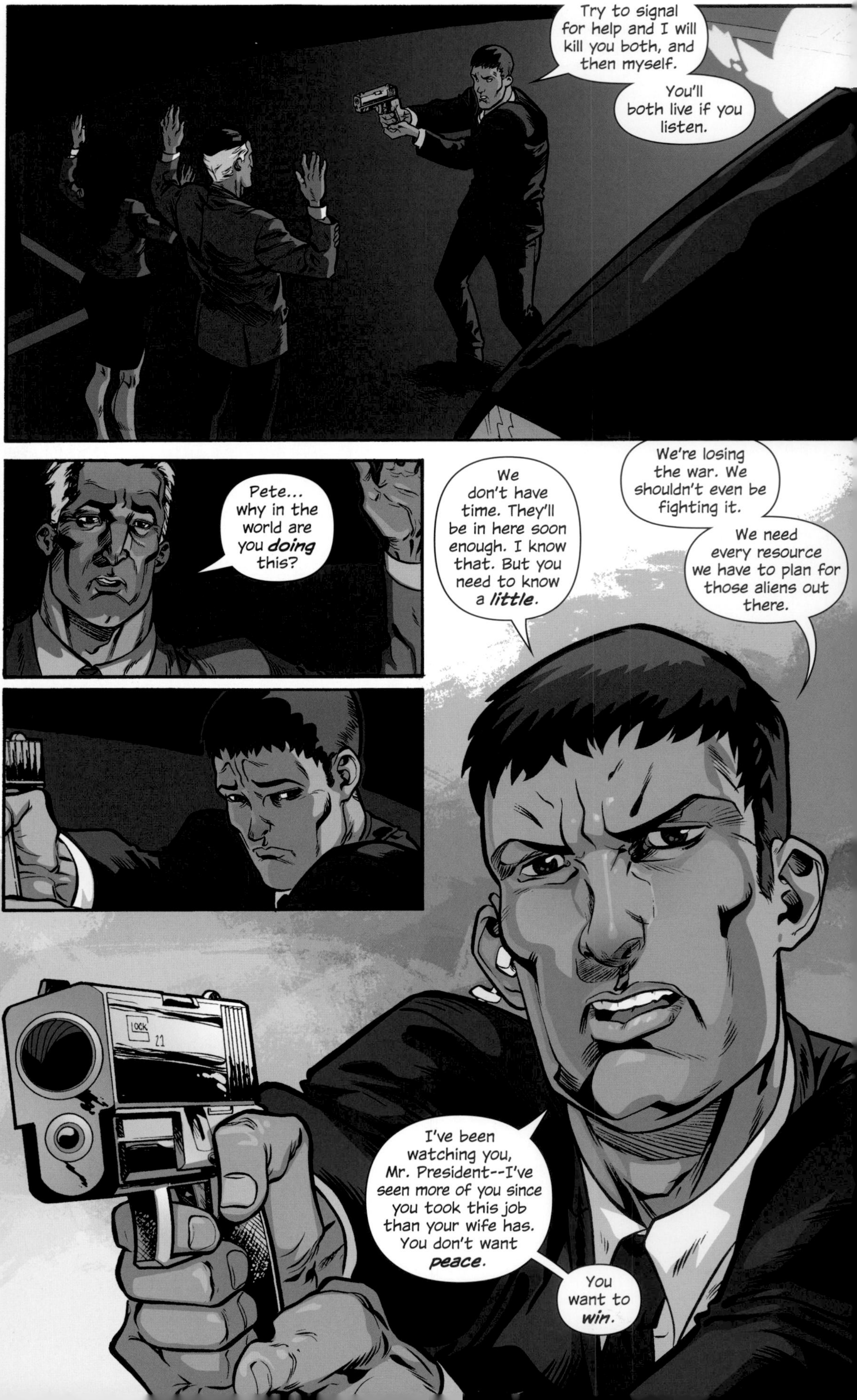
Try to signal for help and I will kill you both, and then myself.
You'll both live if you listen.
Pete... why in the world are you *doing* this?
We don't have time. They'll be in here soon enough. I know that. But you need to know a *little*.
We're losing the war. We shouldn't even be fighting it.
We need every resource we have to plan for those aliens out there.
I've been watching you, Mr. President--I've seen more of you since you took this job than your wife has. You don't want *peace*.
You want to *win*.

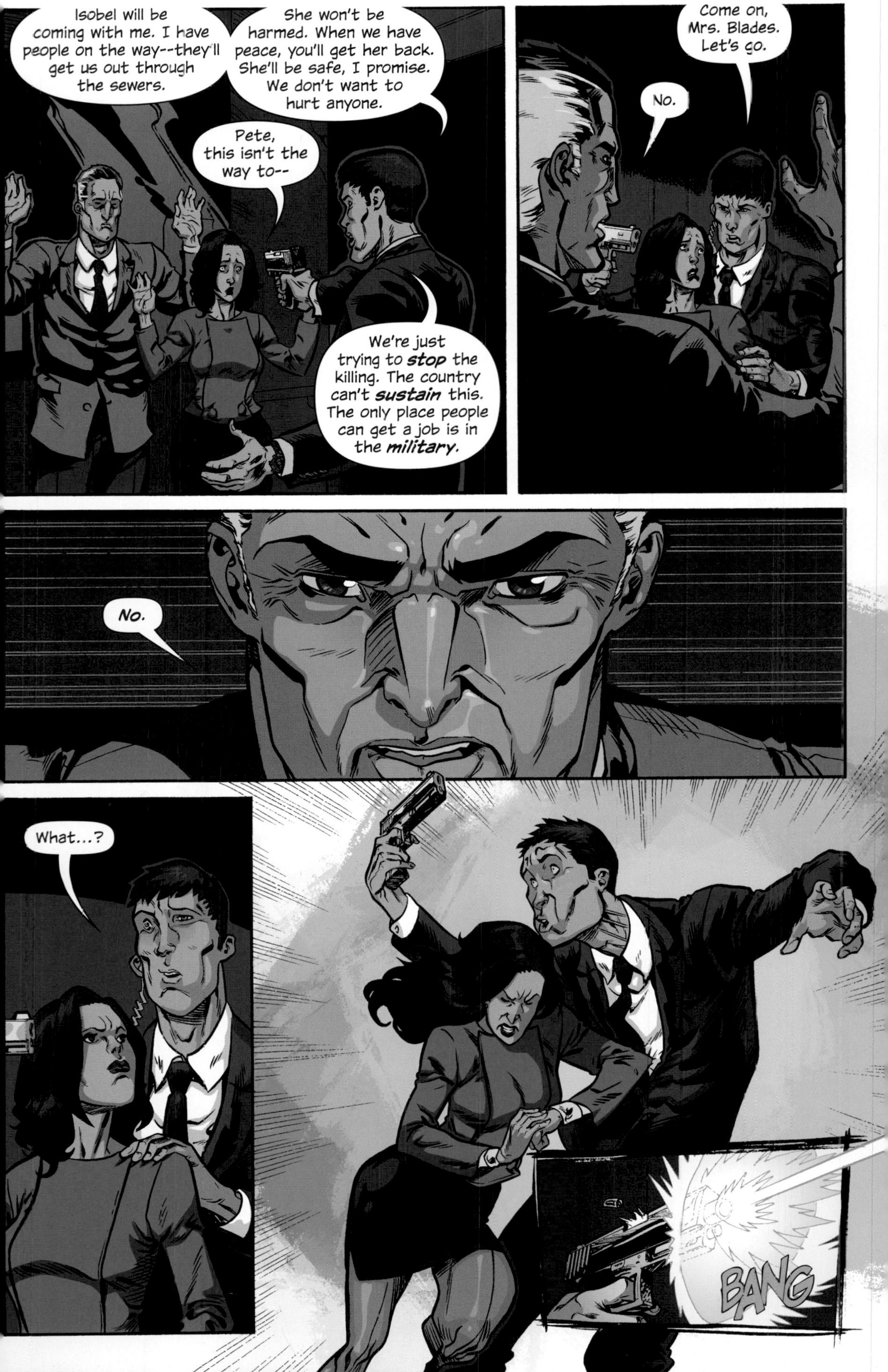
Isobel will be coming with me. I have people on the way--they'll get us out through the sewers.
She won't be harmed. When we have peace, you'll get her back. She'll be safe, I promise. We don't want to hurt anyone.
Pete, this isn't the way to--
We're just trying to *stop* the killing. The country can't *sustain* this. The only place people can get a job is in the *military*.
Come on, Mrs. Blades. Let's go.
No.
No.
What...?
BANG

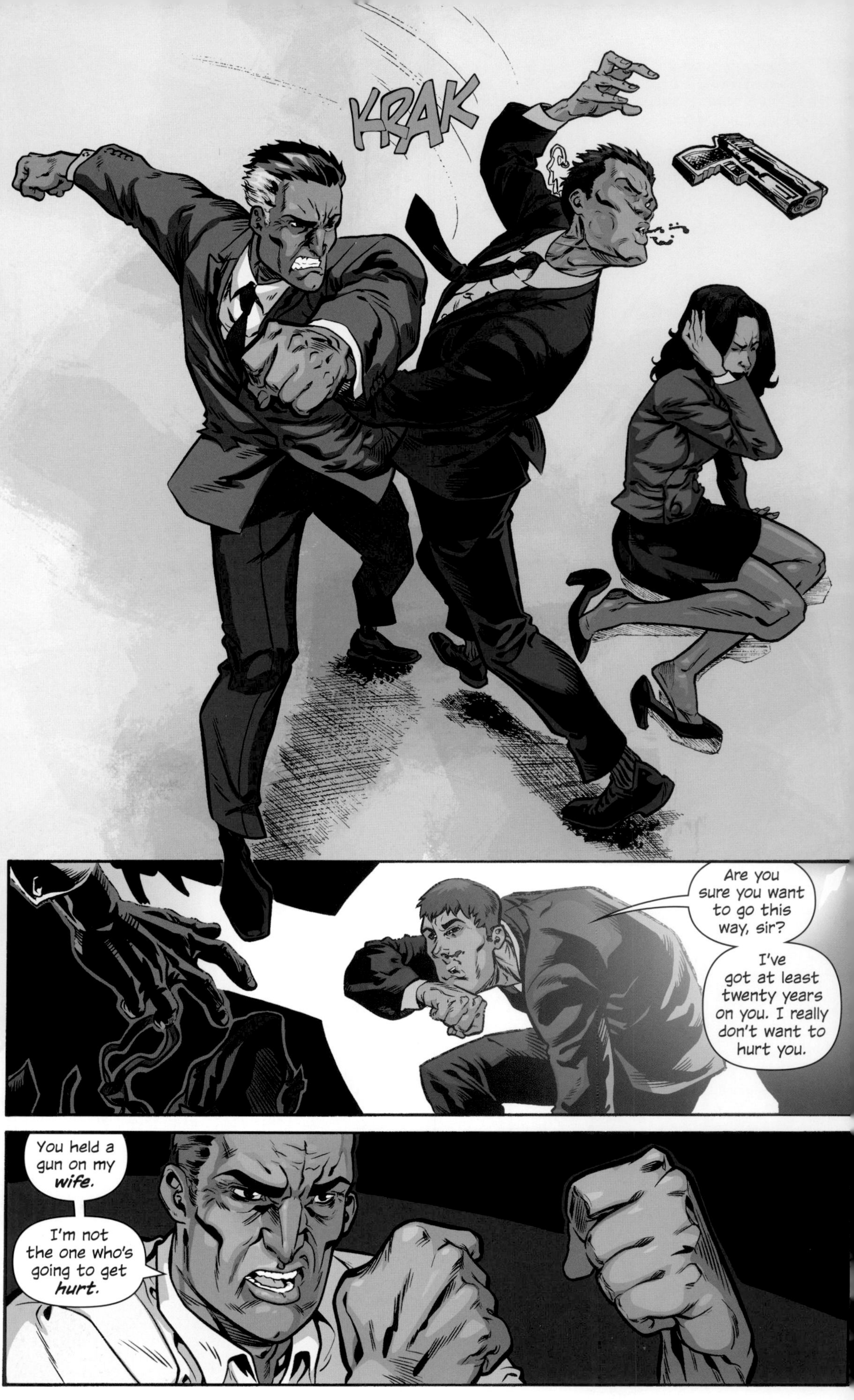
KRAK
Are you sure you want to go this way, sir?
I've got at least twenty years on you. I really don't want to hurt you.
You held a gun on my *wife.*
I'm not the one who's going to get *hurt.*

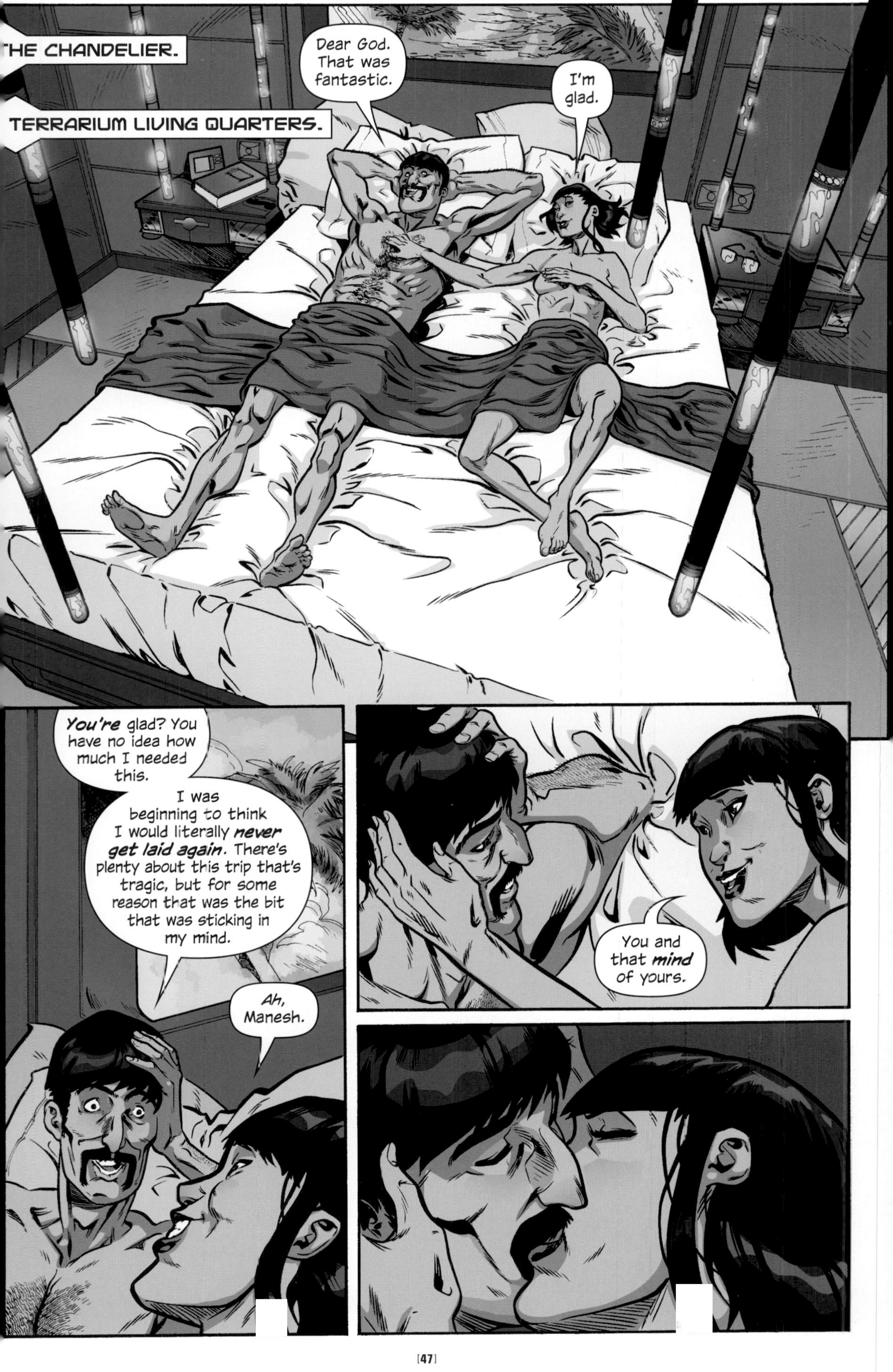
THE CHANDELIER.
TERRARIUM LIVING QUARTERS.
Dear God. That was fantastic.
I'm glad.
You're glad? You have no idea how much I needed this.
I was beginning to think I would literally never get laid again. There's plenty about this trip that's tragic, but for some reason that was the bit that was sticking in my mind.
Ah, Manesh.
You and that mind of yours.

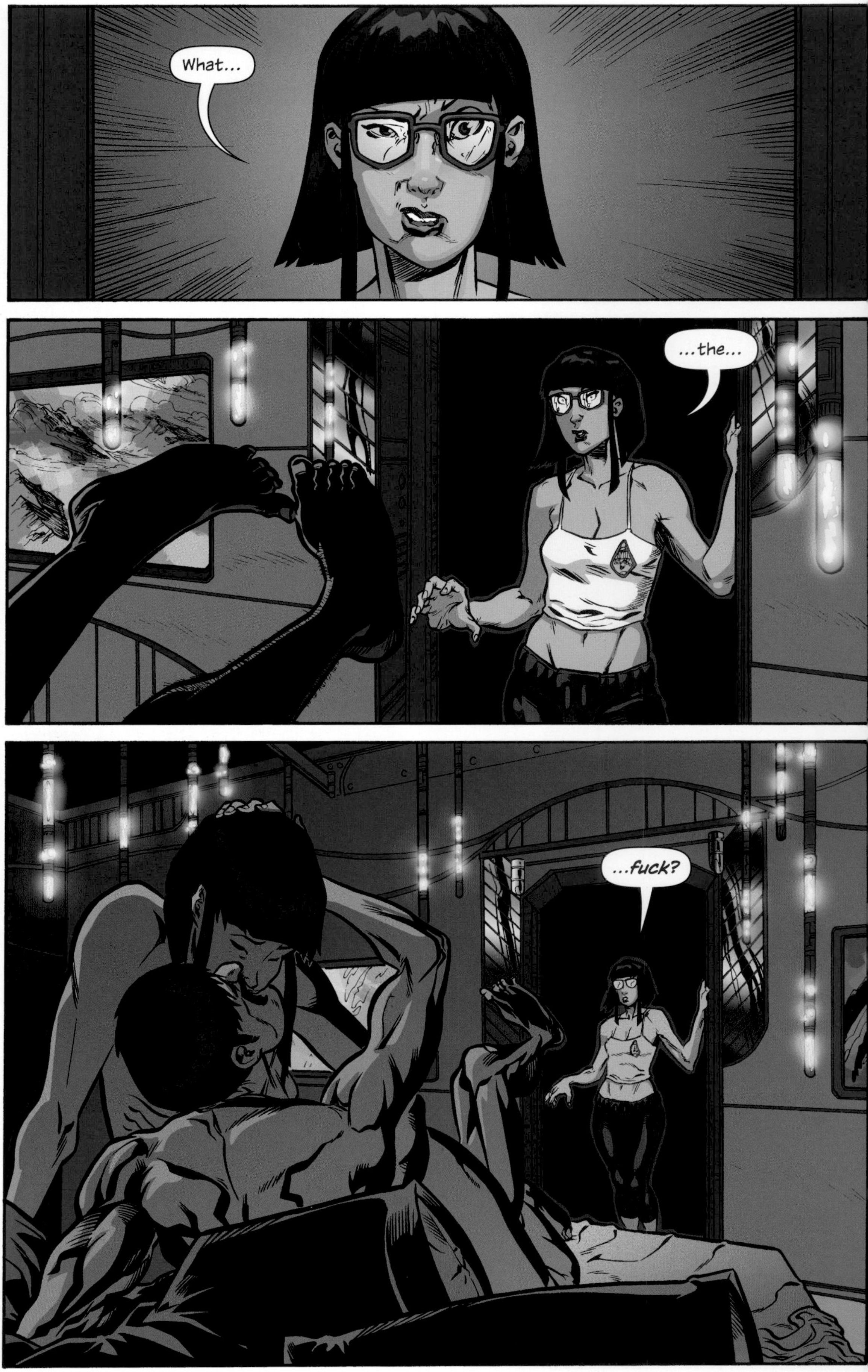
What...
...the...
...fuck?

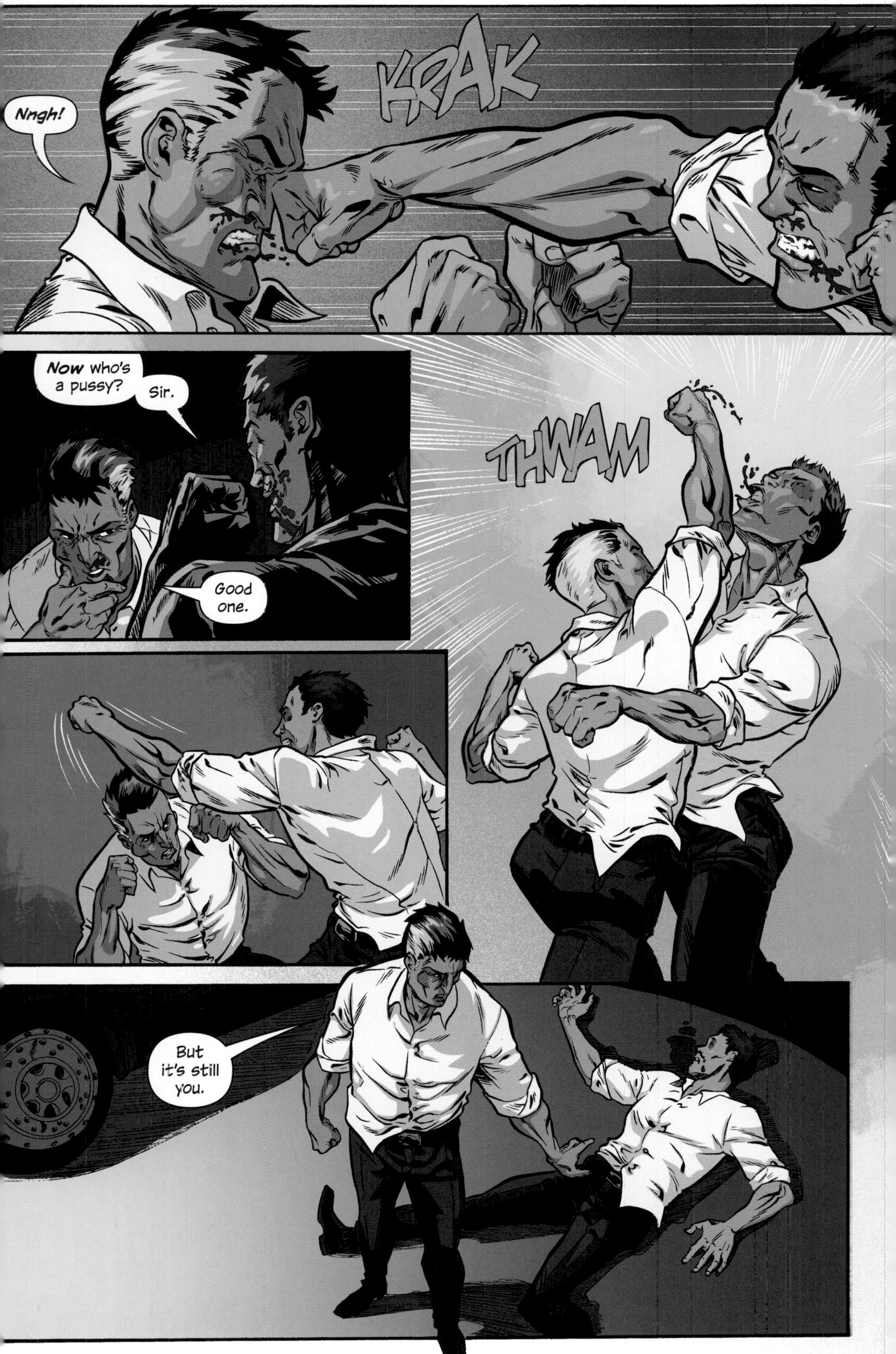
Nngh!
KRAK
Now who's a pussy?
Sir.
Good one.
THWAM
But it's still you.

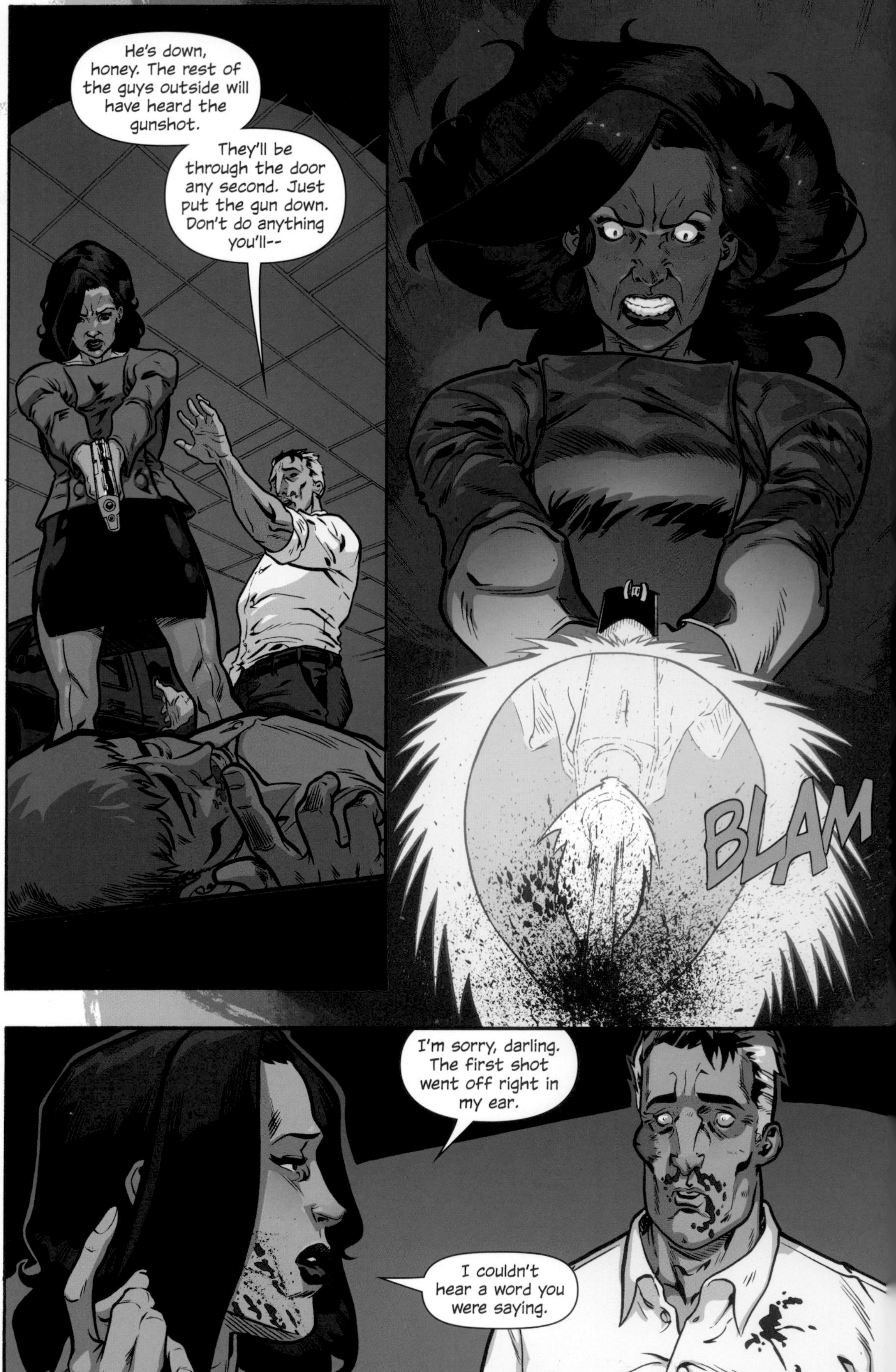
He's down, honey. The rest of the guys outside will have heard the gunshot.
They'll be through the door any second. Just put the gun down. Don't do anything you'll--
BLAM
I'm sorry, darling. The first shot went off right in my ear.
I couldn't hear a word you were saying.

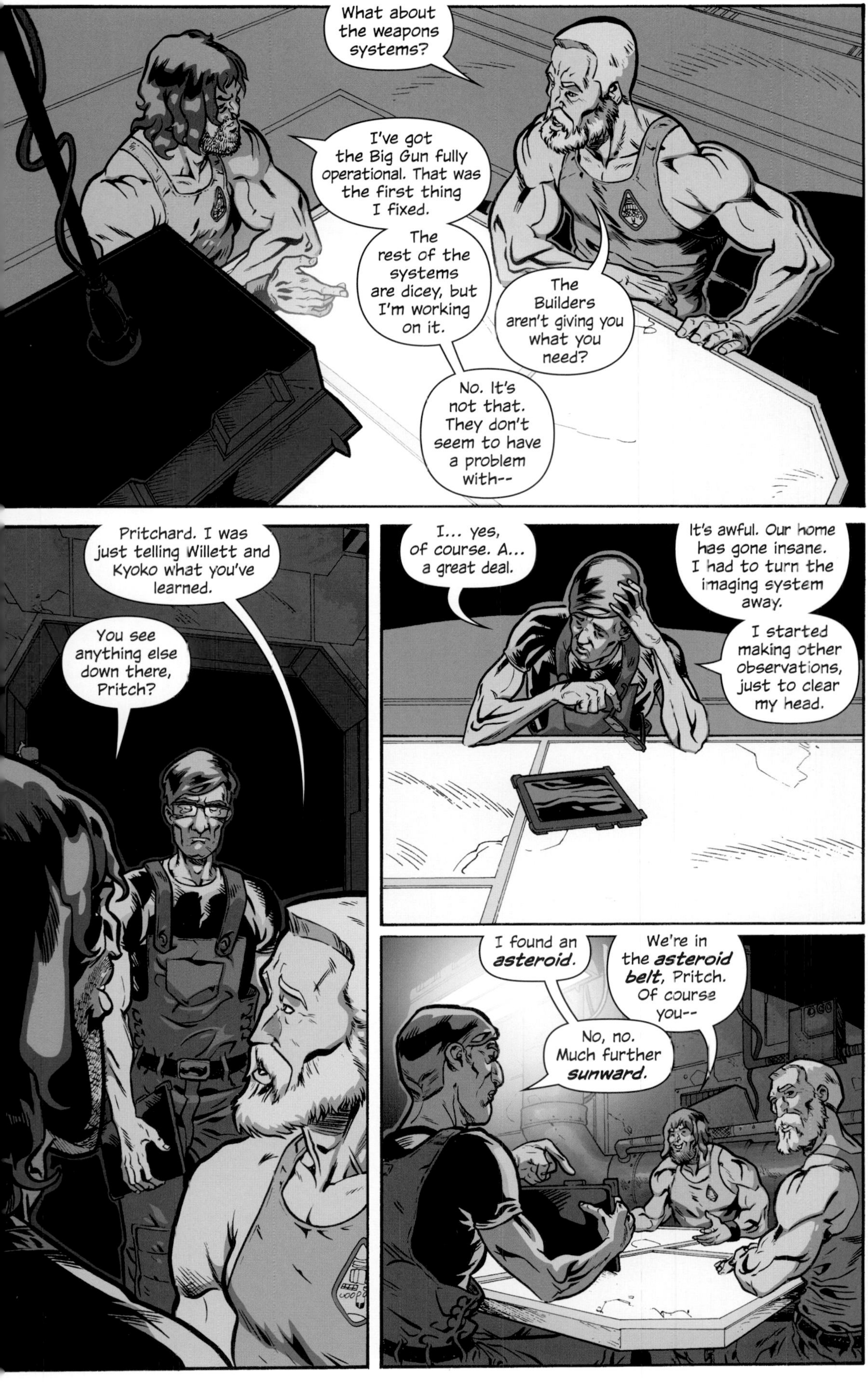
What about the weapons systems?
I've got the Big Gun fully operational. That was the first thing I fixed.
The rest of the systems are dicey, but I'm working on it.
The Builders aren't giving you what you need?
No. It's not that. They don't seem to have a problem with--
Pritchard. I was just telling Willett and Kyoko what you've learned.
You see anything else down there, Pritch?
I... yes, of course. A... a great deal.
It's awful. Our home has gone insane. I had to turn the imaging system away.
I started making other observations, just to clear my head.
I found an *asteroid*.
We're in the *asteroid belt*, Pritch. Of course you--
No, no. Much further *sunward*.

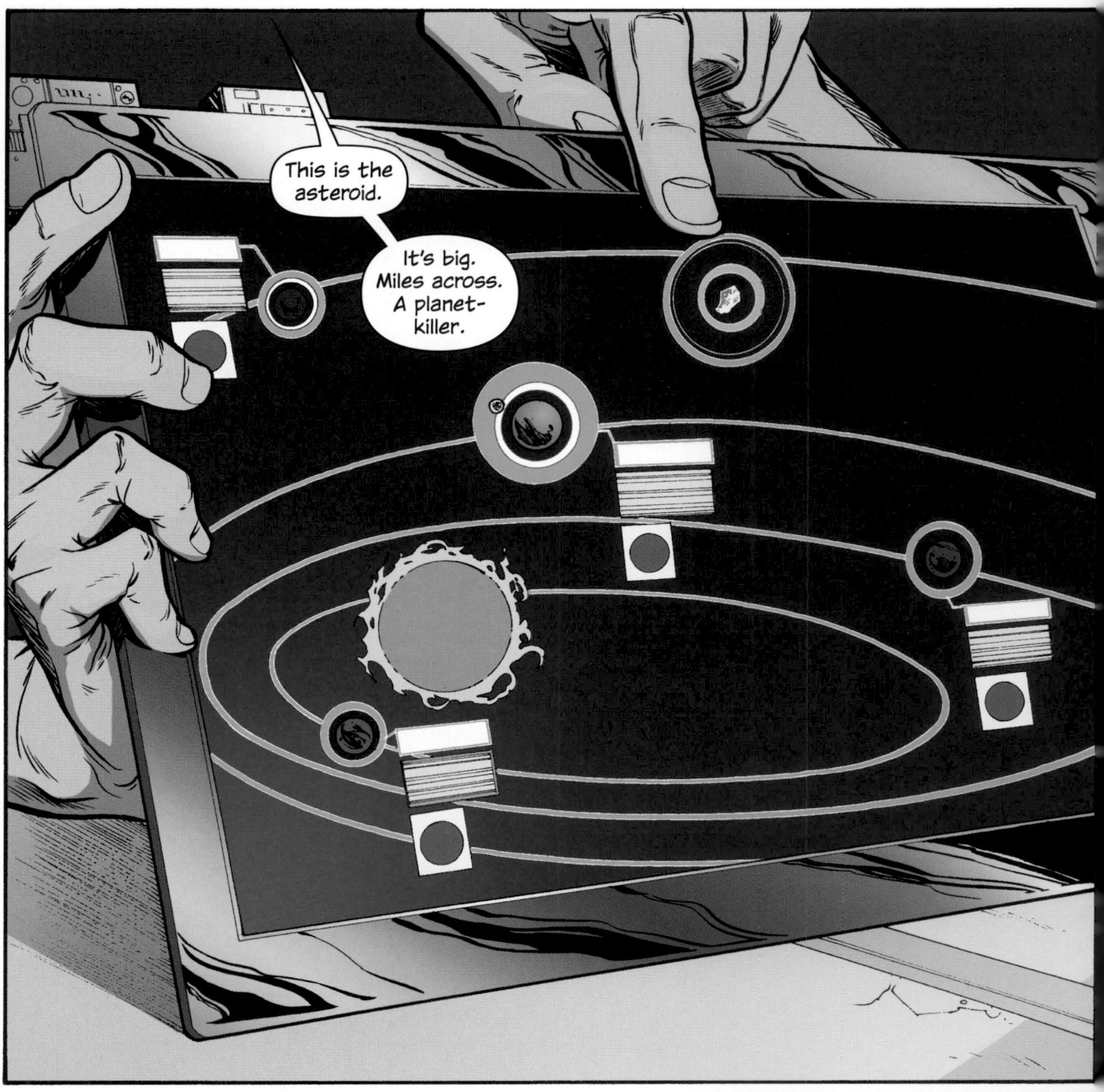
This is the asteroid.
It's big. Miles across. A planet-killer.

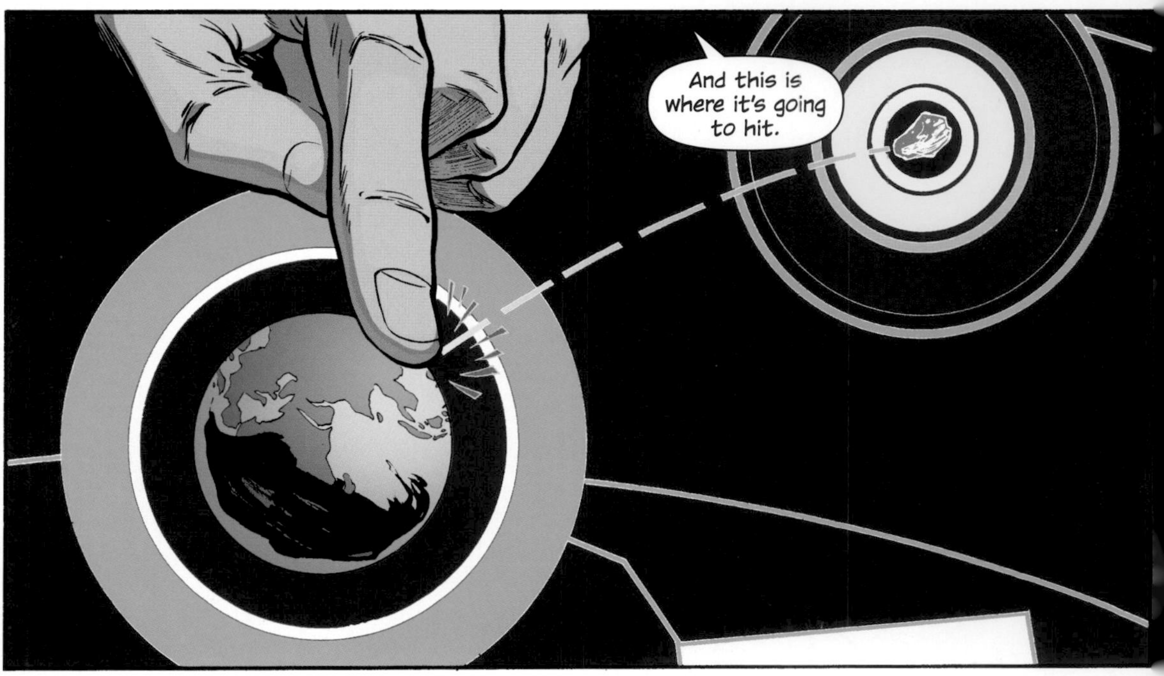
And this is where it's going to hit.

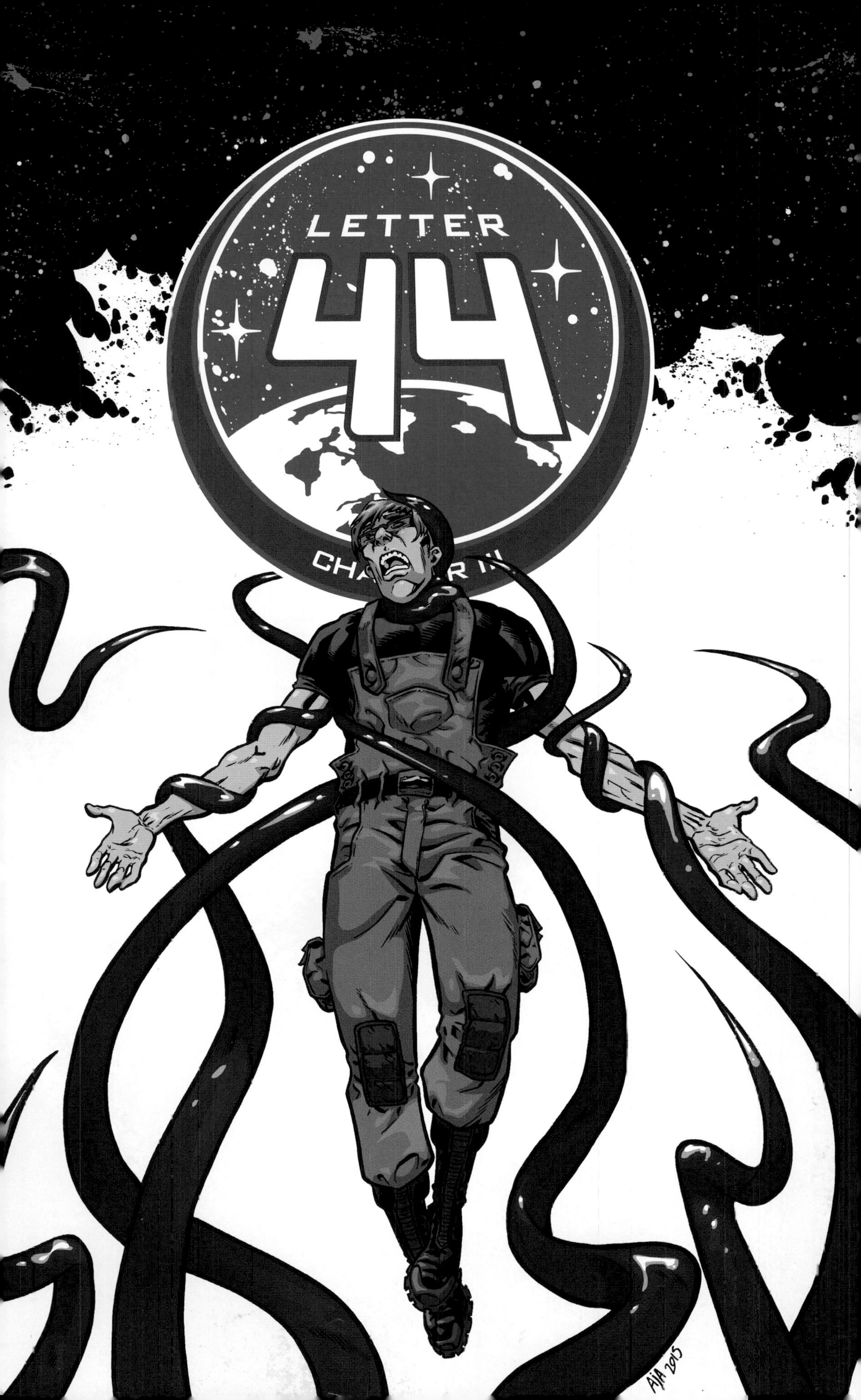
LETTER
44

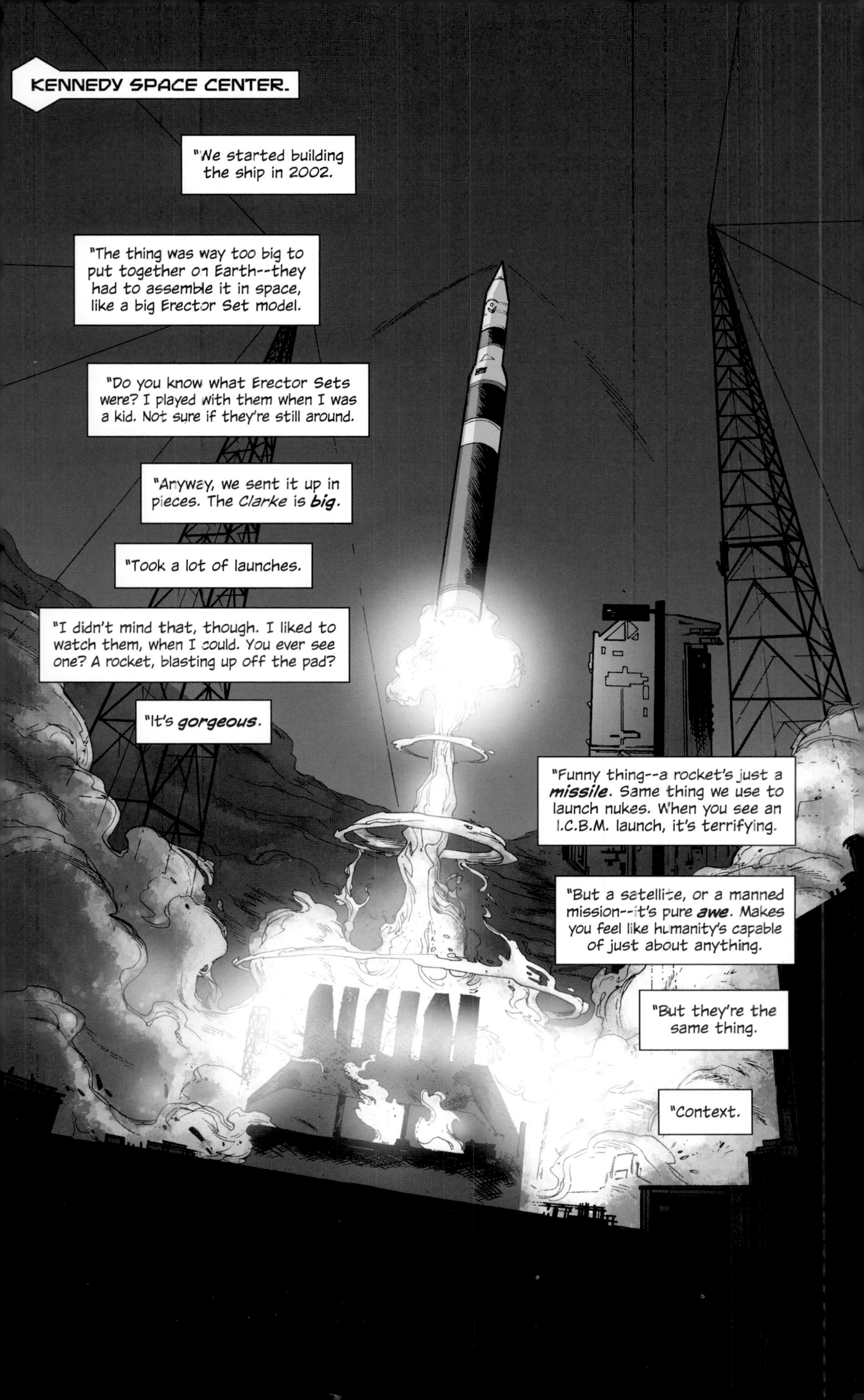
KENNEDY SPACE CENTER.
"We started building the ship in 2002.
"The thing was way too big to put together on Earth--they had to assemble it in space, like a big Erector Set model.
"Do you know what Erector Sets were? I played with them when I was a kid. Not sure if they're still around.
"Anyway, we sent it up in pieces. The *Clarke* is ***big.***
"Took a lot of launches.
"I didn't mind that, though. I liked to watch them, when I could. You ever see one? A rocket, blasting up off the pad?
"It's ***gorgeous.***
"Funny thing--a rocket's just a ***missile.*** Same thing we use to launch nukes. When you see an I.C.B.M. launch, it's terrifying.
"But a satellite, or a manned mission--it's pure ***awe.*** Makes you feel like humanity's capable of just about anything.
"But they're the same thing.
"Context.

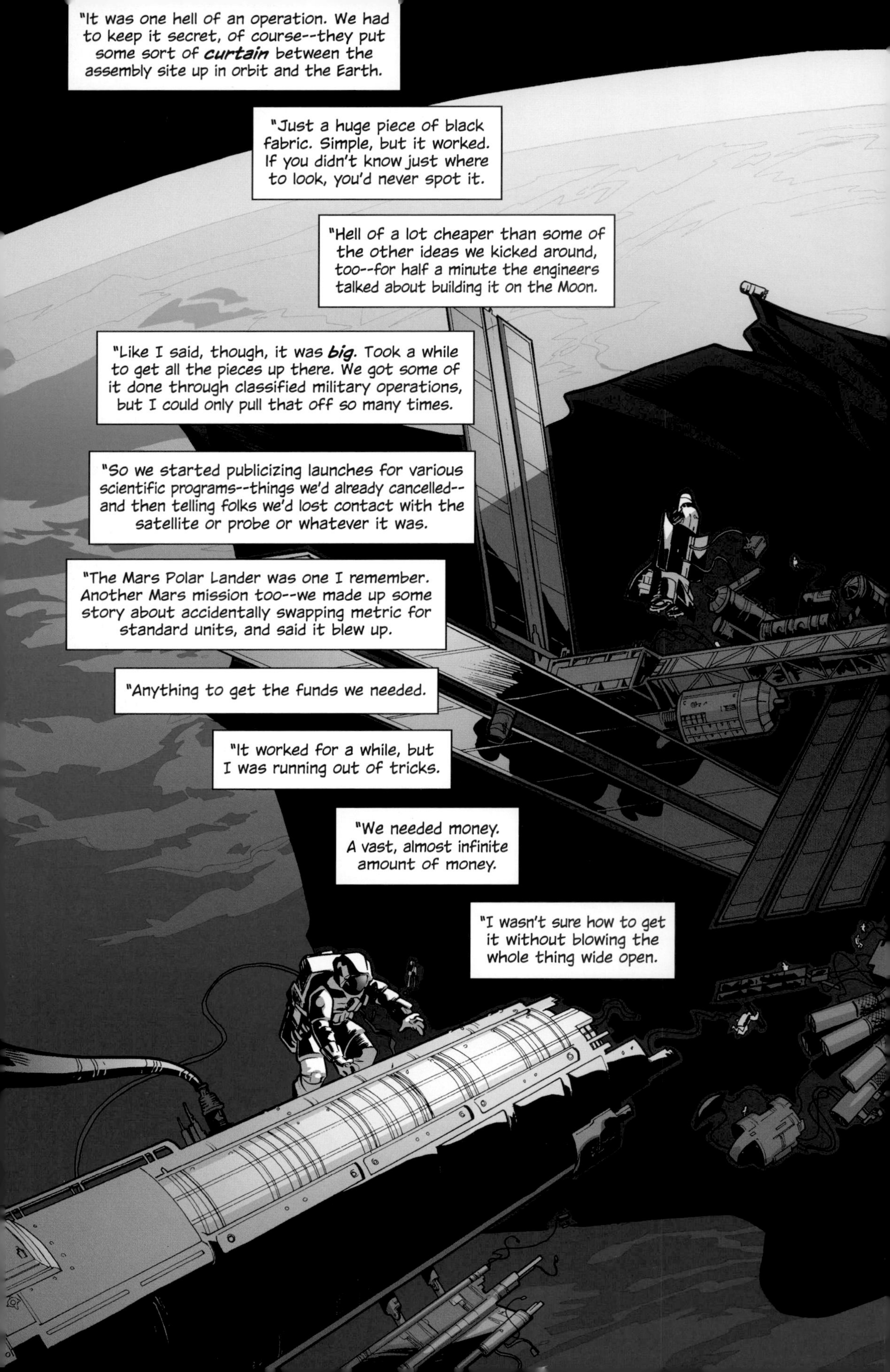
"It was one hell of an operation. We had to keep it secret, of course--they put some sort of *curtain* between the assembly site up in orbit and the Earth.
"Just a huge piece of black fabric. Simple, but it worked. If you didn't know just where to look, you'd never spot it.
"Hell of a lot cheaper than some of the other ideas we kicked around, too--for half a minute the engineers talked about building it on the Moon.
"Like I said, though, it was *big*. Took a while to get all the pieces up there. We got some of it done through classified military operations, but I could only pull that off so many times.
"So we started publicizing launches for various scientific programs--things we'd already cancelled--and then telling folks we'd lost contact with the satellite or probe or whatever it was.
"The Mars Polar Lander was one I remember. Another Mars mission too--we made up some story about accidentally swapping metric for standard units, and said it blew up.
"Anything to get the funds we needed.
"It worked for a while, but I was running out of tricks.
"We needed money. A vast, almost infinite amount of money.
"I wasn't sure how to get it without blowing the whole thing wide open.

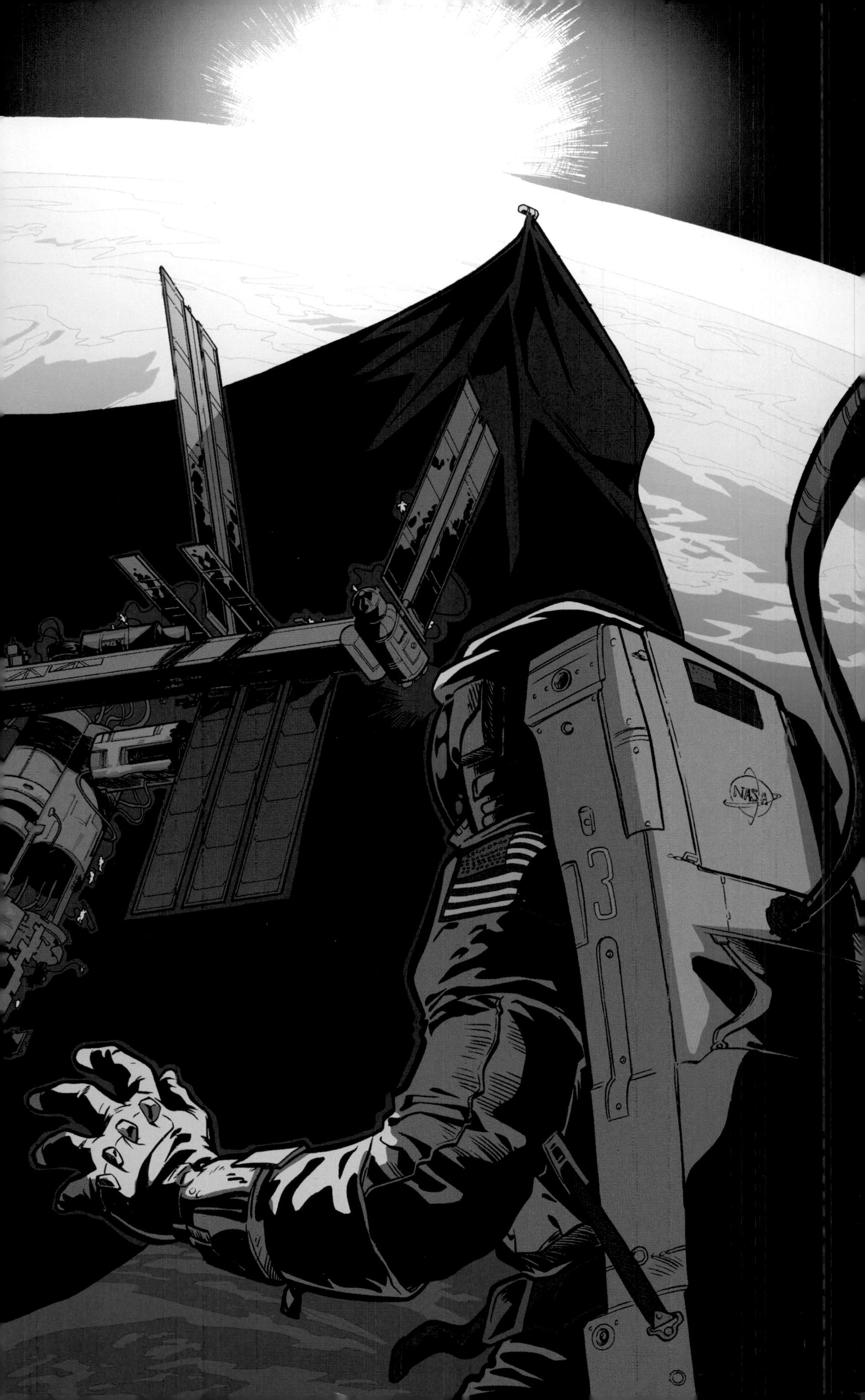
NASA

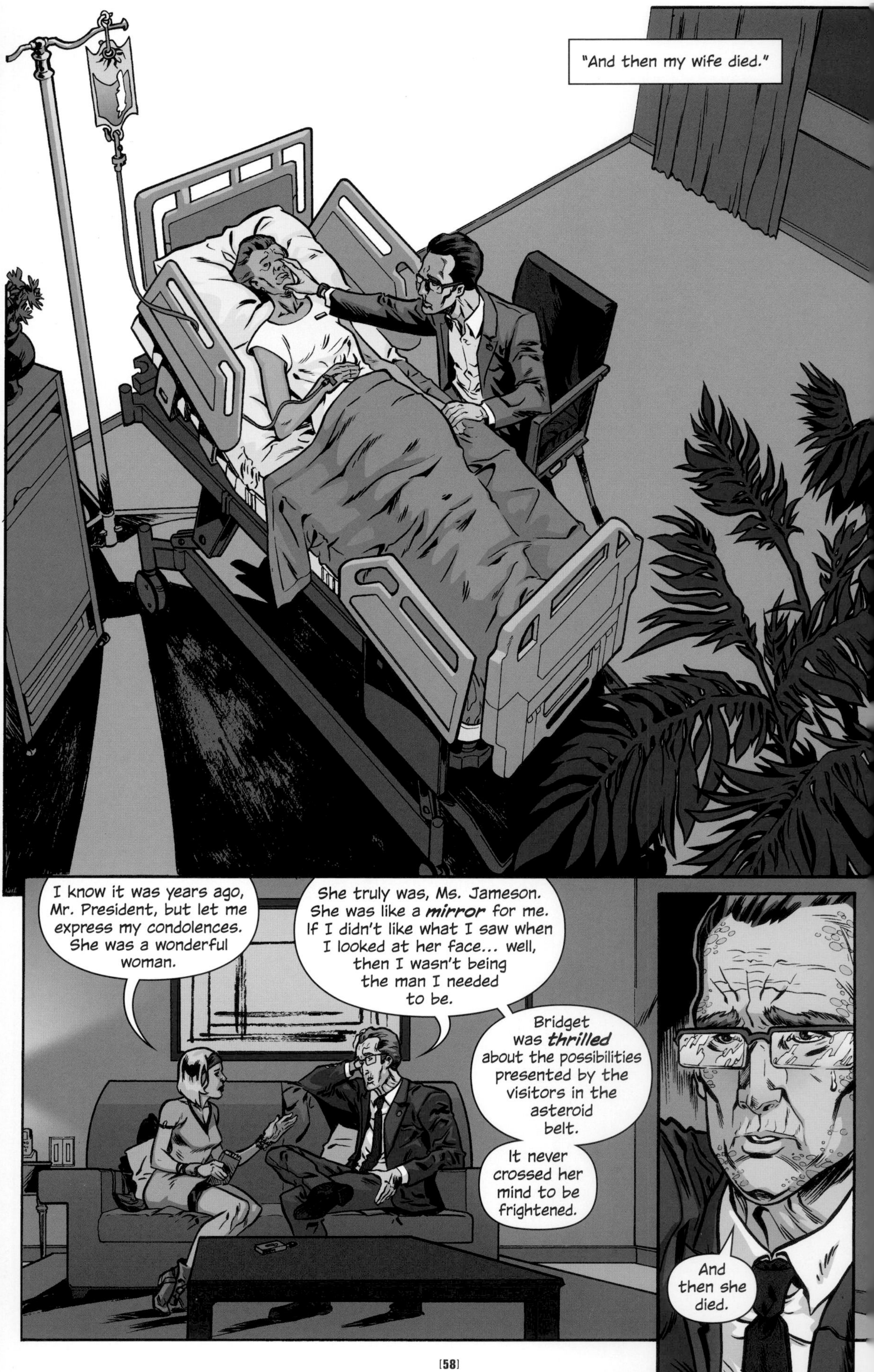
"And then my wife died."
I know it was years ago, Mr. President, but let me express my condolences. She was a wonderful woman.
She truly was, Ms. Jameson. She was like a *mirror* for me. If I didn't like what I saw when I looked at her face... well, then I wasn't being the man I needed to be.
Bridget was *thrilled* about the possibilities presented by the visitors in the asteroid belt.
It never crossed her mind to be frightened.
And then she died.

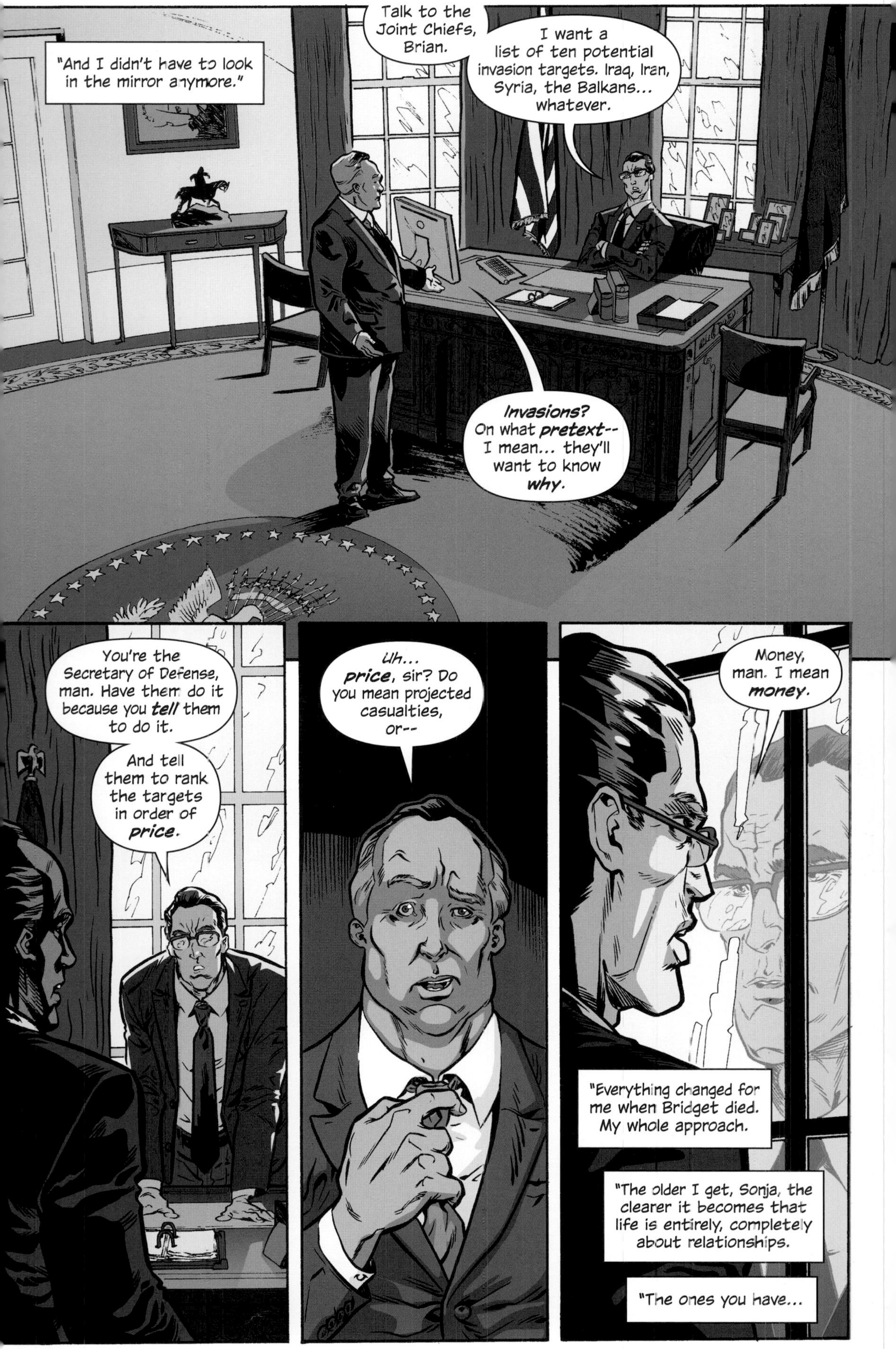
"And I didn't have to look in the mirror anymore."
Talk to the Joint Chiefs, Brian.
I want a list of ten potential invasion targets. Iraq, Iran, Syria, the Balkans... whatever.
Invasions? On what *pretext*-- I mean... they'll want to know *why*.
You're the Secretary of Defense, man. Have them do it because you *tell* them to do it.
And tell them to rank the targets in order of *price*.
Uh... price, sir? Do you mean projected casualties, or--
Money, man. I mean *money*.
"Everything changed for me when Bridget died. My whole approach.
"The older I get, Sonja, the clearer it becomes that life is entirely, completely about relationships.
"The ones you have...

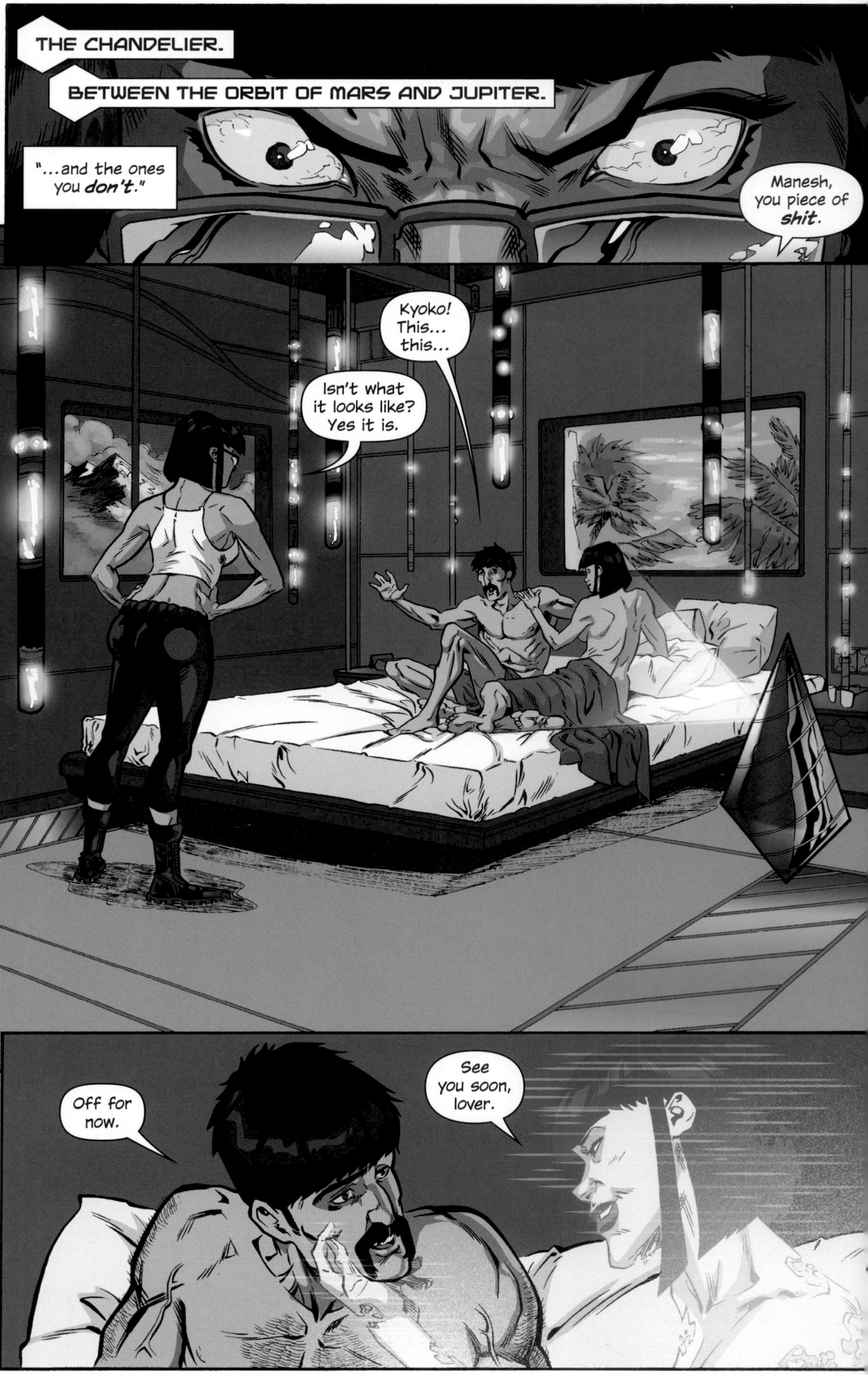
THE CHANDELIER.
BETWEEN THE ORBIT OF MARS AND JUPITER.
"...and the ones you *don't*."
Manesh, you piece of *shit*.
Kyoko! This... this...
Isn't what it looks like? Yes it is.
Off for now.
See you soon, lover.

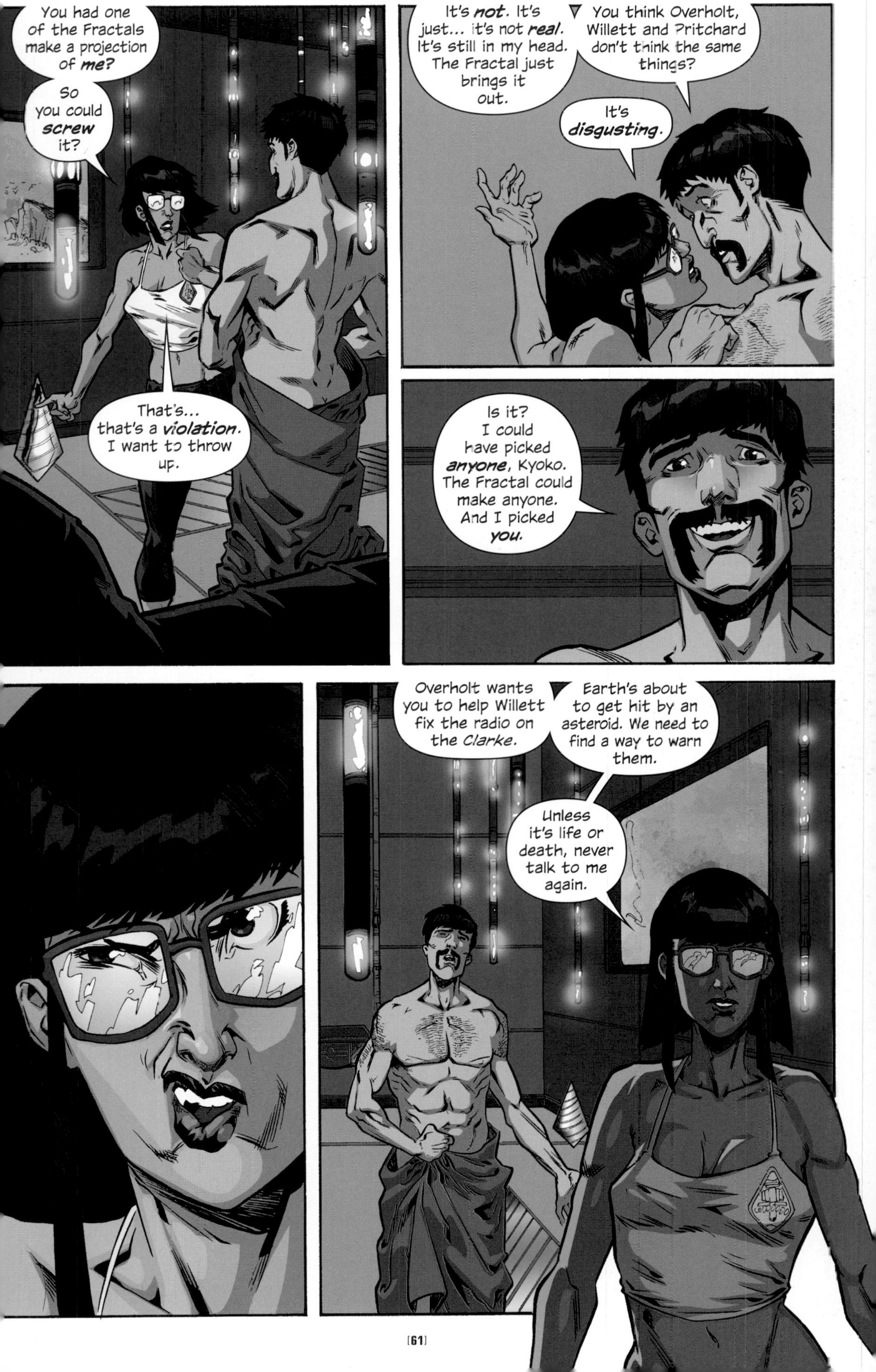

You had one of the Fractals make a projection of *me?*
So you could *screw* it?
That's... that's a *violation*. I want to throw up.
It's *not*. It's just... it's not *real*. It's still in my head. The Fractal just brings it out.
You think Overholt, Willett and Pritchard don't think the same things?
It's *disgusting*.
Is it? I could have picked *anyone*, Kyoko. The Fractal could make anyone. And I picked *you*.
Overholt wants you to help Willett fix the radio on the *Clarke*.
Earth's about to get hit by an asteroid. We need to find a way to warn them.
Unless it's life or death, never talk to me again.

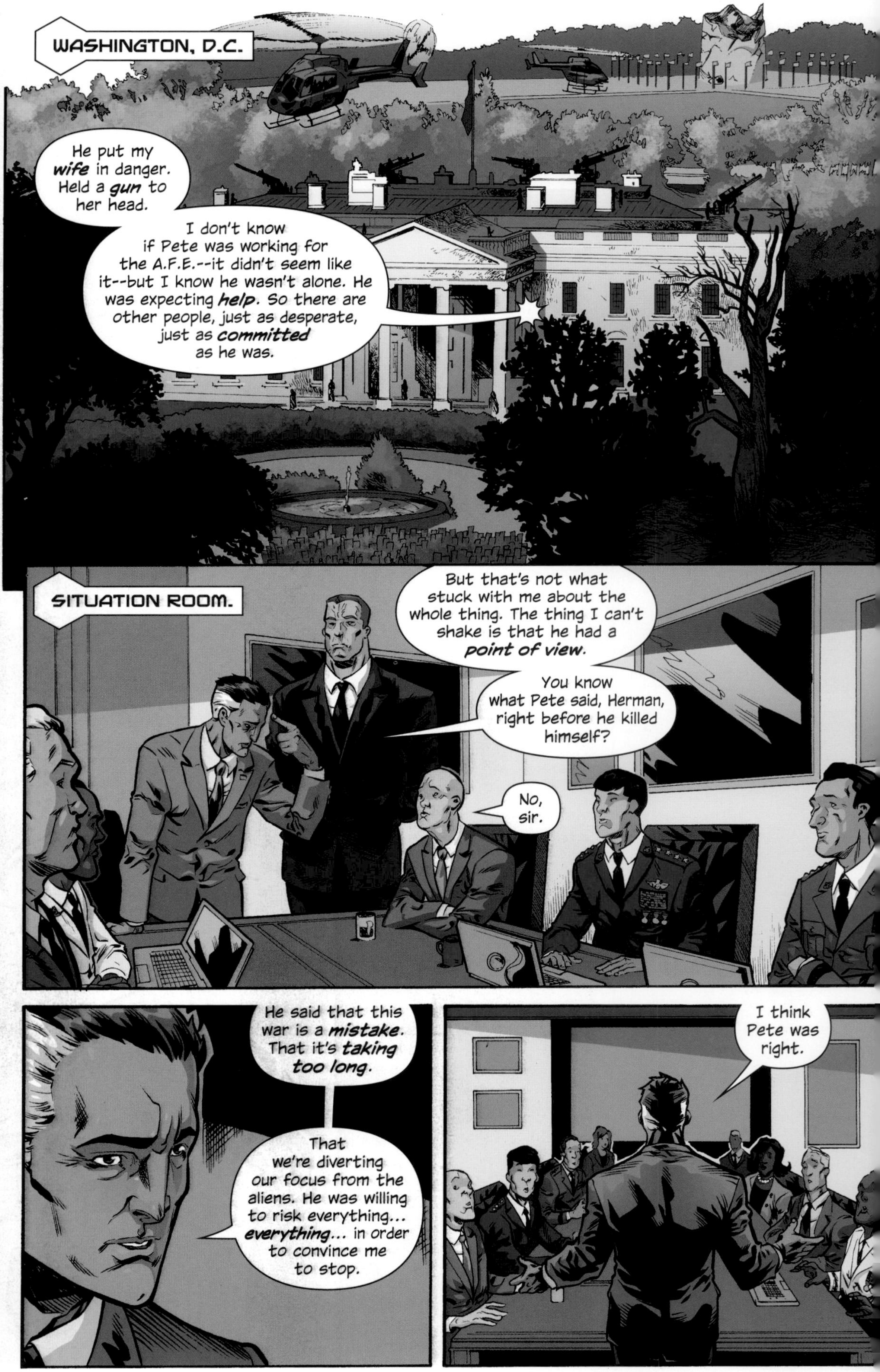
WASHINGTON, D.C.
He put my wife in danger. Held a gun to her head.
I don't know if Pete was working for the A.F.E.--it didn't seem like it--but I know he wasn't alone. He was expecting help. So there are other people, just as desperate, just as committed as he was.
SITUATION ROOM.
But that's not what stuck with me about the whole thing. The thing I can't shake is that he had a point of view.
You know what Pete said, Herman, right before he killed himself?
No, sir.
He said that this war is a mistake. That it's taking too long.
That we're diverting our focus from the aliens. He was willing to risk everything... everything... in order to convince me to stop.
I think Pete was right.

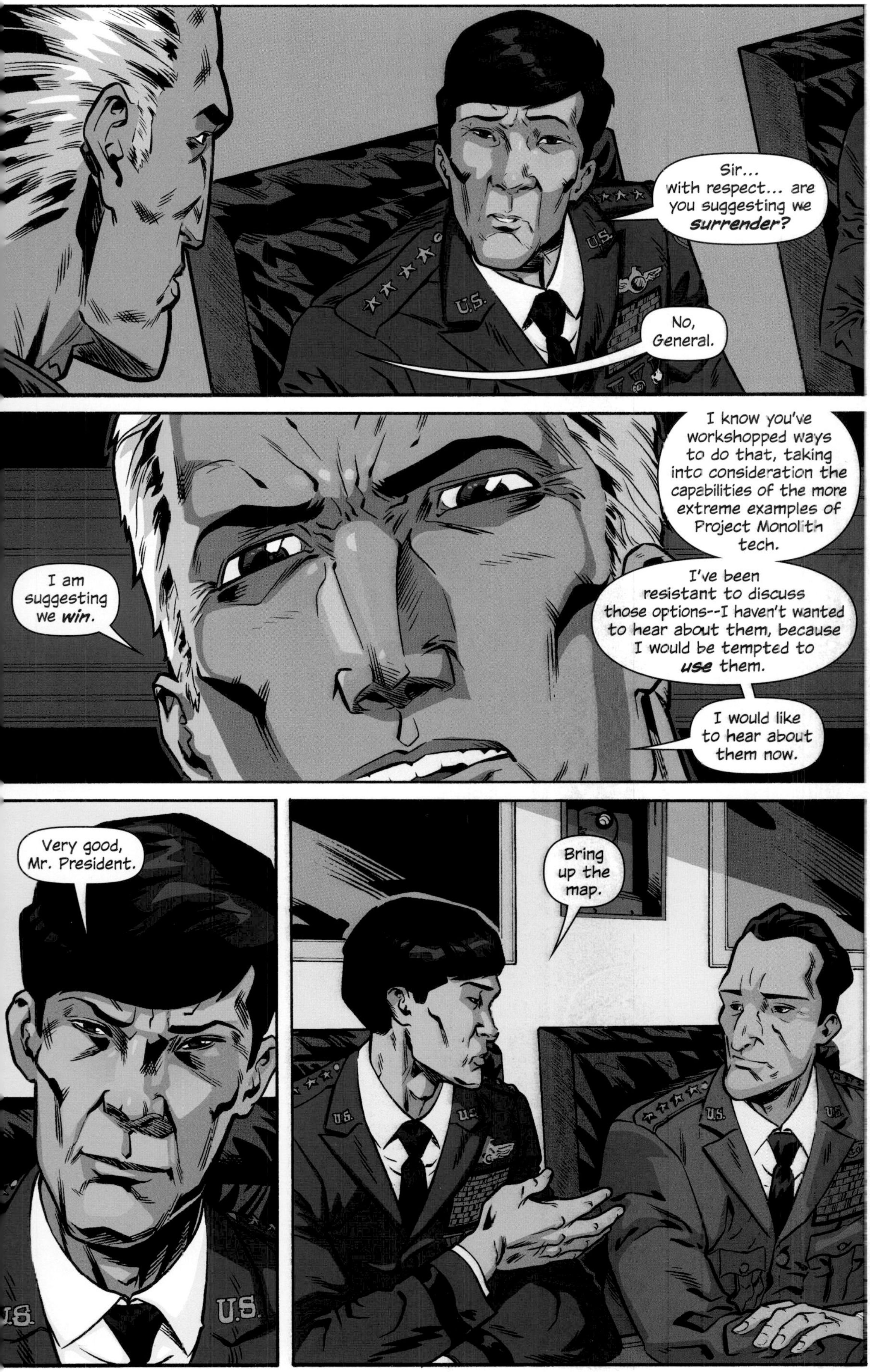
Sir... with respect... are you suggesting we *surrender?*
No, General.
I know you've workshopped ways to do that, taking into consideration the capabilities of the more extreme examples of Project Monolith tech.
I am suggesting we *win*.
I've been resistant to discuss those options--I haven't wanted to hear about them, because I would be tempted to *use* them.
I would like to hear about them now.
Very good, Mr. President.
Bring up the map.
U.S.
U.S.

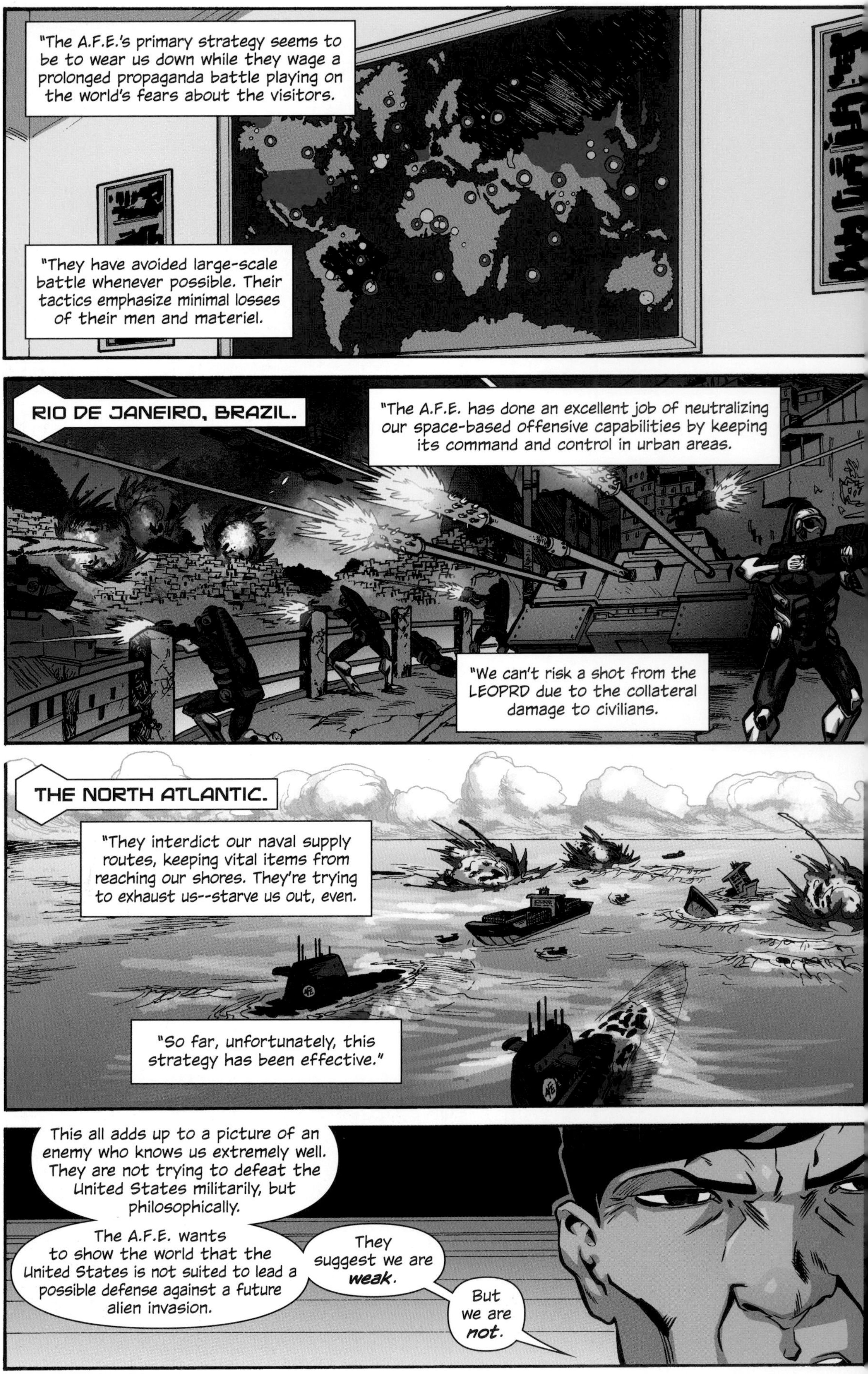
"The A.F.E.'s primary strategy seems to be to wear us down while they wage a prolonged propaganda battle playing on the world's fears about the visitors.
"They have avoided large-scale battle whenever possible. Their tactics emphasize minimal losses of their men and materiel.
RIO DE JANEIRO, BRAZIL.
"The A.F.E. has done an excellent job of neutralizing our space-based offensive capabilities by keeping its command and control in urban areas.
"We can't risk a shot from the LEOPRD due to the collateral damage to civilians.
THE NORTH ATLANTIC.
"They interdict our naval supply routes, keeping vital items from reaching our shores. They're trying to exhaust us--starve us out, even.
"So far, unfortunately, this strategy has been effective."
This all adds up to a picture of an enemy who knows us extremely well. They are not trying to defeat the United States militarily, but philosophically.
The A.F.E. wants to show the world that the United States is not suited to lead a possible defense against a future alien invasion.
They suggest we are *weak*.
But we are *not*.

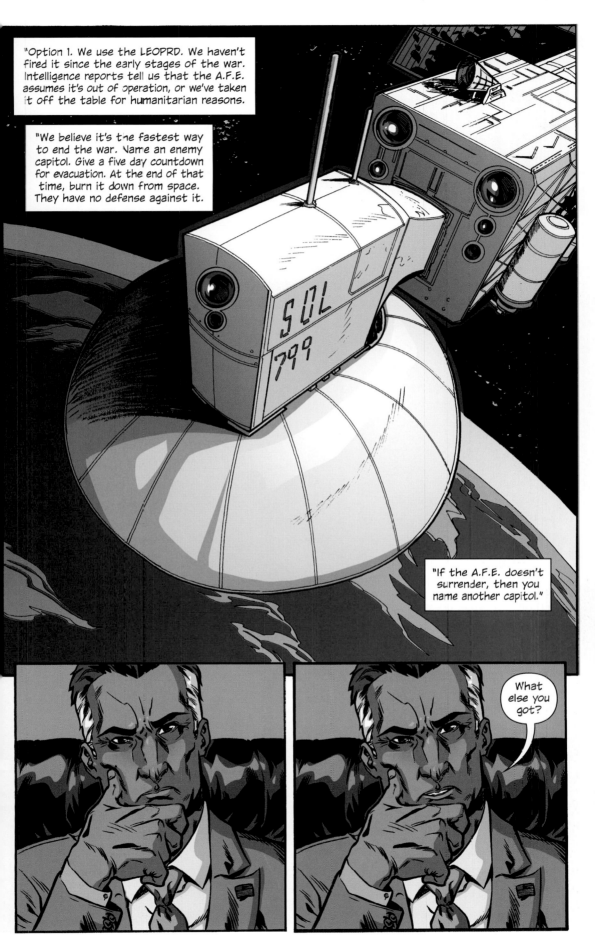

"Option 1. We use the LEOPRD. We haven't fired it since the early stages of the war. Intelligence reports tell us that the A.F.E. assumes it's out of operation, or we've taken it off the table for humanitarian reasons.

"We believe it's the fastest way to end the war. Name an enemy capitol. Give a five day countdown for evacuation. At the end of that time, burn it down from space. They have no defense against it.

"If the A.F.E. doesn't surrender, then you name another capitol."

What else you got?

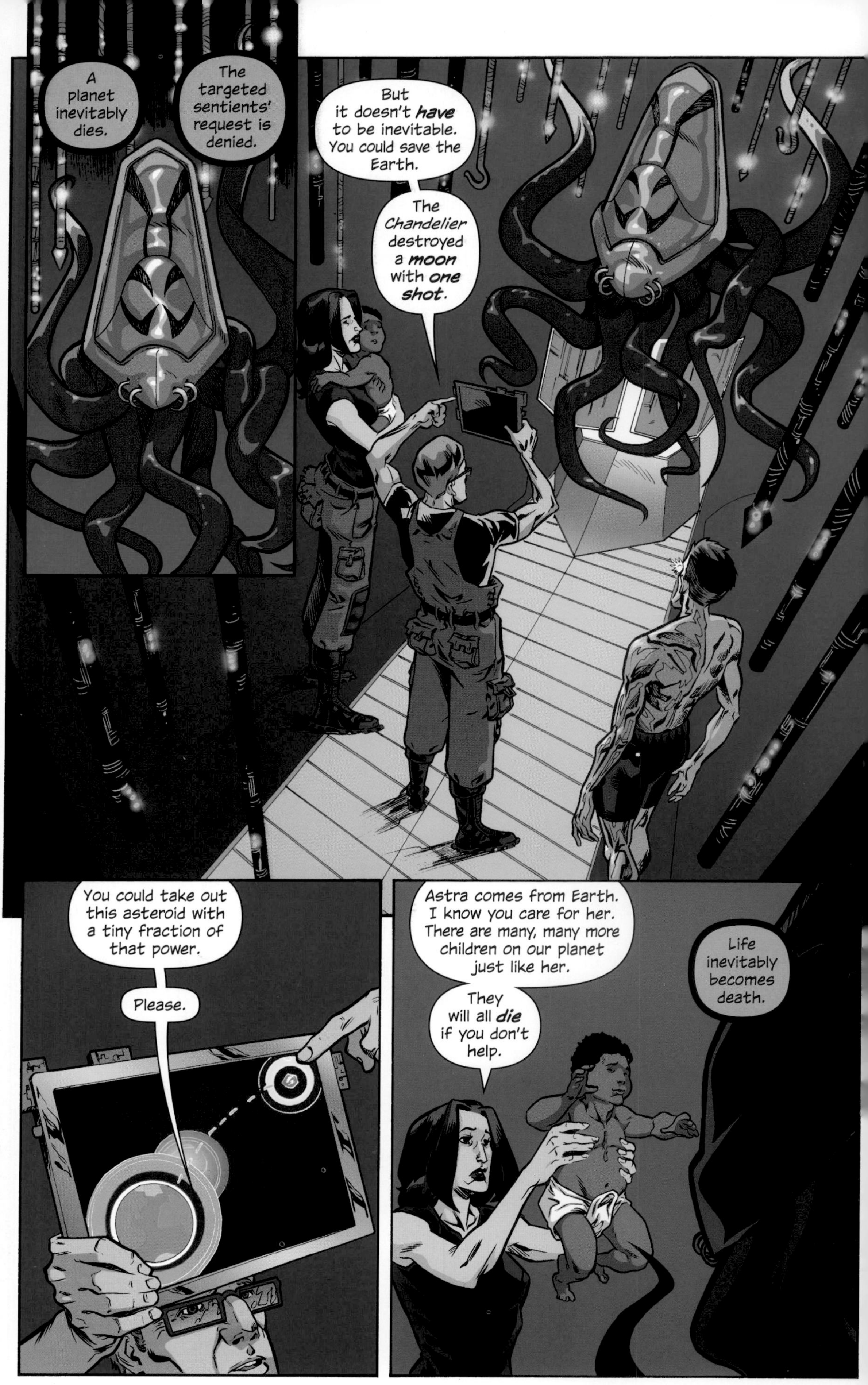
A planet inevitably dies.
The targeted sentients' request is denied.
But it doesn't *have* to be inevitable. You could save the Earth.
The *Chandelier* destroyed a *moon* with *one shot*.
You could take out this asteroid with a tiny fraction of that power.
Please.
Astra comes from Earth. I know you care for her. There are many, many more children on our planet just like her.
They will all *die* if you don't help.
Life inevitably becomes death.

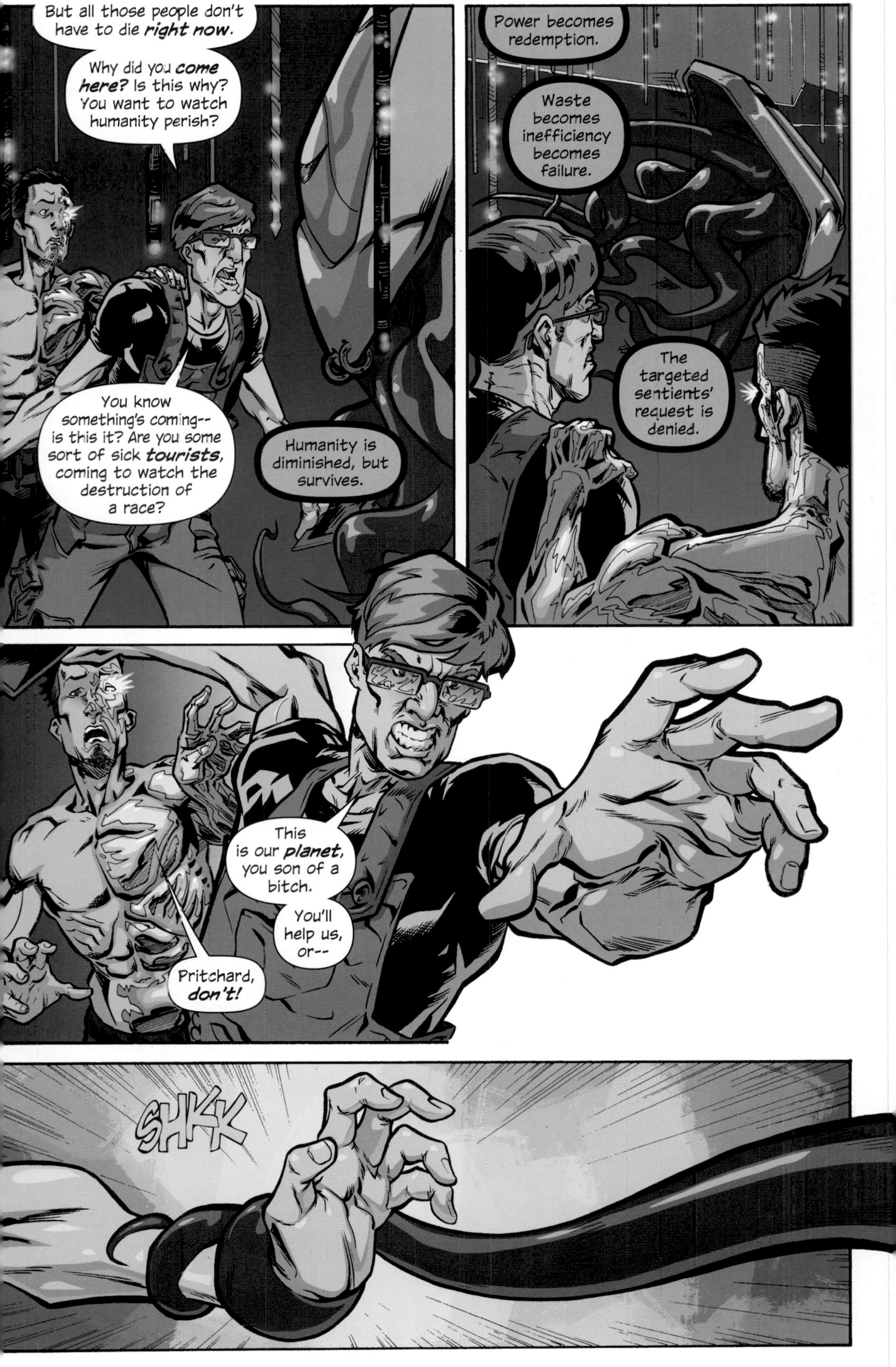
But all those people don't have to die ***right now.***
Why did you ***come here?*** Is this why? You want to watch humanity perish?
You know something's coming-- is this it? Are you some sort of sick ***tourists,*** coming to watch the destruction of a race?
Humanity is diminished, but survives.
Power becomes redemption.
Waste becomes inefficiency becomes failure.
The targeted sentients' request is denied.
This is our ***planet,*** you son of a bitch.
You'll help us, or--
Pritchard, ***don't!***
SHKK

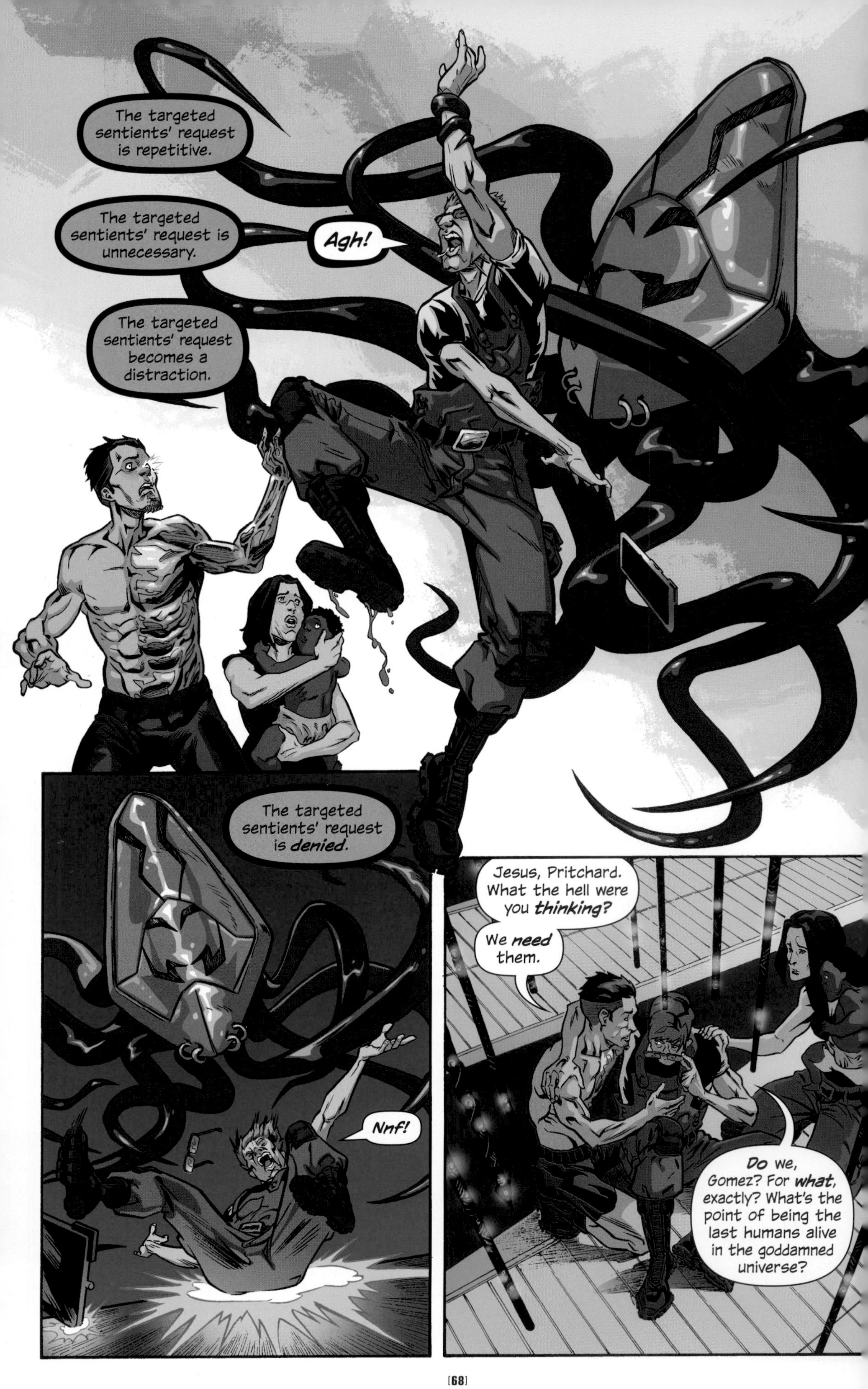
The targeted sentients' request is repetitive.
The targeted sentients' request is unnecessary.
Agh!
The targeted sentients' request becomes a distraction.
The targeted sentients' request is ***denied.***
Nnf!
Jesus, Pritchard. What the hell were you ***thinking?***
We ***need*** them.
Do we, Gomez? For ***what,*** exactly? What's the point of being the last humans alive in the goddamned universe?

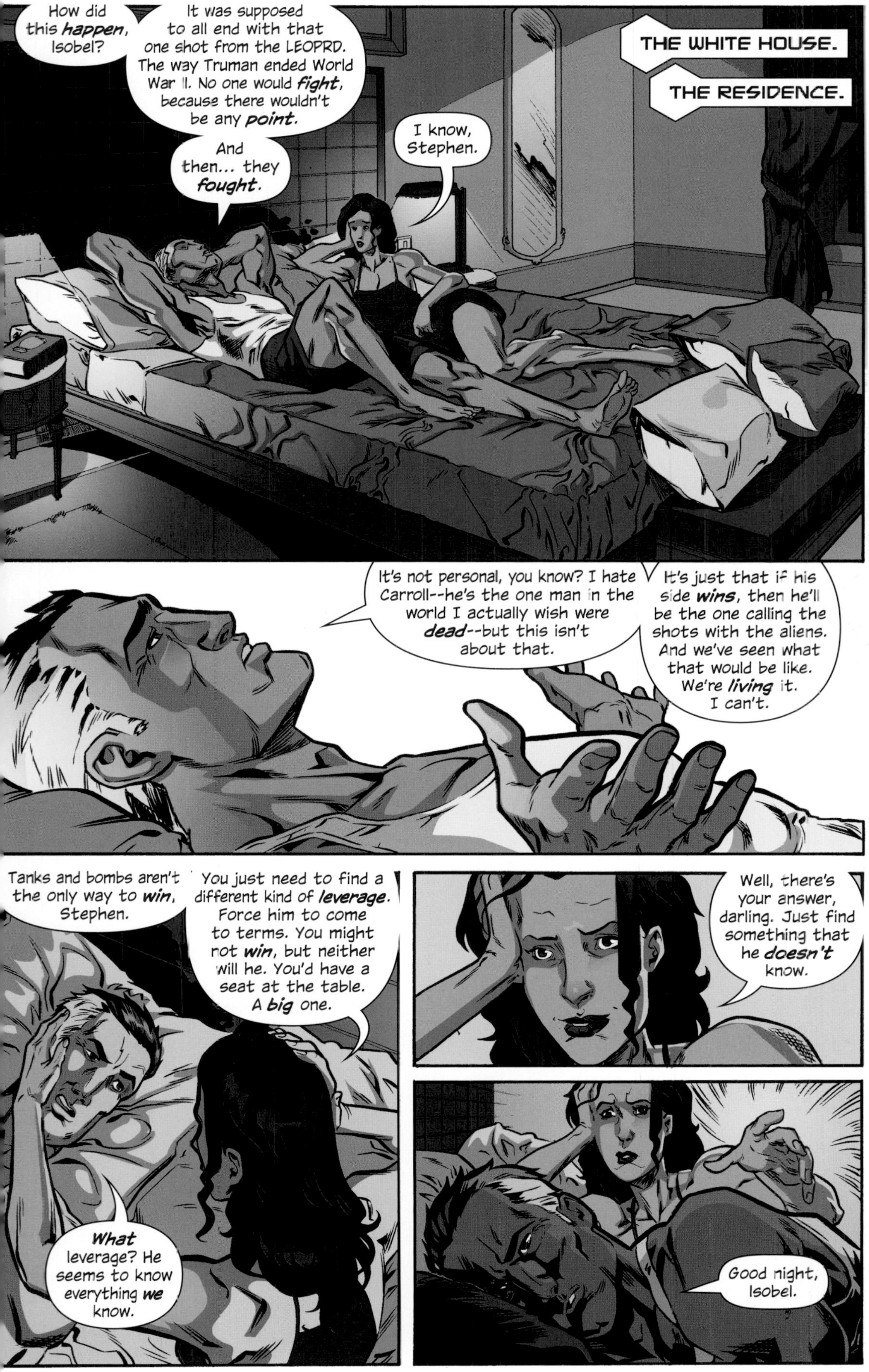

THE WHITE HOUSE.
THE RESIDENCE.
How did this *happen*, Isobel?
It was supposed to all end with that one shot from the LEOPRD. The way Truman ended World War II. No one would *fight*, because there wouldn't be any *point*.
And then... they *fought*.
I know, Stephen.
It's not personal, you know? I hate Carroll--he's the one man in the world I actually wish were *dead*--but this isn't about that.
It's just that if his side *wins*, then he'll be the one calling the shots with the aliens. And we've seen what that would be like. We're *living* it. I can't.
Tanks and bombs aren't the only way to *win*, Stephen.
You just need to find a different kind of *leverage*. Force him to come to terms. You might not *win*, but neither will he. You'd have a seat at the table. A *big* one.
What leverage? He seems to know everything *we* know.
Well, there's your answer, darling. Just find something that he *doesn't* know.
Good night, Isobel.

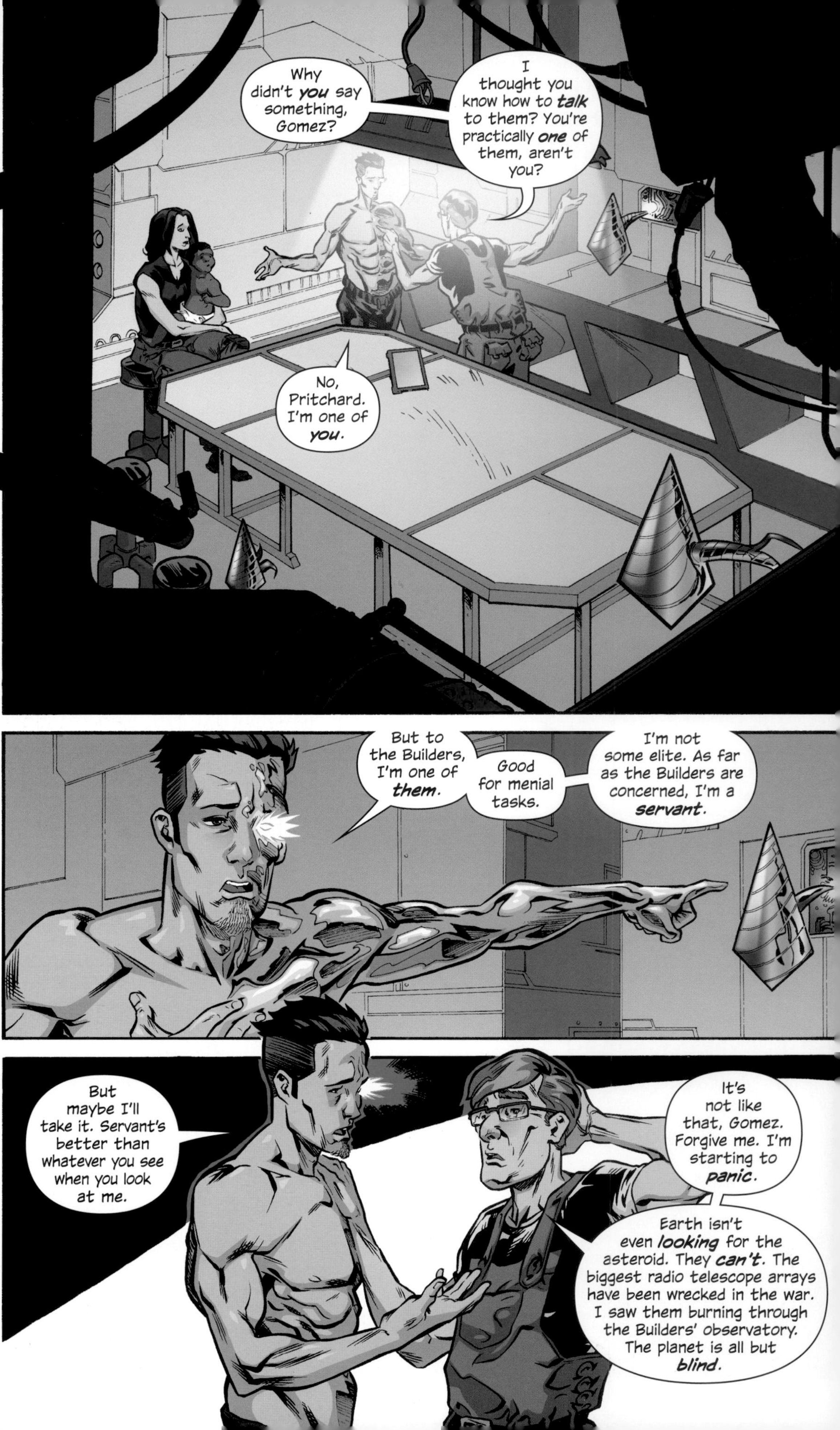
Why didn't *you* say something, Gomez?
I thought you know how to *talk* to them? You're practically *one* of them, aren't you?
No, Pritchard. I'm one of *you*.
But to the Builders, I'm one of *them*.
Good for menial tasks.
I'm not some elite. As far as the Builders are concerned, I'm a *servant*.
But maybe I'll take it. Servant's better than whatever you see when you look at me.
It's not like that, Gomez. Forgive me. I'm starting to *panic*.
Earth isn't even *looking* for the asteroid. They *can't*. The biggest radio telescope arrays have been wrecked in the war. I saw them burning through the Builders' observatory. The planet is all but *blind*.

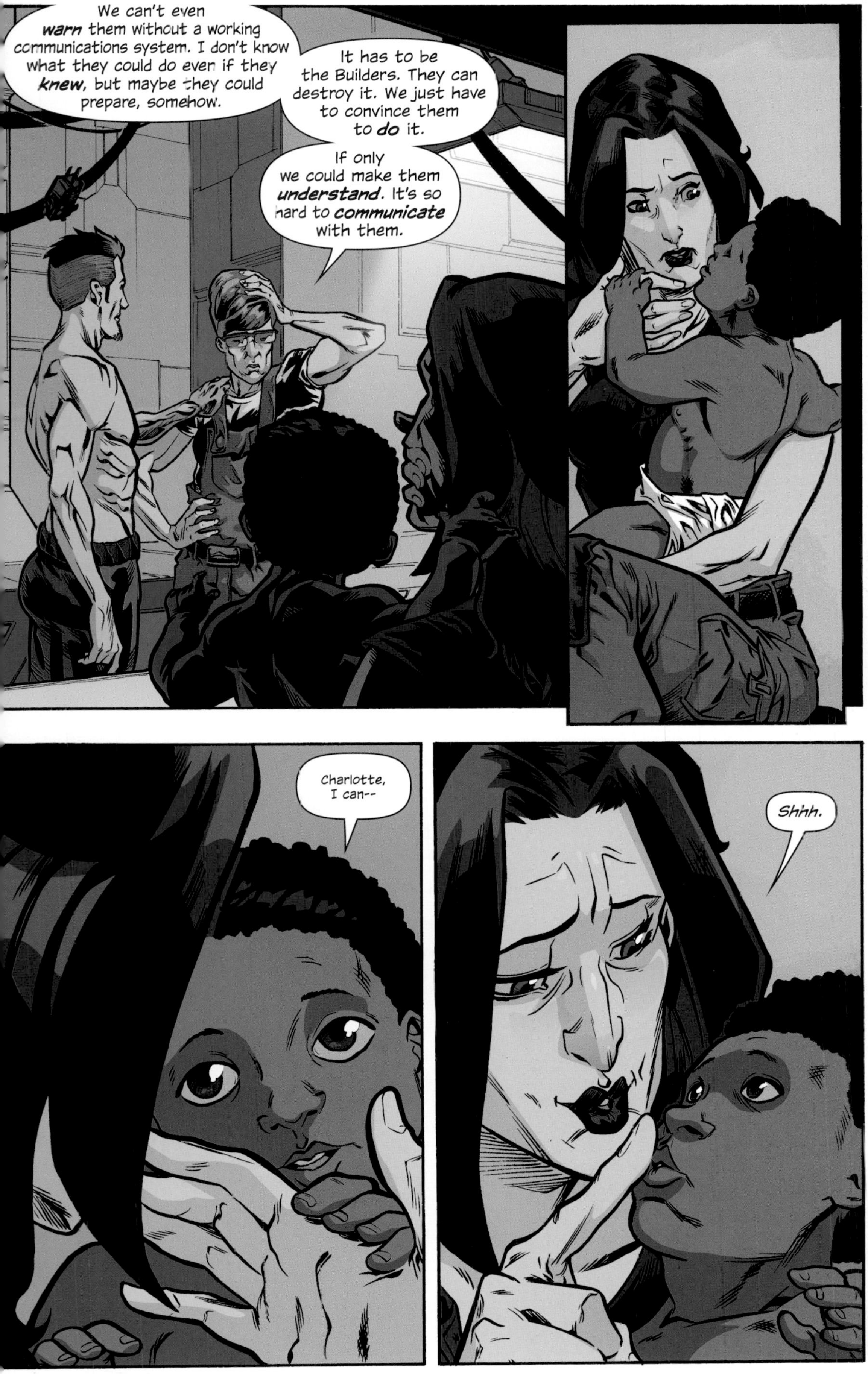
We can't even warn them without a working communications system. I don't know what they could do even if they knew, but maybe they could prepare, somehow.
It has to be the Builders. They can destroy it. We just have to convince them to do it.
If only we could make them understand. It's so hard to communicate with them.
Charlotte, I can--
Shhh.

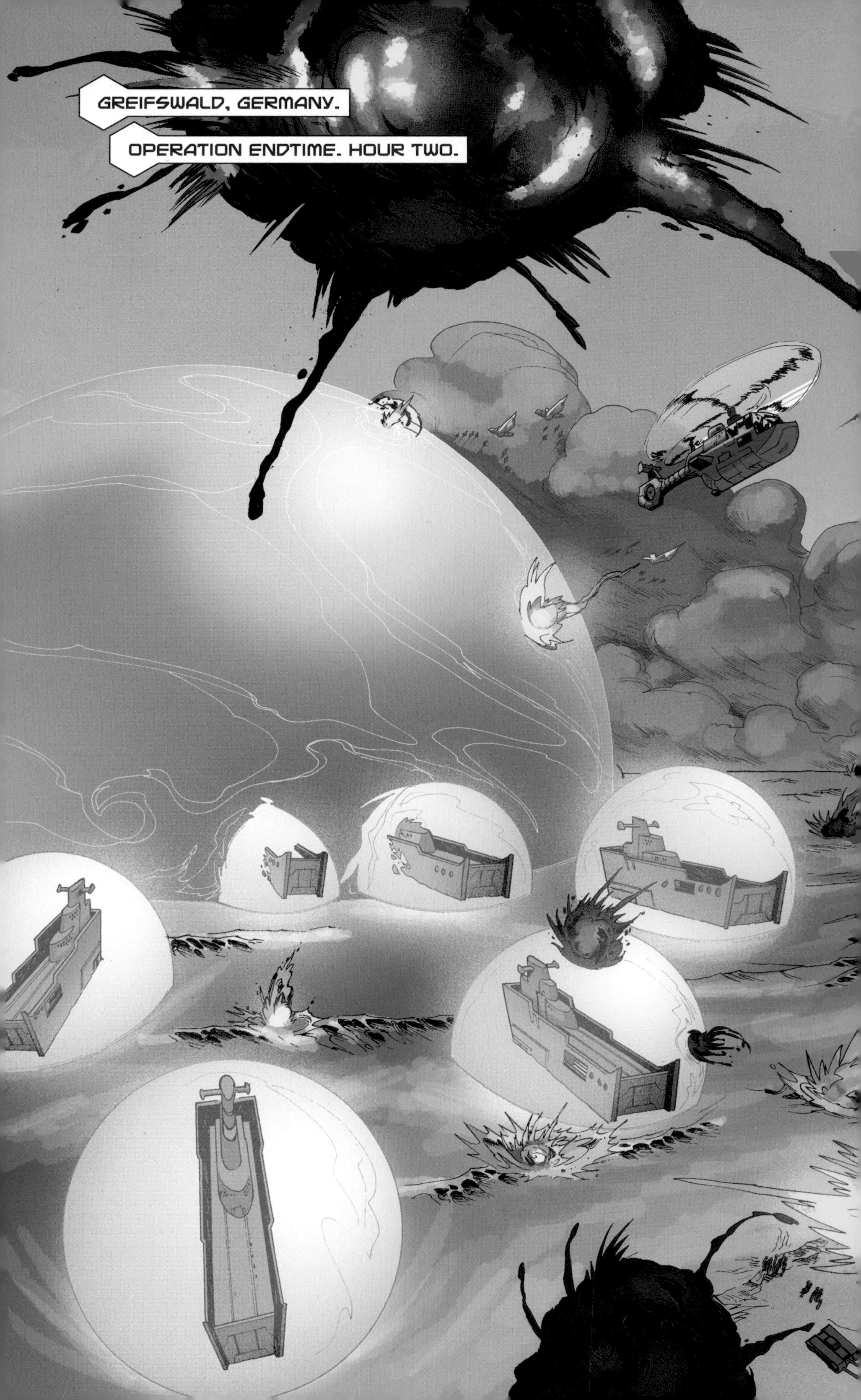
GREIFSWALD, GERMANY.
OPERATION ENDTIME. HOUR TWO.

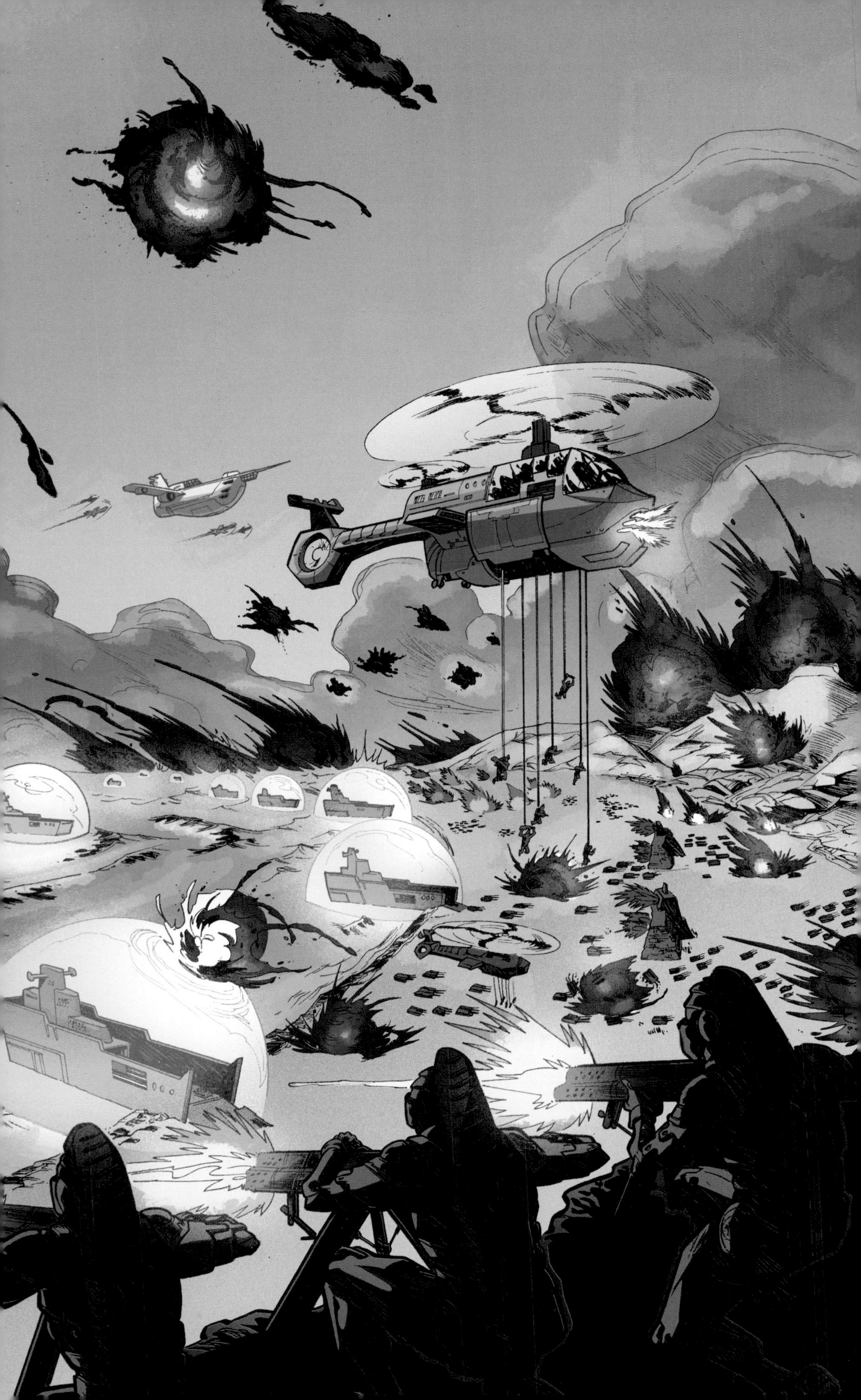

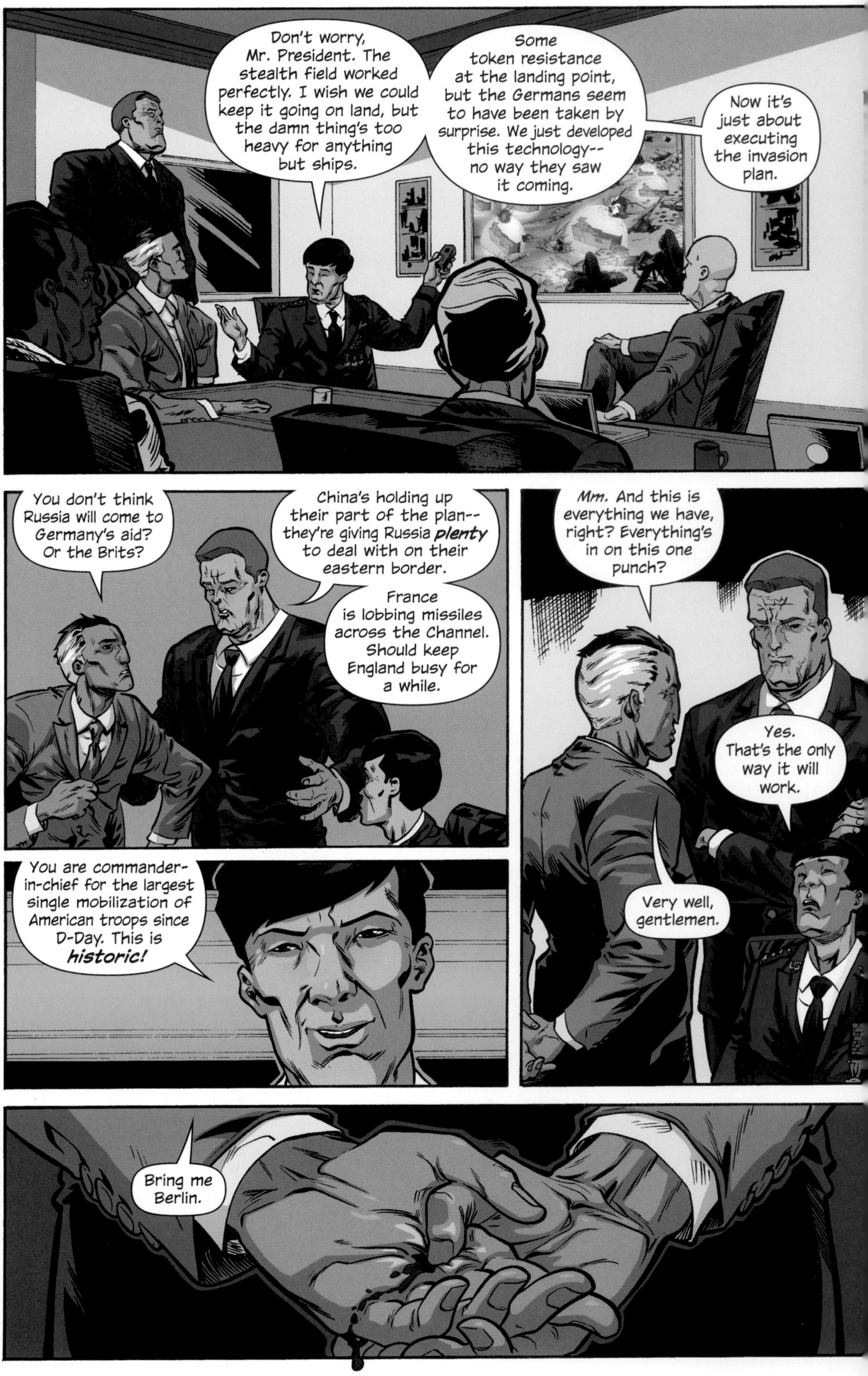

Don't worry, Mr. President. The stealth field worked perfectly. I wish we could keep it going on land, but the damn thing's too heavy for anything but ships.
Some token resistance at the landing point, but the Germans seem to have been taken by surprise. We just developed this technology-- no way they saw it coming.
Now it's just about executing the invasion plan.
You don't think Russia will come to Germany's aid? Or the Brits?
China's holding up their part of the plan-- they're giving Russia *plenty* to deal with on their eastern border.
France is lobbing missiles across the Channel. Should keep England busy for a while.
You are commander-in-chief for the largest single mobilization of American troops since D-Day. This is ***historic!***
Mm. And this is everything we have, right? Everything's in on this one punch?
Yes. That's the only way it will work.
Very well, gentlemen.
Bring me Berlin.

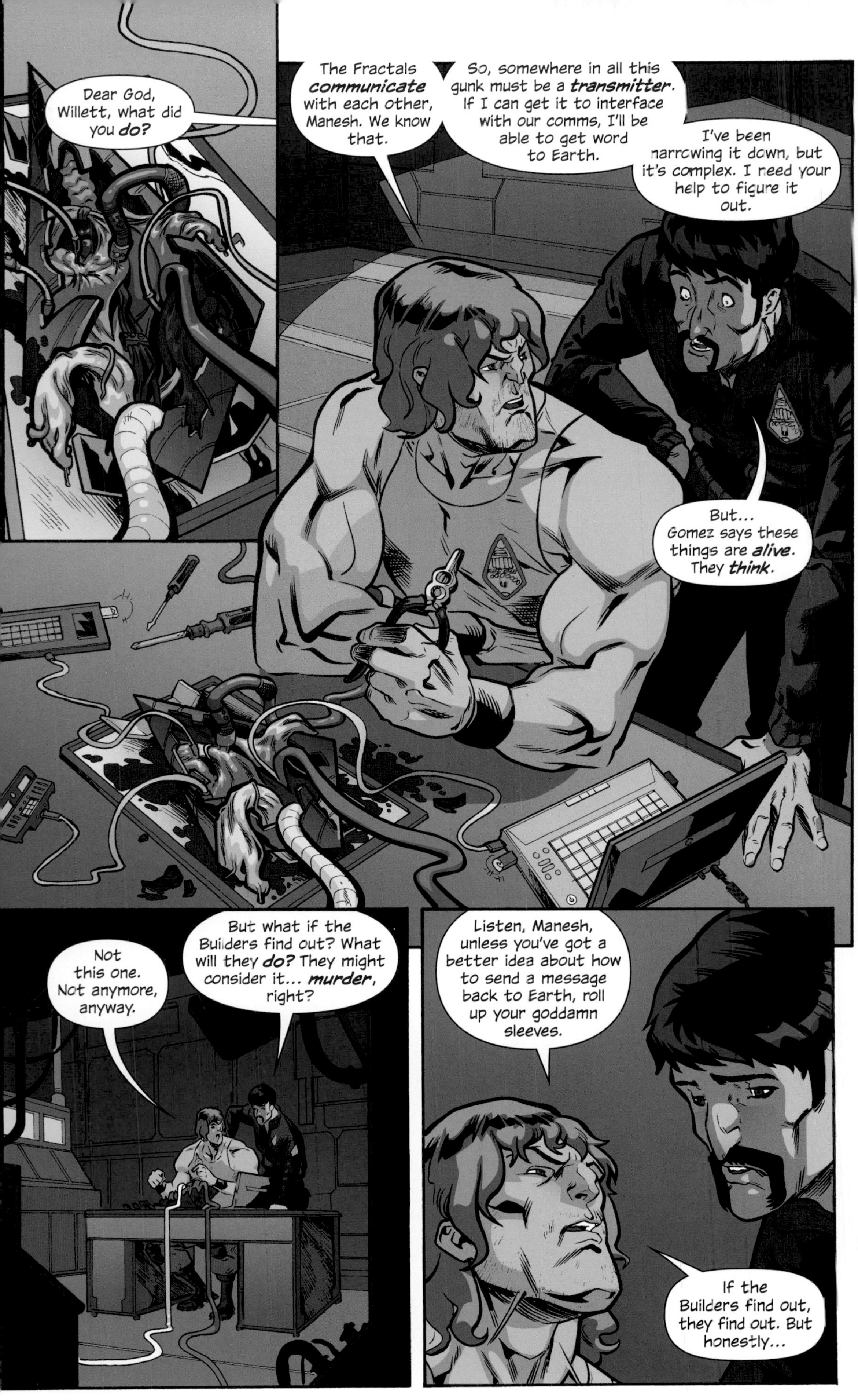
Dear God, Willett, what did you *do?*
The Fractals ***communicate*** with each other, Manesh. We know that.
So, somewhere in all this gunk must be a ***transmitter***. If I can get it to interface with our comms, I'll be able to get word to Earth.
I've been narrowing it down, but it's complex. I need your help to figure it out.
But... Gomez says these things are ***alive***. They ***think***.
Not this one. Not anymore, anyway.
But what if the Builders find out? What will they ***do?*** They might consider it... ***murder***, right?
Listen, Manesh, unless you've got a better idea about how to send a message back to Earth, roll up your goddamn sleeves.
If the Builders find out, they find out. But honestly...

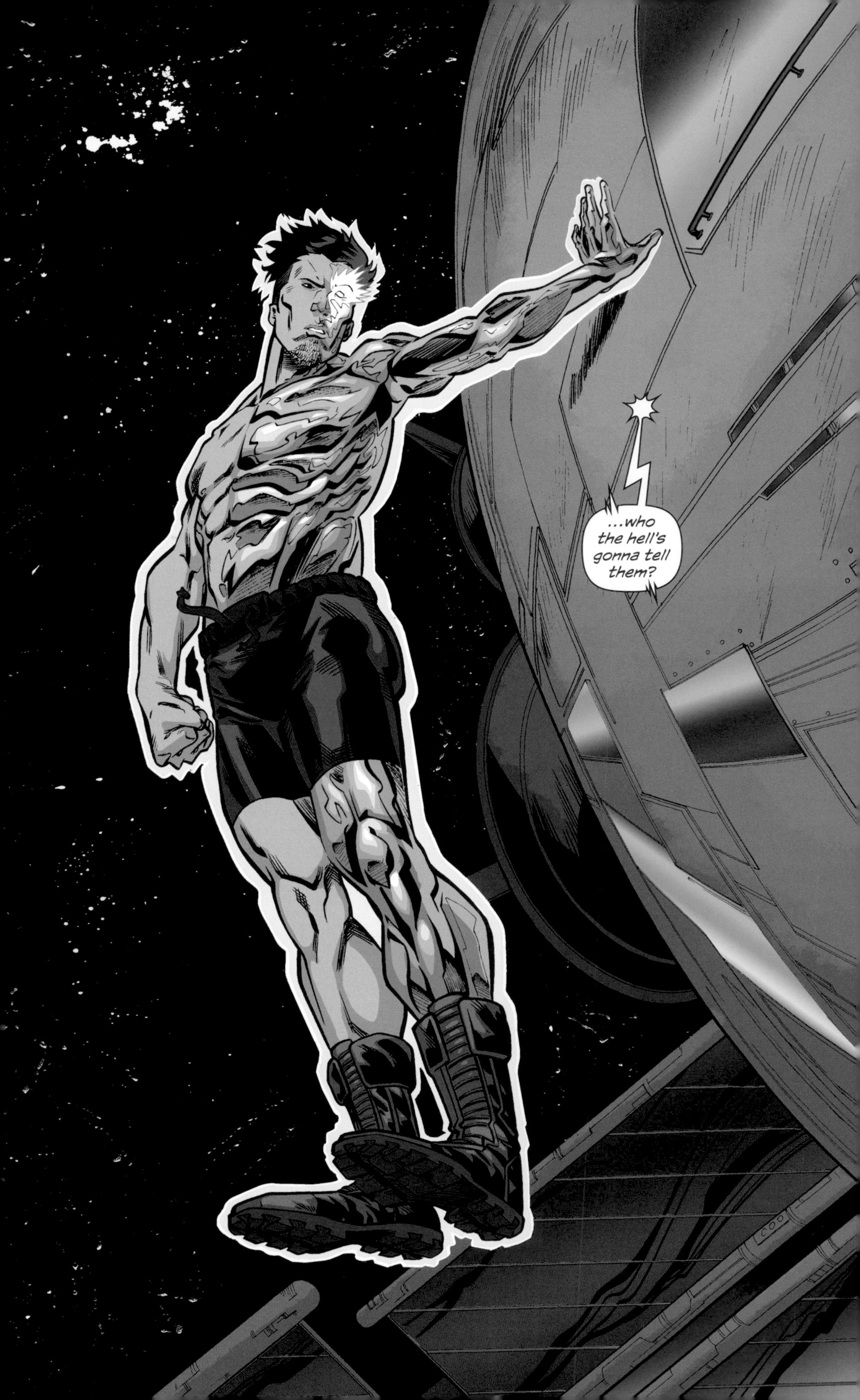
...who the hell's gonna tell them?

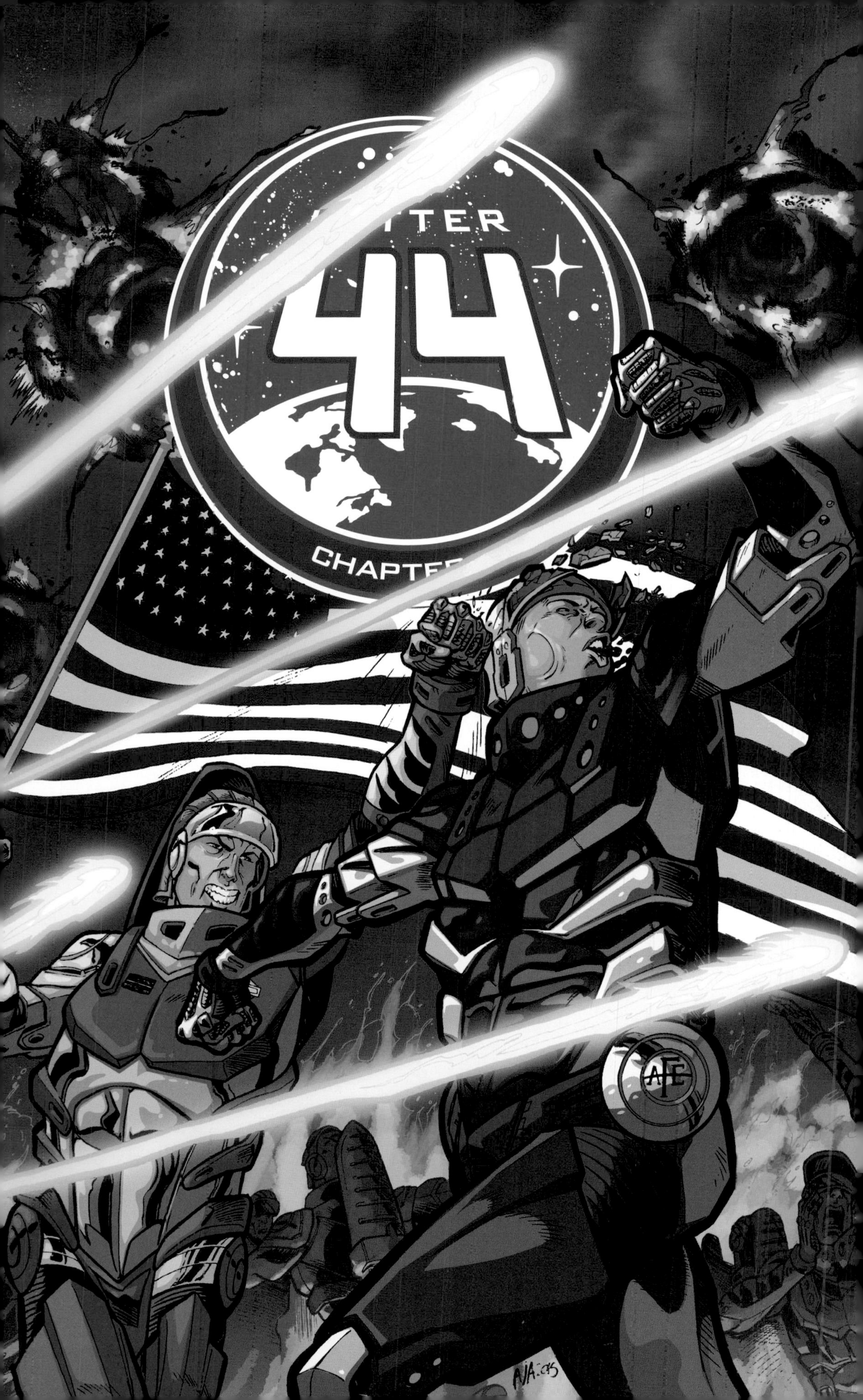
44

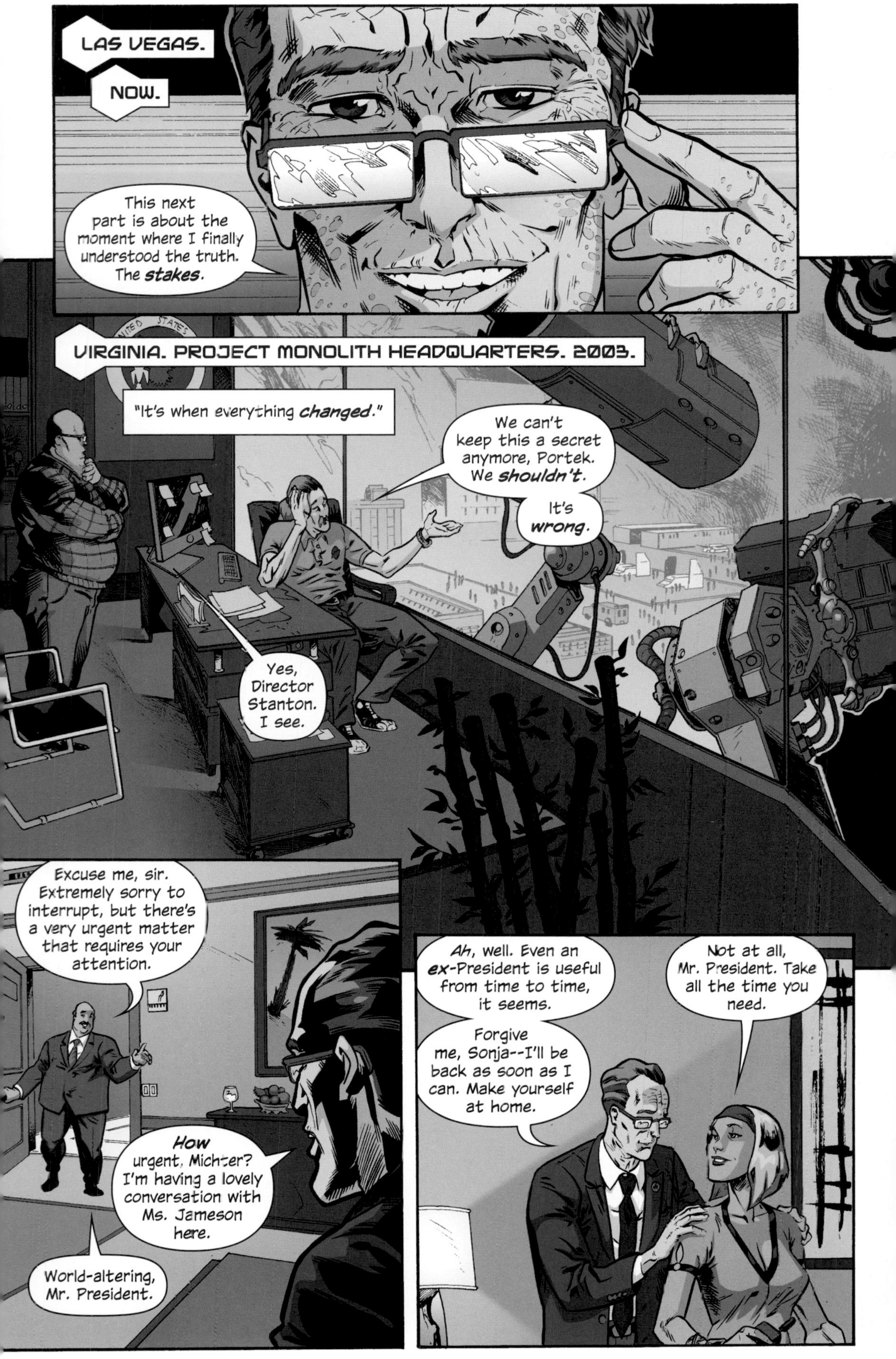

LAS VEGAS.
NOW.
This next part is about the moment where I finally understood the truth. The stakes.
VIRGINIA. PROJECT MONOLITH HEADQUARTERS. 2003.
"It's when everything changed."
We can't keep this a secret anymore, Portek. We shouldn't.
It's wrong.
Yes, Director Stanton. I see.
Excuse me, sir. Extremely sorry to interrupt, but there's a very urgent matter that requires your attention.
How urgent, Michter? I'm having a lovely conversation with Ms. Jameson here.
World-altering, Mr. President.
Ah, well. Even an ex-President is useful from time to time, it seems.
Not at all, Mr. President. Take all the time you need.
Forgive me, Sonja--I'll be back as soon as I can. Make yourself at home.

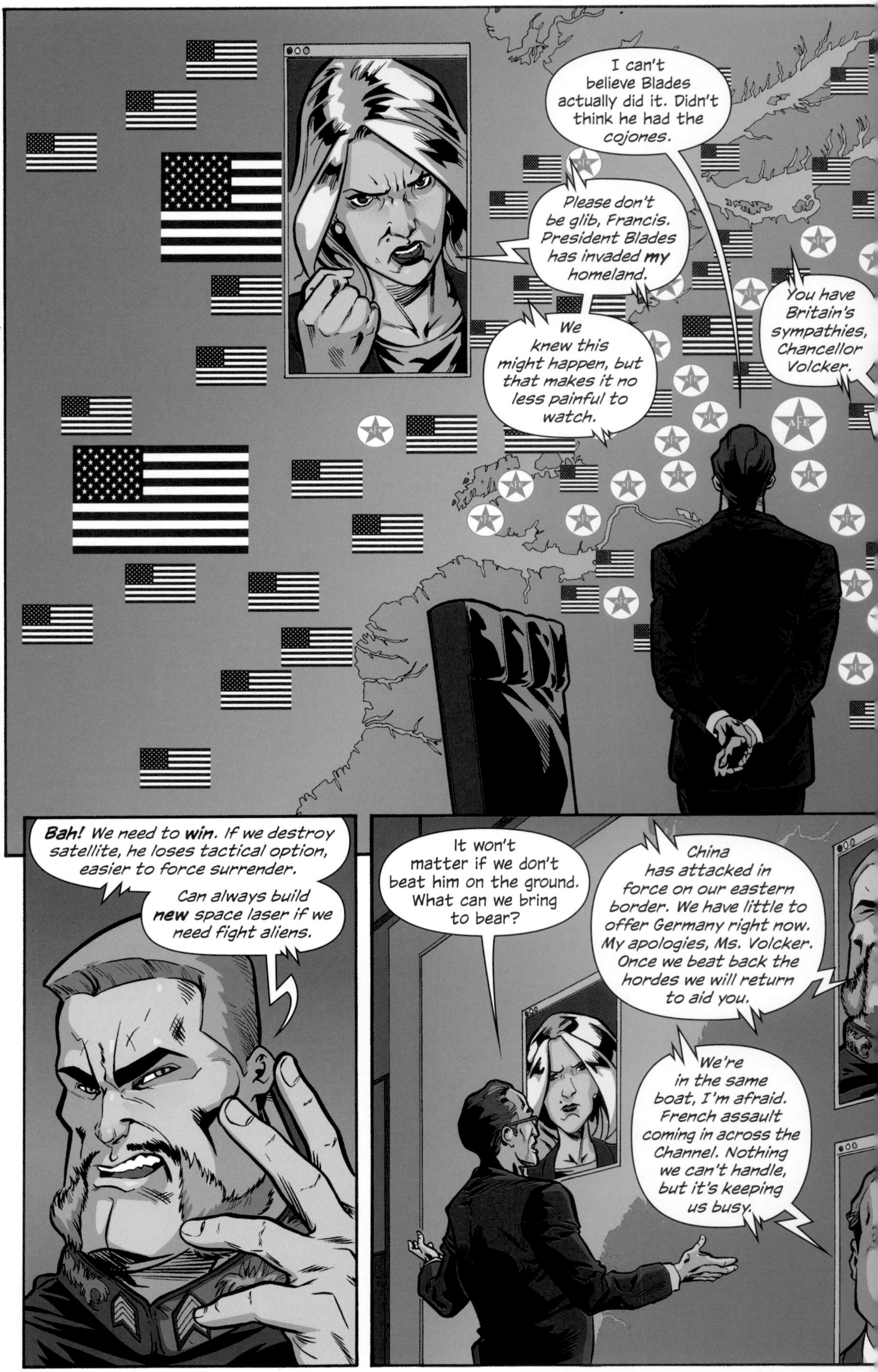

I can't believe Blades actually did it. Didn't think he had the cojones.
Please don't be glib, Francis. President Blades has invaded my homeland.
We knew this might happen, but that makes it no less painful to watch.
You have Britain's sympathies, Chancellor Volcker.
Bah! We need to win. If we destroy satellite, he loses tactical option, easier to force surrender.
Can always build new space laser if we need fight aliens.
It won't matter if we don't beat him on the ground. What can we bring to bear?
China has attacked in force on our eastern border. We have little to offer Germany right now. My apologies, Ms. Volcker. Once we beat back the hordes we will return to aid you.
We're in the same boat, I'm afraid. French assault coming in across the Channel. Nothing we can't handle, but it's keeping us busy.

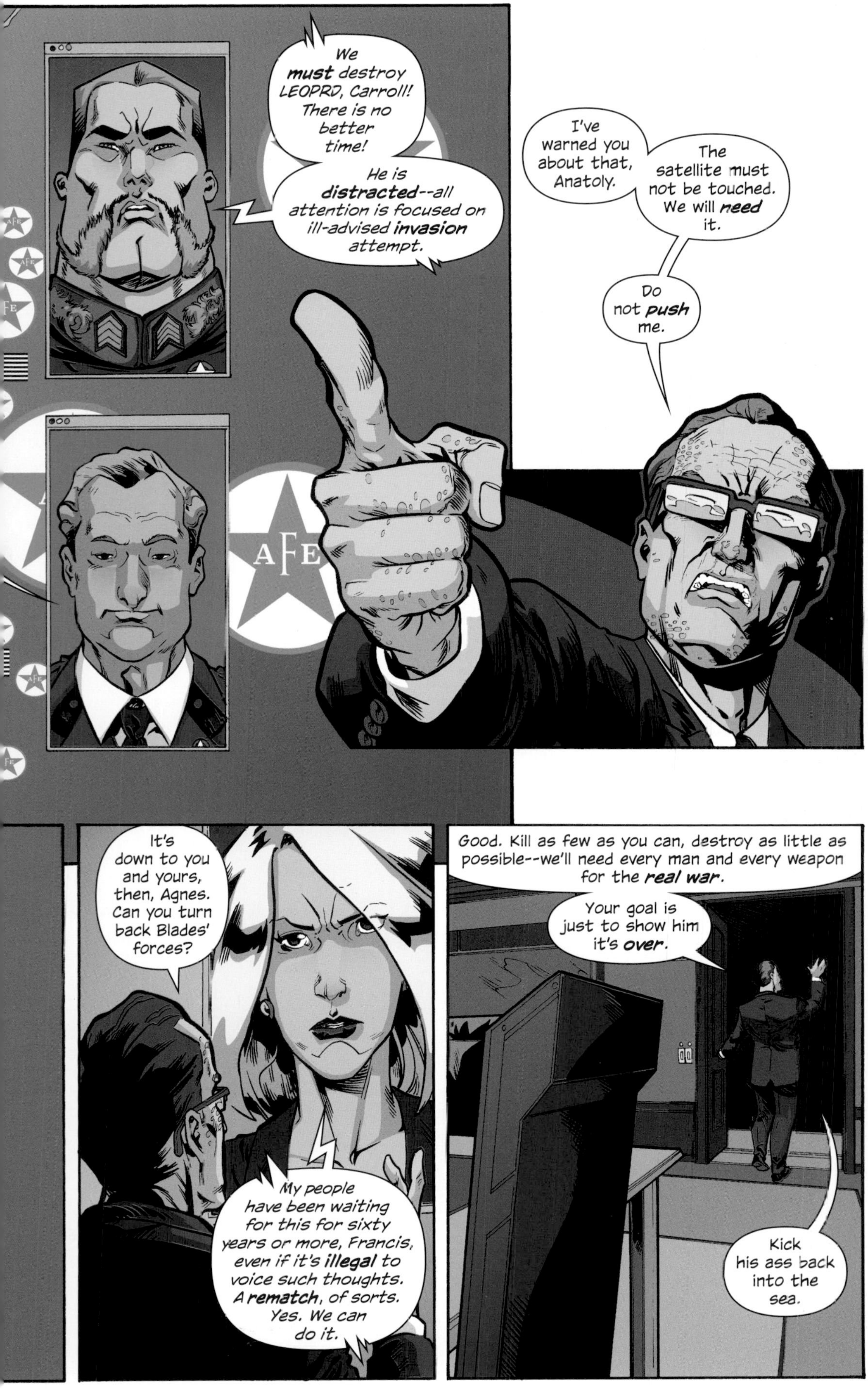

We must destroy LEOPRD, Carroll! There is no better time!
He is distracted--all attention is focused on ill-advised invasion attempt.
I've warned you about that, Anatoly.
The satellite must not be touched. We will need it.
Do not push me.
It's down to you and yours, then, Agnes. Can you turn back Blades' forces?
My people have been waiting for this for sixty years or more, Francis, even if it's illegal to voice such thoughts. A rematch, of sorts. Yes. We can do it.
Good. Kill as few as you can, destroy as little as possible--we'll need every man and every weapon for the real war.
Your goal is just to show him it's over.
Kick his ass back into the sea.

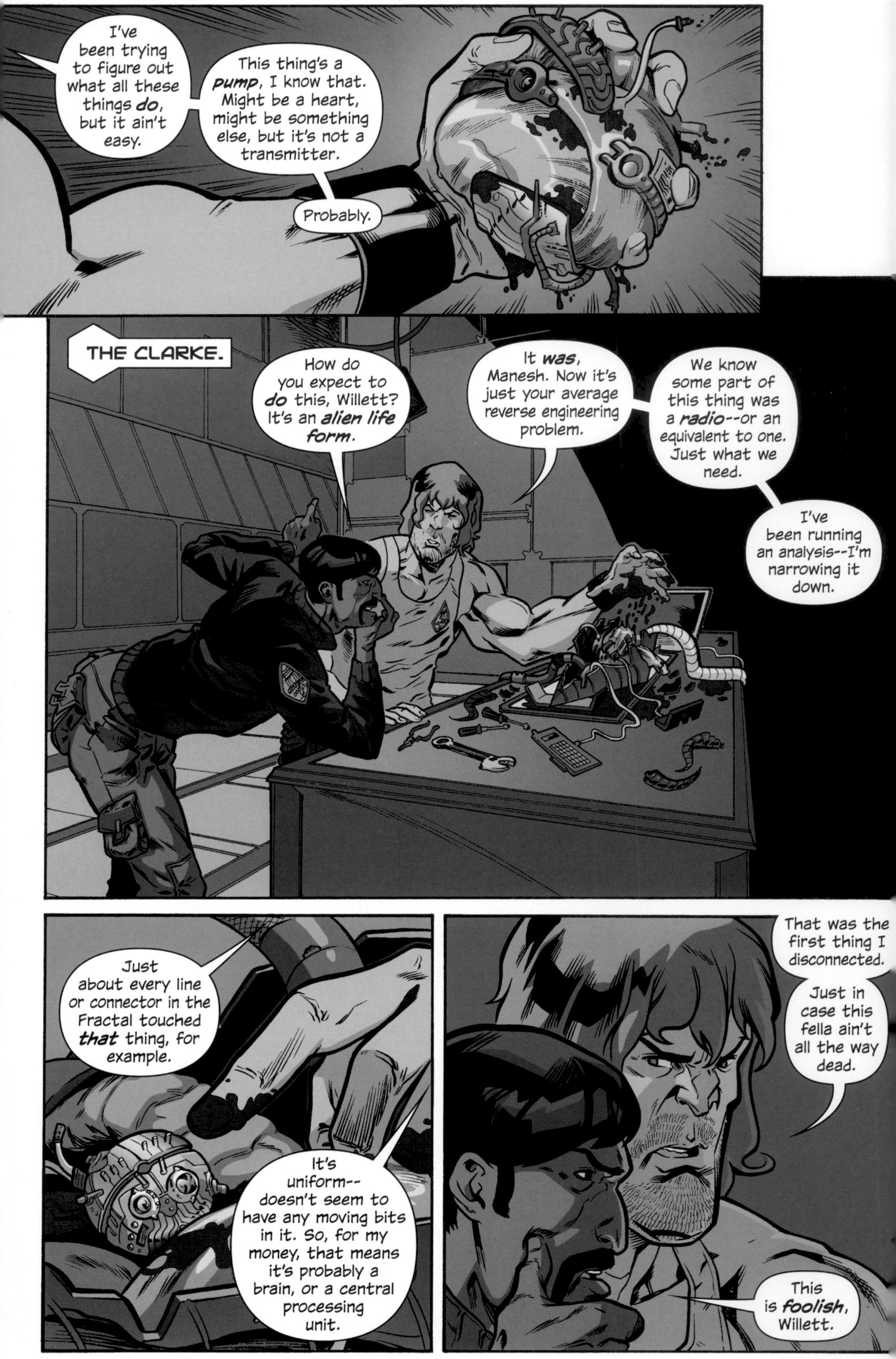
I've been trying to figure out what all these things *do*, but it ain't easy.
This thing's a *pump*, I know that. Might be a heart, might be something else, but it's not a transmitter.
Probably.
THE CLARKE.
How do you expect to *do* this, Willett? It's an *alien life form*.
It *was*, Manesh. Now it's just your average reverse engineering problem.
We know some part of this thing was a *radio*--or an equivalent to one. Just what we need.
I've been running an analysis--I'm narrowing it down.
Just about every line or connector in the Fractal touched *that* thing, for example.
It's uniform--doesn't seem to have any moving bits in it. So, for my money, that means it's probably a brain, or a central processing unit.
That was the first thing I disconnected.
Just in case this fella ain't all the way dead.
This is *foolish*, Willett.

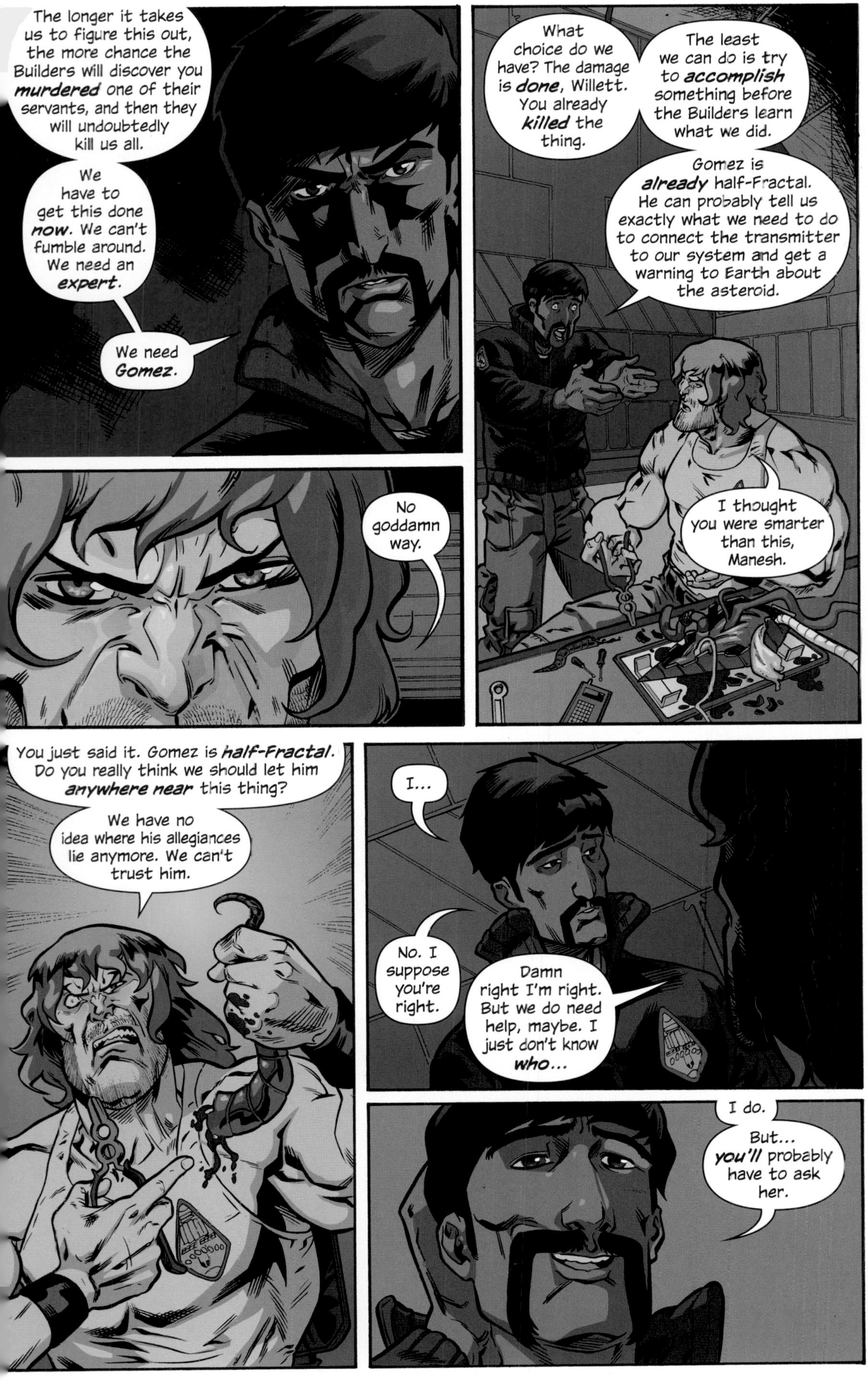
The longer it takes us to figure this out, the more chance the Builders will discover you murdered one of their servants, and then they will undoubtedly kill us all.
We have to get this done now. We can't fumble around. We need an expert.
We need Gomez.
What choice do we have? The damage is done, Willett. You already killed the thing.
The least we can do is try to accomplish something before the Builders learn what we did.
Gomez is already half-Fractal. He can probably tell us exactly what we need to do to connect the transmitter to our system and get a warning to Earth about the asteroid.
No goddamn way.
I thought you were smarter than this, Manesh.
You just said it. Gomez is half-Fractal. Do you really think we should let him anywhere near this thing?
We have no idea where his allegiances lie anymore. We can't trust him.
I...
No. I suppose you're right.
Damn right I'm right. But we do need help, maybe. I just don't know who...
I do.
But... you'll probably have to ask her.

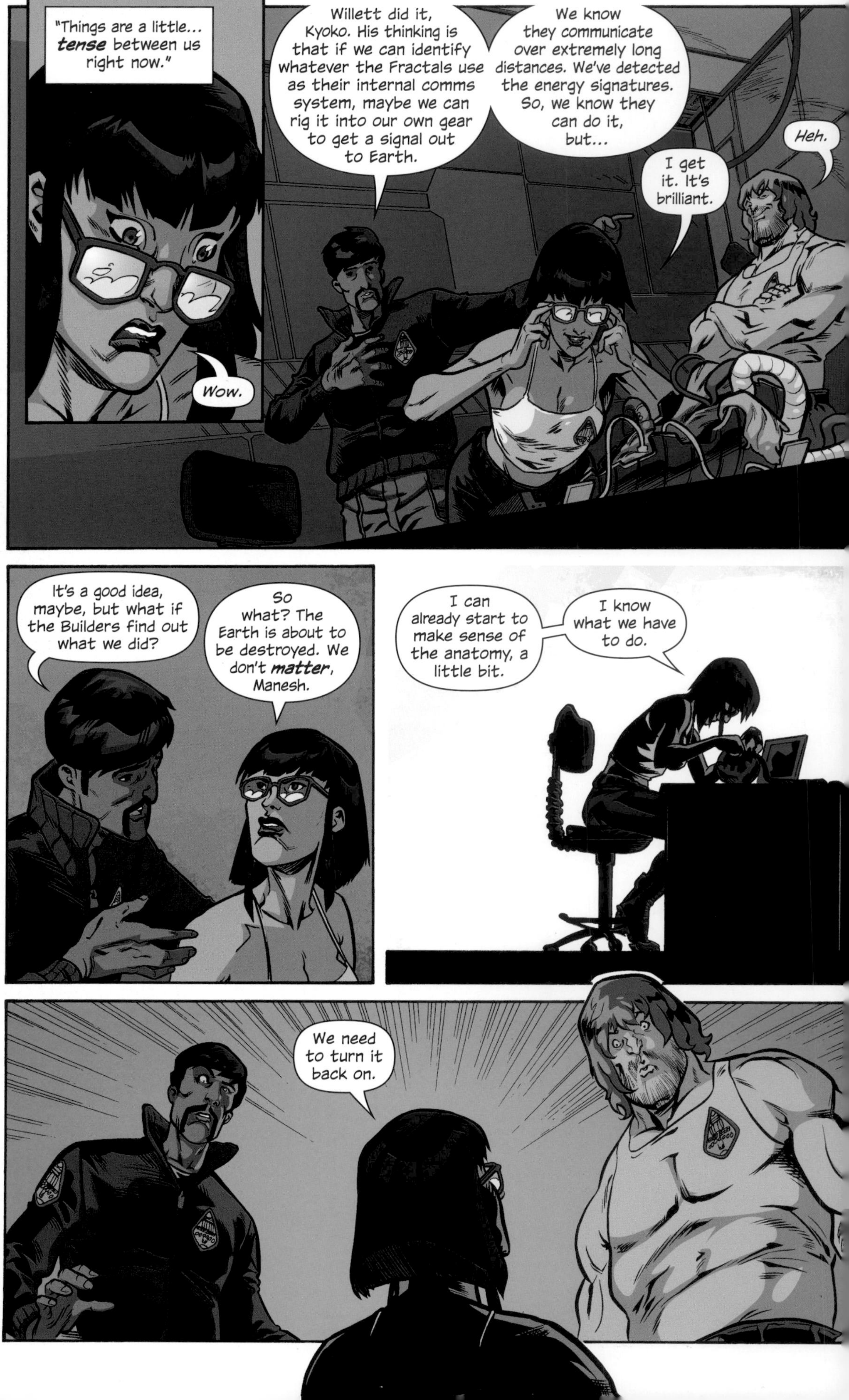
"Things are a little... ***tense*** between us right now."
Wow.
Willett did it, Kyoko. His thinking is that if we can identify whatever the Fractals use as their internal comms system, maybe we can rig it into our own gear to get a signal out to Earth.
We know they communicate over extremely long distances. We've detected the energy signatures. So, we know they can do it, but...
I get it. It's brilliant.
Heh.
It's a good idea, maybe, but what if the Builders find out what we did?
So what? The Earth is about to be destroyed. We don't ***matter***, Manesh.
I can already start to make sense of the anatomy, a little bit.
I know what we have to do.
We need to turn it back on.

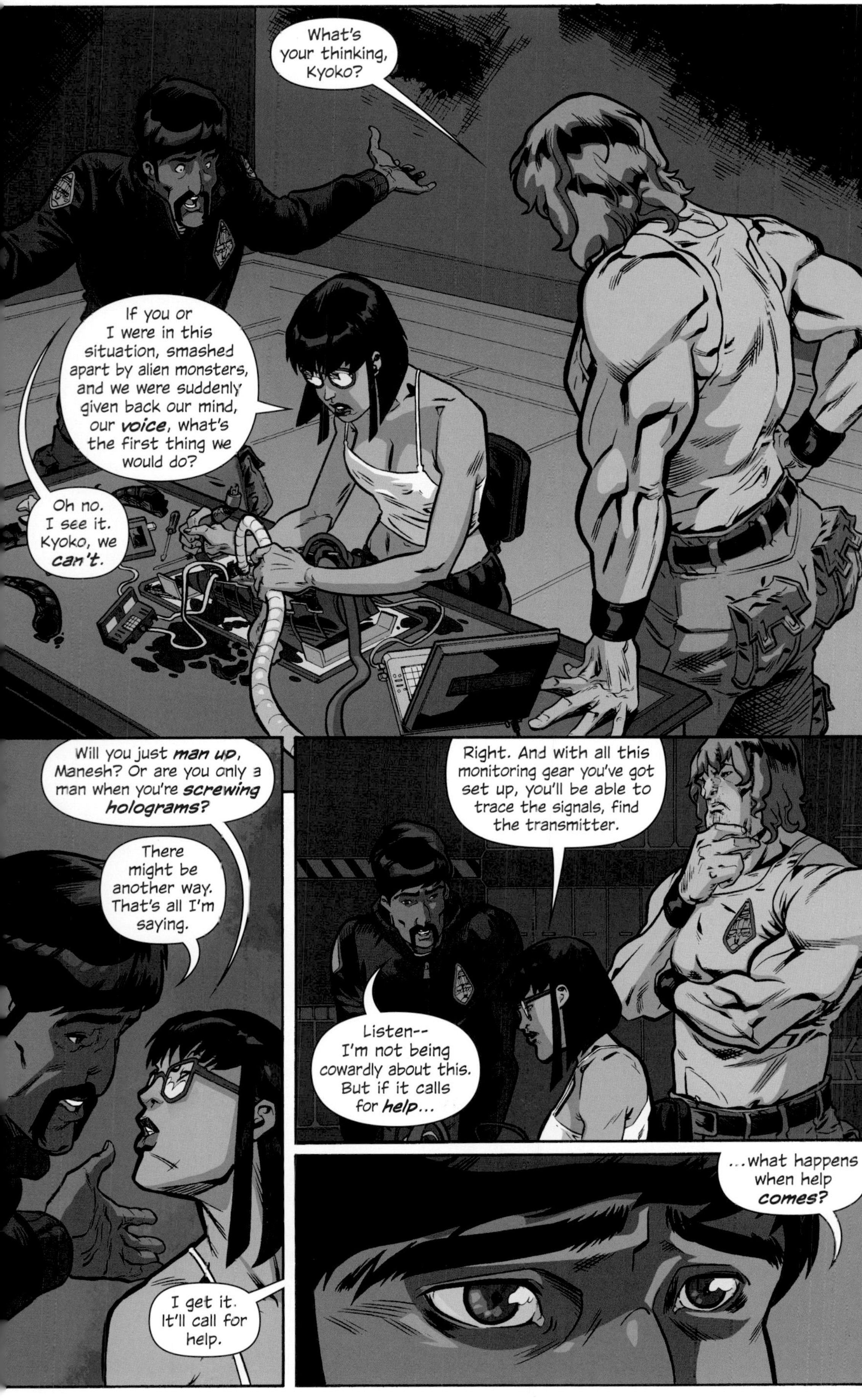
What's your thinking, Kyoko?
If you or I were in this situation, smashed apart by alien monsters, and we were suddenly given back our mind, our *voice*, what's the first thing we would do?
Oh no. I see it. Kyoko, we *can't*.
Will you just *man up*, Manesh? Or are you only a man when you're *screwing holograms?*
There might be another way. That's all I'm saying.
I get it. It'll call for help.
Right. And with all this monitoring gear you've got set up, you'll be able to trace the signals, find the transmitter.
Listen-- I'm not being cowardly about this. But if it calls for *help*...
...what happens when help *comes?*

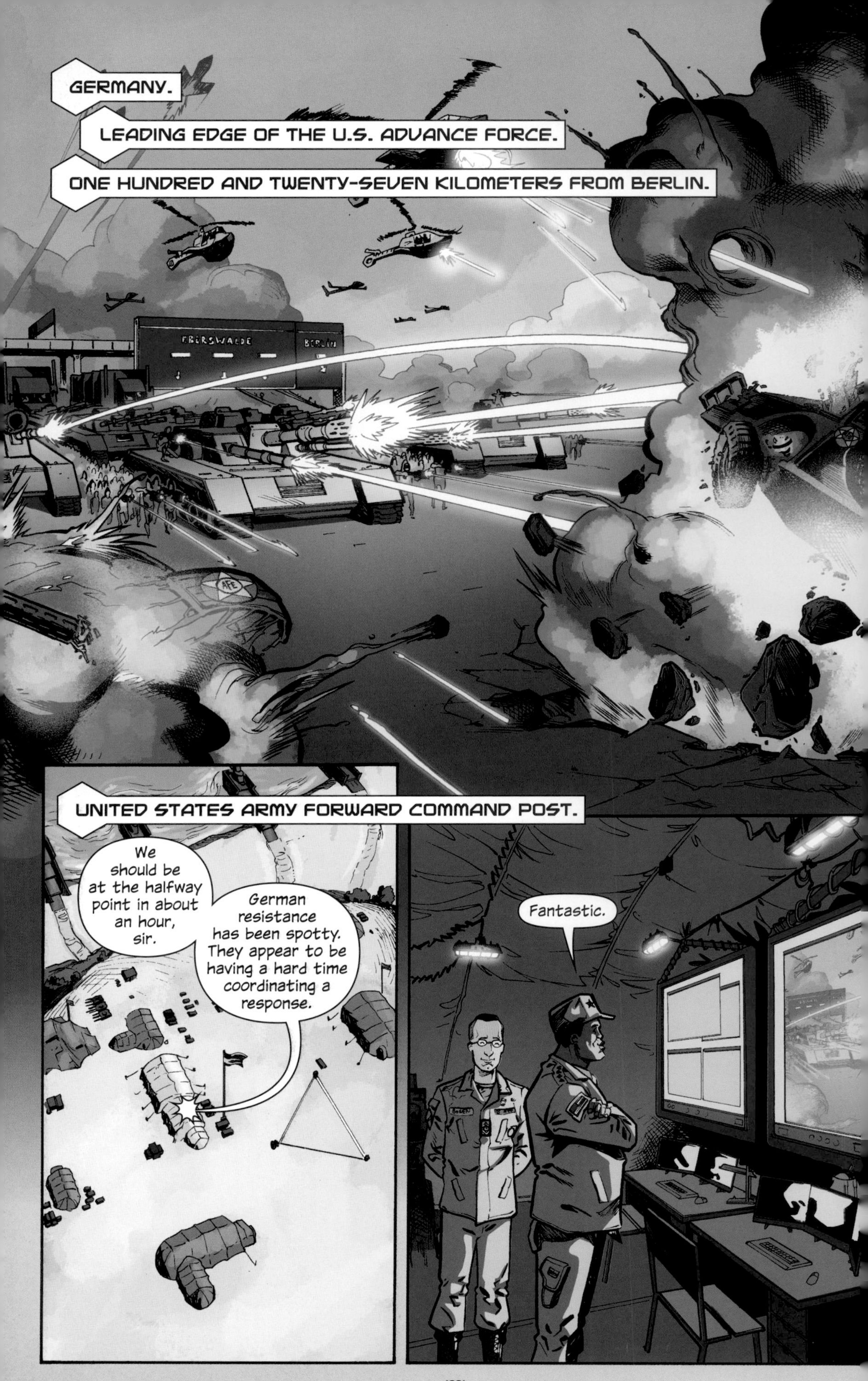
GERMANY.
LEADING EDGE OF THE U.S. ADVANCE FORCE.
ONE HUNDRED AND TWENTY-SEVEN KILOMETERS FROM BERLIN.
EBERSWALDE
BERLIN
UNITED STATES ARMY FORWARD COMMAND POST.
We should be at the halfway point in about an hour, sir.
German resistance has been spotty. They appear to be having a hard time coordinating a response.
Fantastic.

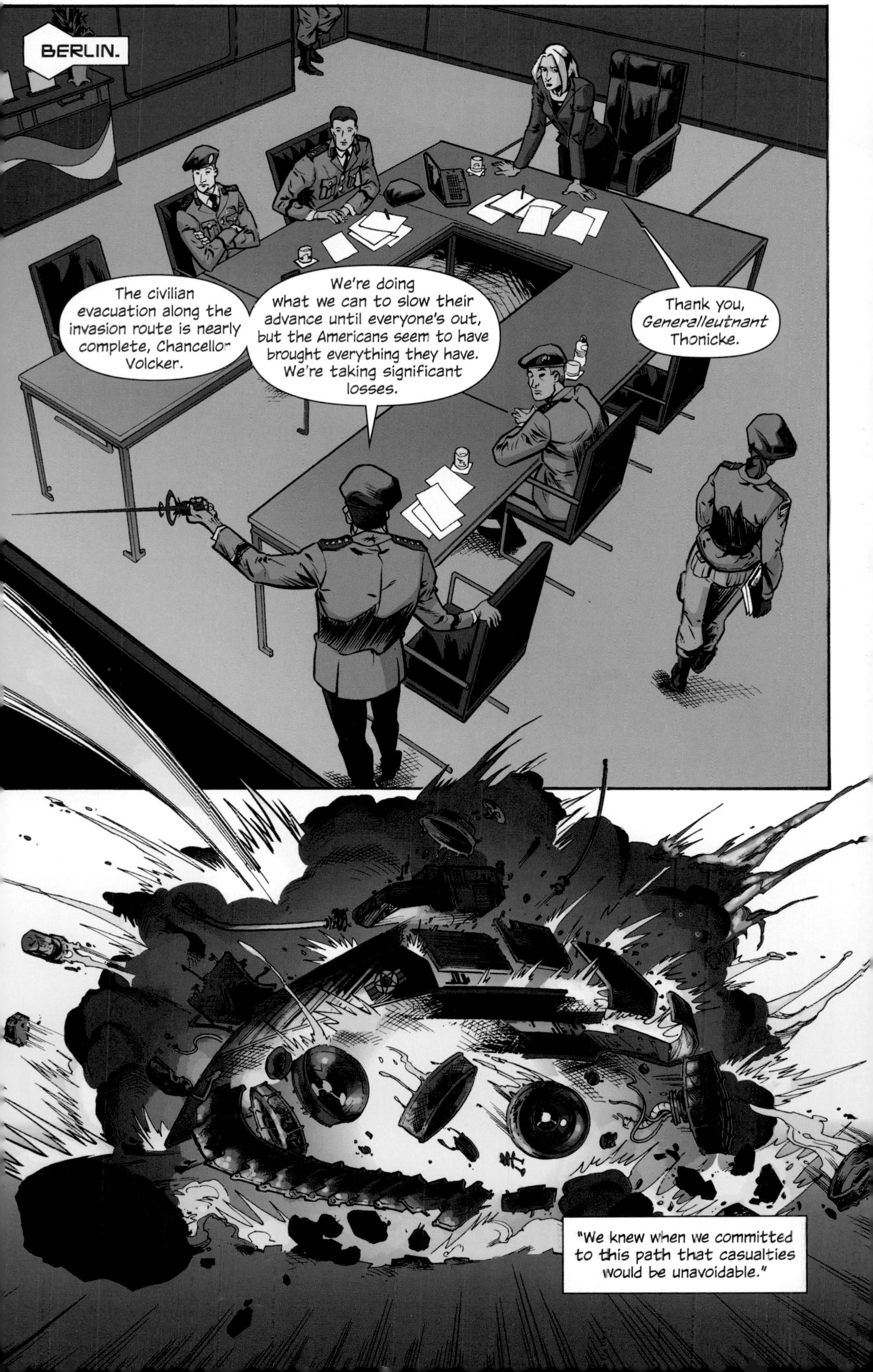
BERLIN.
The civilian evacuation along the invasion route is nearly complete, Chancellor Volcker.
We're doing what we can to slow their advance until everyone's out, but the Americans seem to have brought everything they have. We're taking significant losses.
Thank you, Generalleutnant Thonicke.
"We knew when we committed to this path that casualties would be unavoidable."

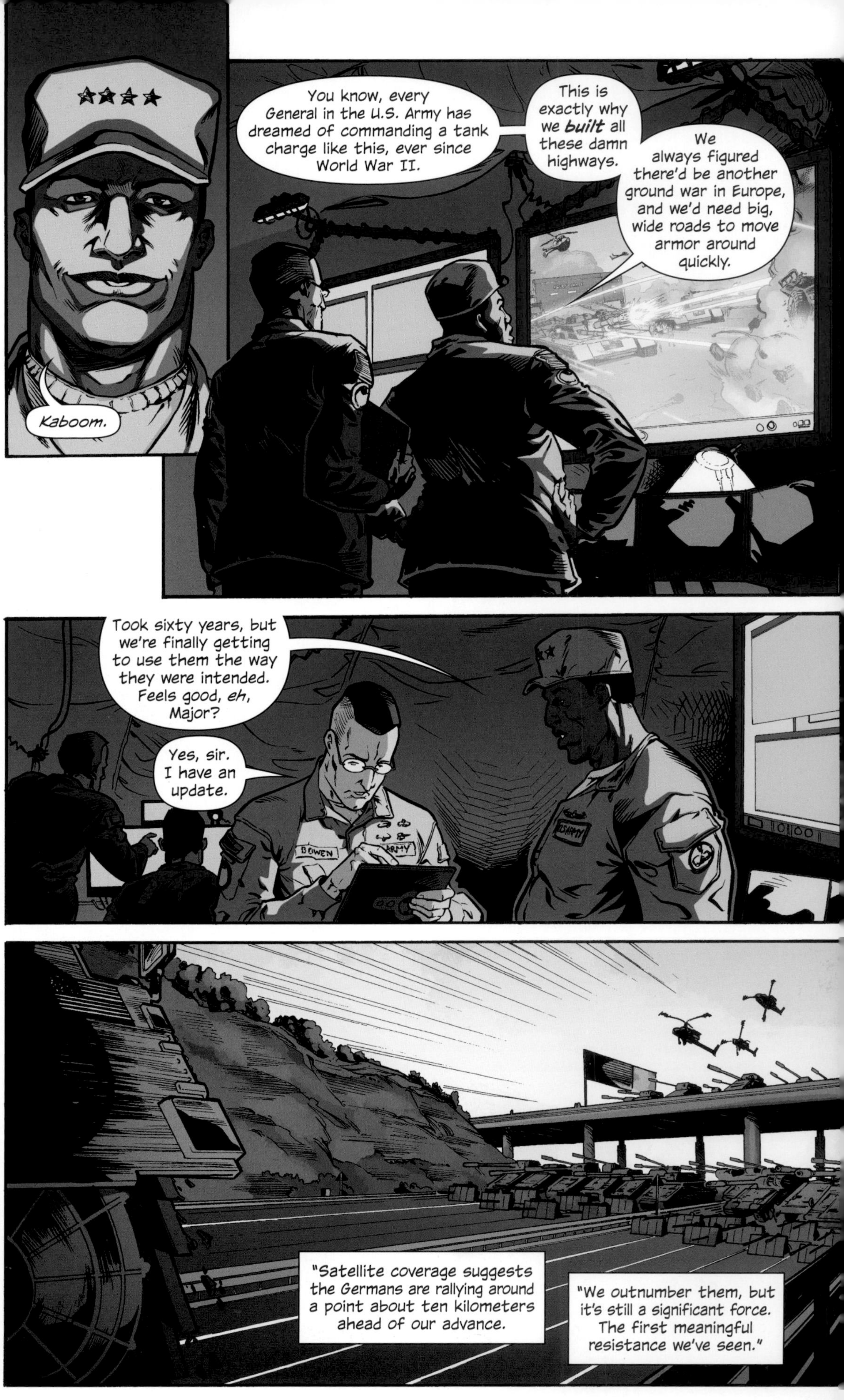
You know, every General in the U.S. Army has dreamed of commanding a tank charge like this, ever since World War II.
This is exactly why we **built** all these damn highways.
We always figured there'd be another ground war in Europe, and we'd need big, wide roads to move armor around quickly.
Kaboom.
Took sixty years, but we're finally getting to use them the way they were intended. Feels good, *eh*, Major?
Yes, sir. I have an update.
BOWEN
ARMY
US ARMY
"Satellite coverage suggests the Germans are rallying around a point about ten kilometers ahead of our advance.
"We outnumber them, but it's still a significant force. The first meaningful resistance we've seen."

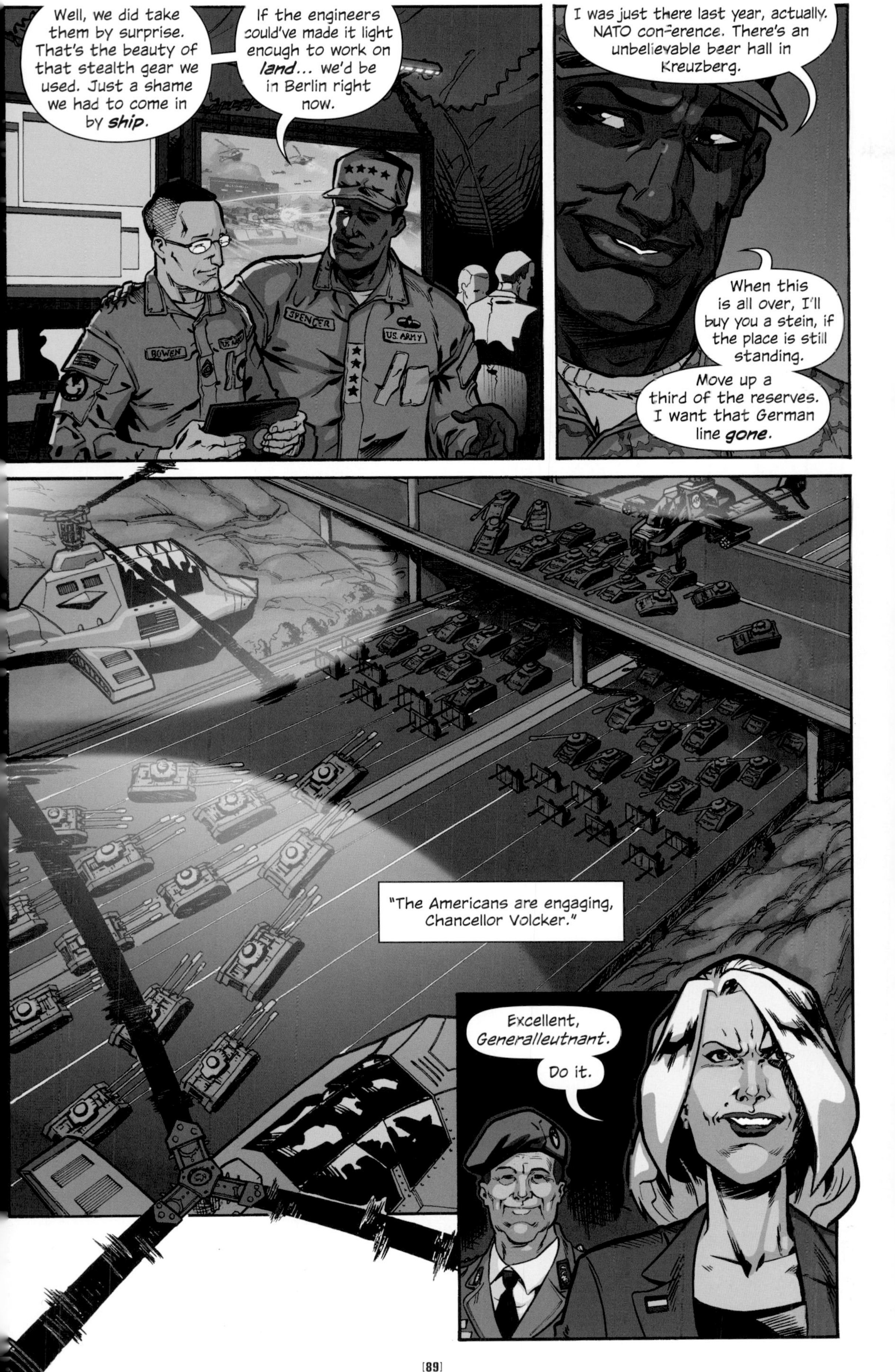
Well, we did take them by surprise. That's the beauty of that stealth gear we used. Just a shame we had to come in by ship.
If the engineers could've made it light enough to work on land... we'd be in Berlin right now.
I was just there last year, actually. NATO conference. There's an unbelievable beer hall in Kreuzberg.
When this is all over, I'll buy you a stein, if the place is still standing.
Move up a third of the reserves. I want that German line gone.
"The Americans are engaging, Chancellor Volcker."
Excellent, Generalleutnant.
Do it.

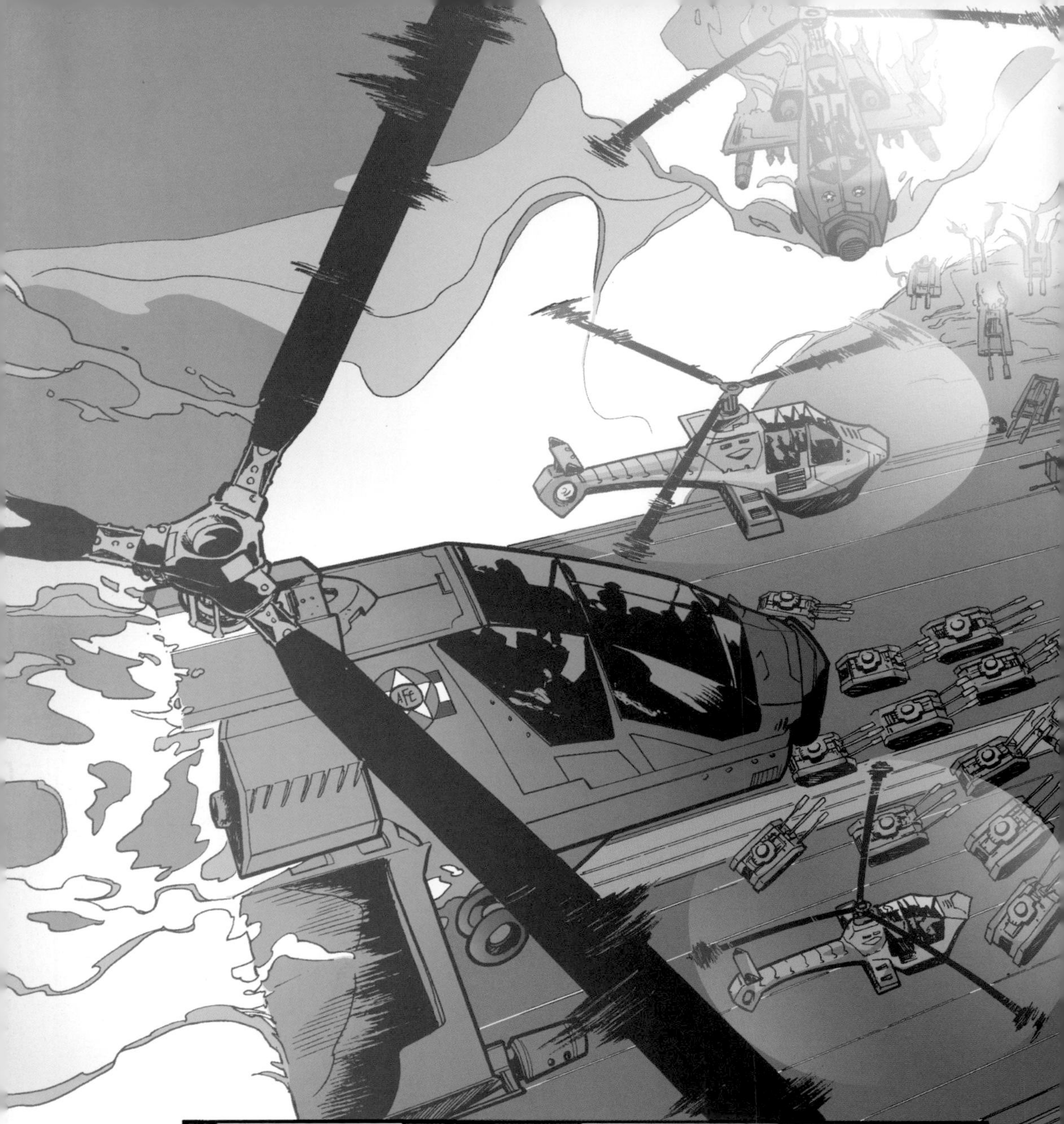

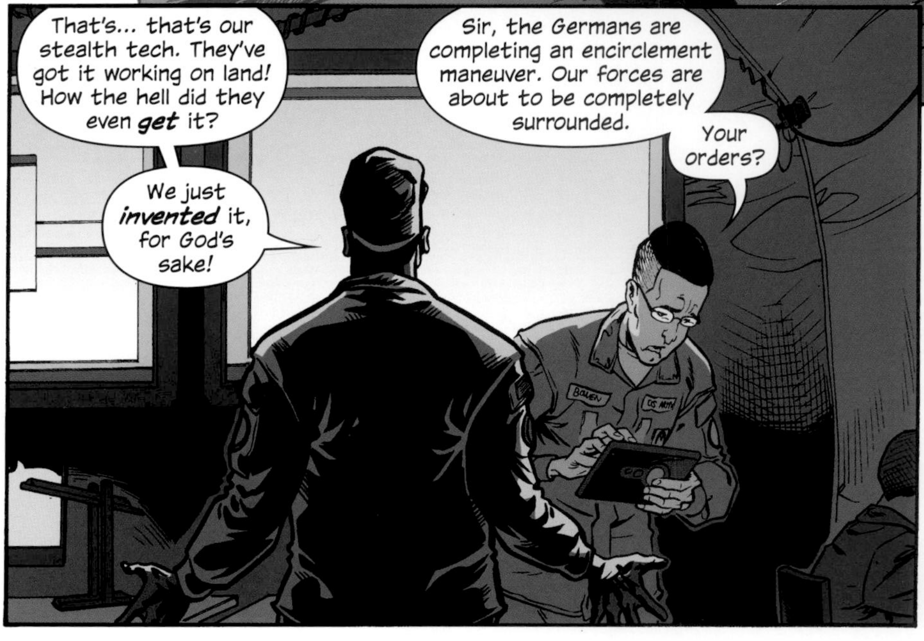
That's... that's our stealth tech. They've got it working on land! How the hell did they even **get** it?
We just **invented** it, for God's sake!
Sir, the Germans are completing an encirclement maneuver. Our forces are about to be completely surrounded.
Your orders?
BOWEN
US ARMY

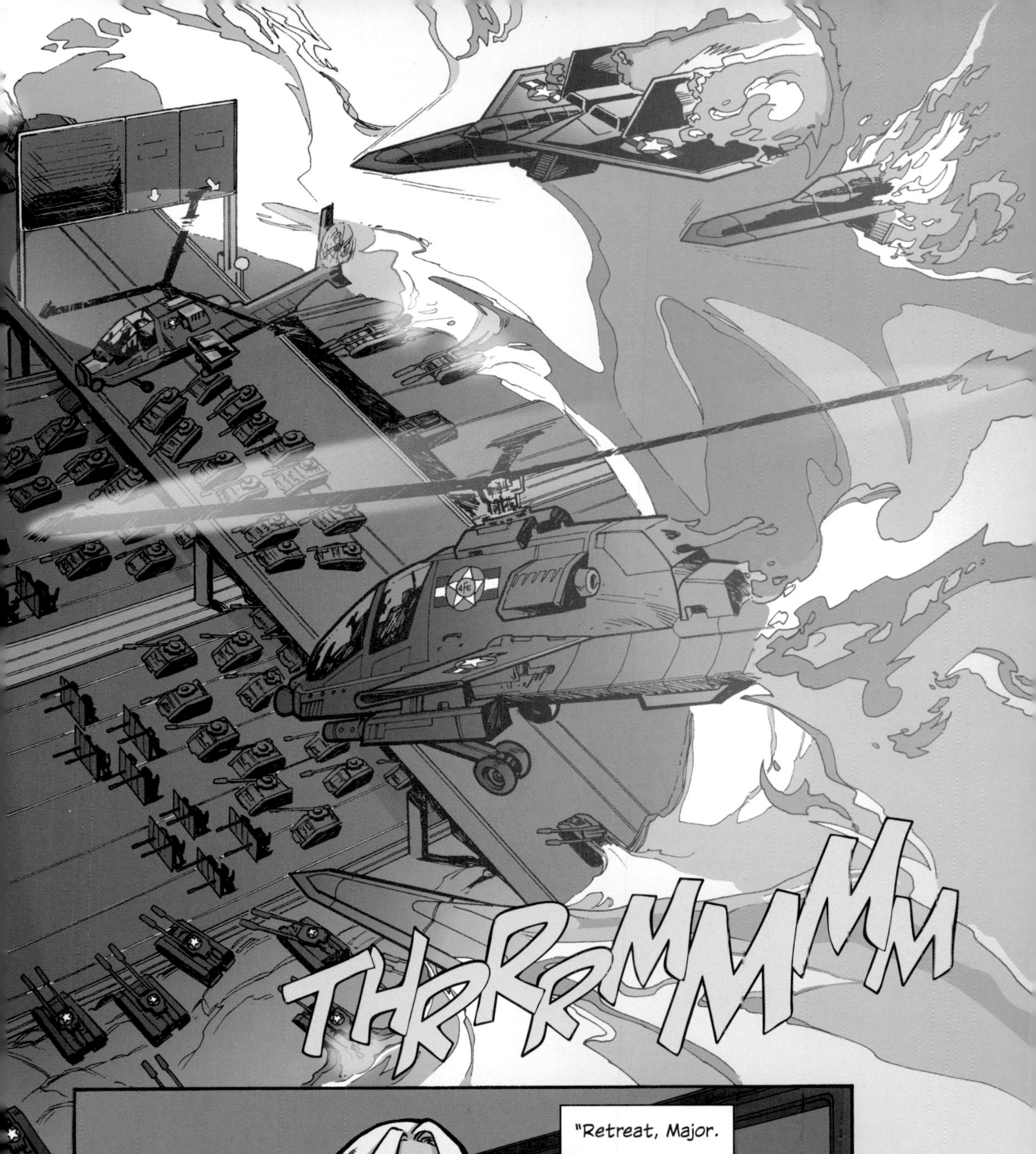
THRRRMMMMMM
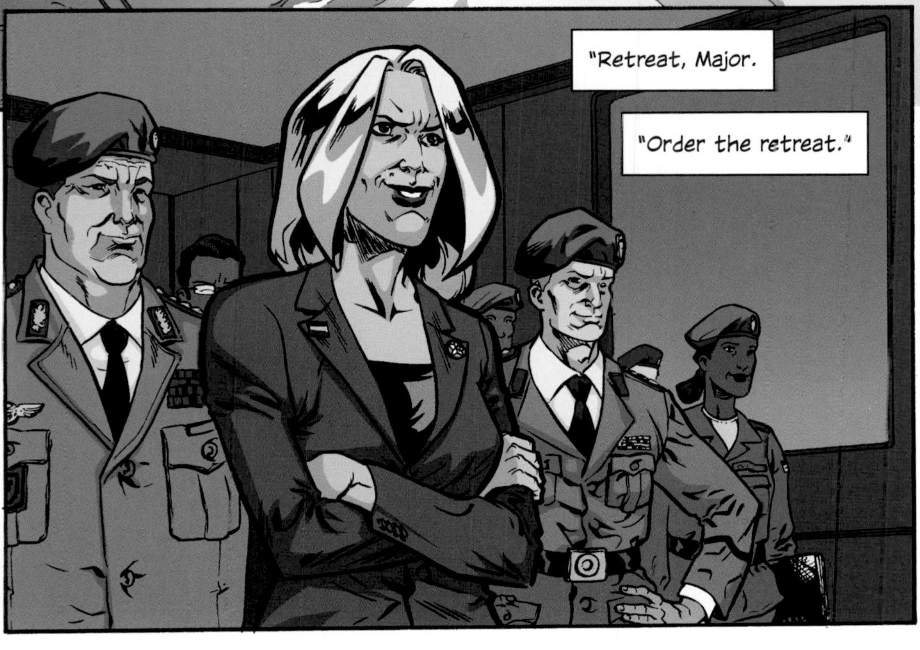
"Retreat, Major.
"Order the retreat."

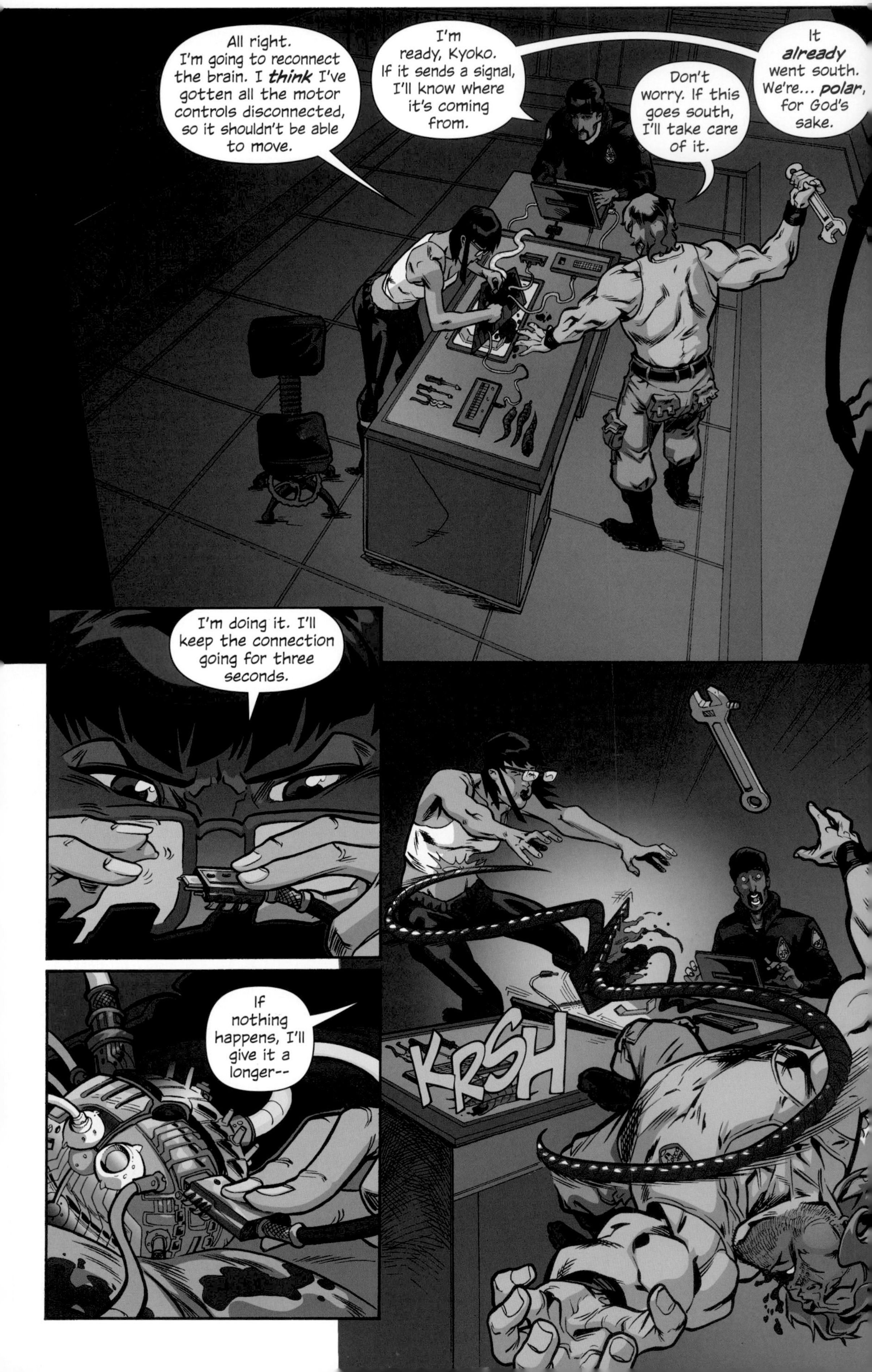
All right. I'm going to reconnect the brain. I *think* I've gotten all the motor controls disconnected, so it shouldn't be able to move.
I'm ready, Kyoko. If it sends a signal, I'll know where it's coming from.
Don't worry. If this goes south, I'll take care of it.
It *already* went south. We're... *polar*, for God's sake.
I'm doing it. I'll keep the connection going for three seconds.
If nothing happens, I'll give it a longer--
KRSH

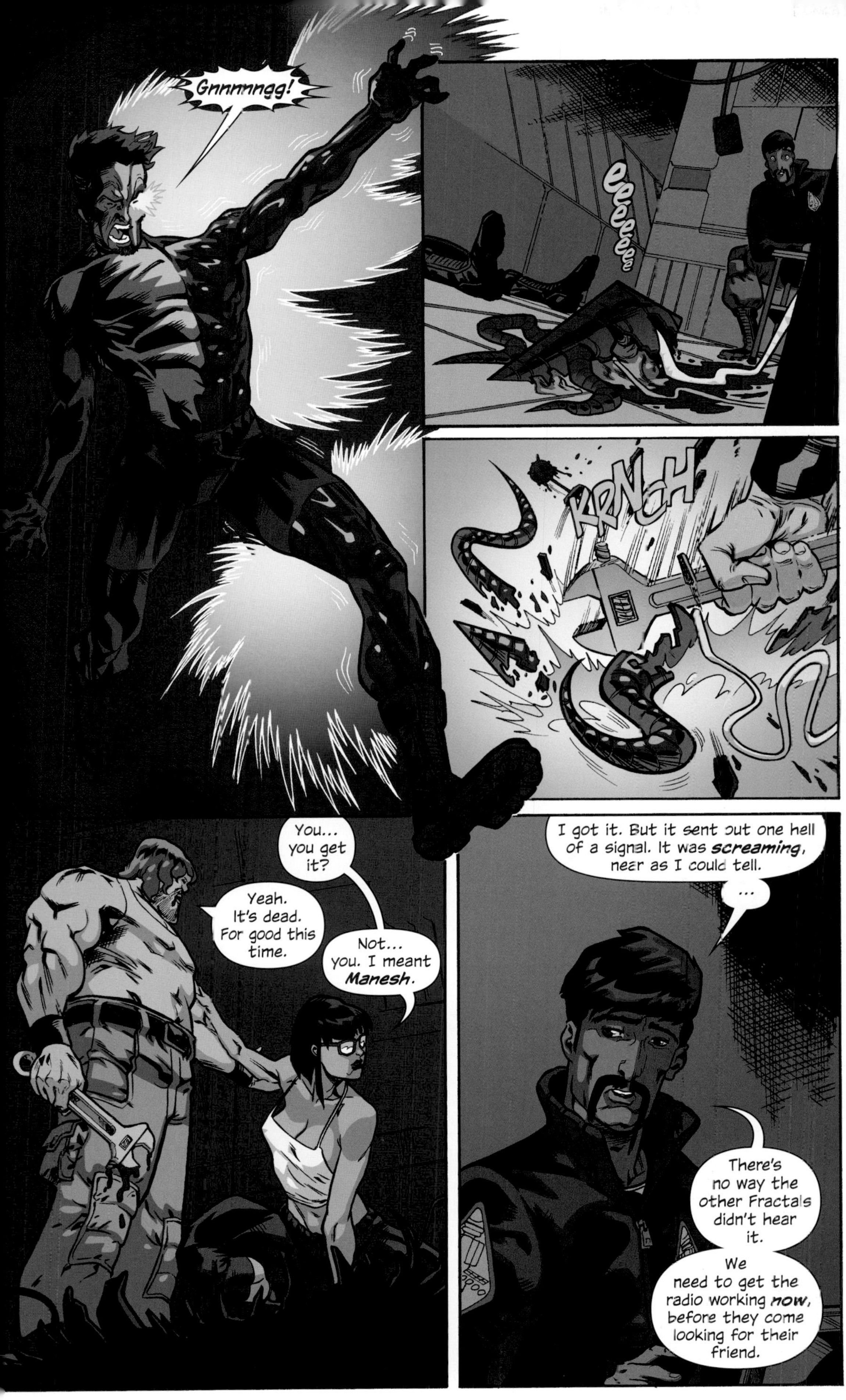

Gnnnnngg!
eeeeeee
KRNCH
You... you get it?
Yeah. It's dead. For good this time.
Not... you. I meant *Manesh*.
I got it. But it sent out one hell of a signal. It was *screaming*, near as I could tell.
...
There's no way the other Fractals didn't hear it.
We need to get the radio working *now*, before they come looking for their friend.

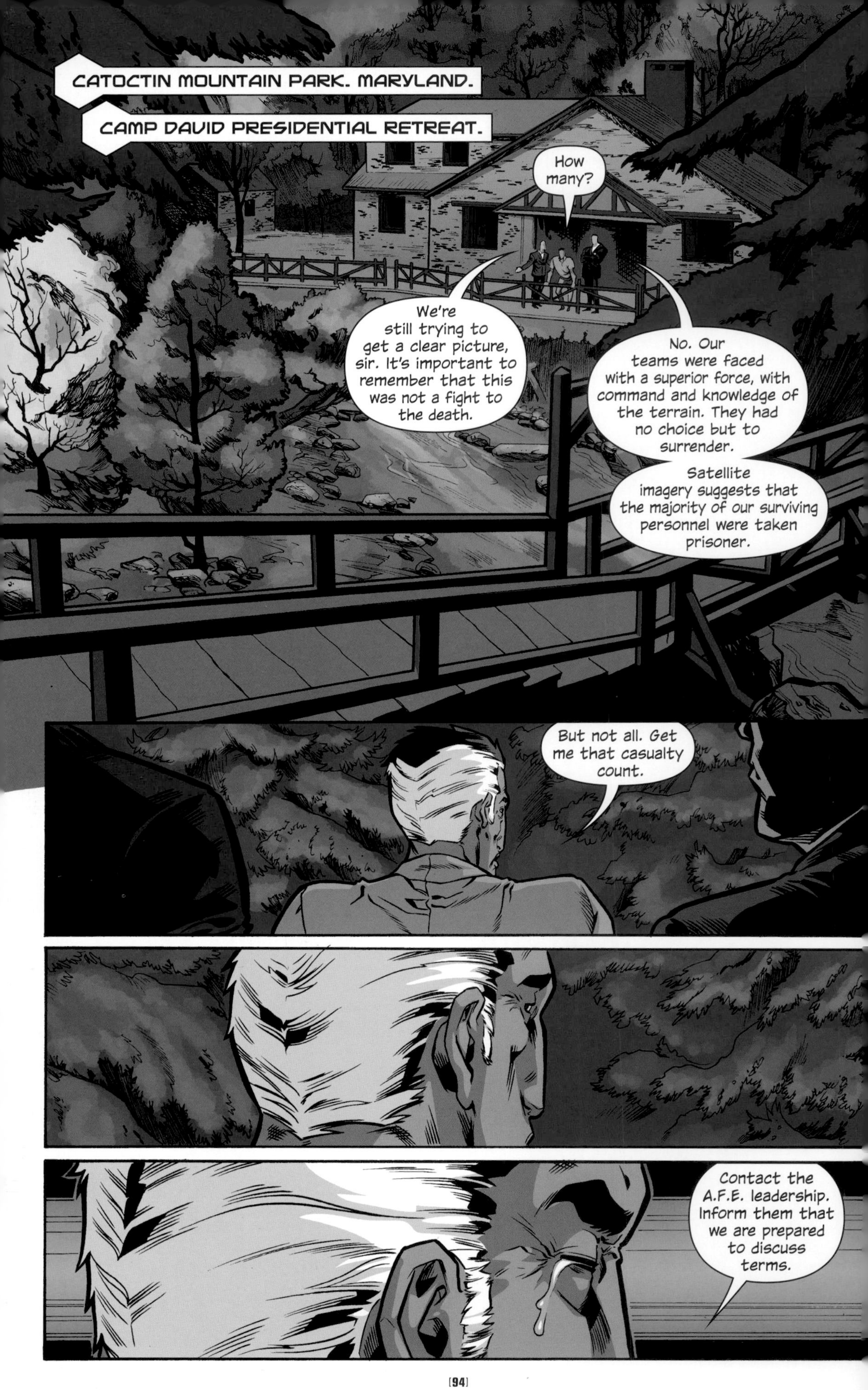
CATOCTIN MOUNTAIN PARK. MARYLAND.
CAMP DAVID PRESIDENTIAL RETREAT.
How many?
We're still trying to get a clear picture, sir. It's important to remember that this was not a fight to the death.
No. Our teams were faced with a superior force, with command and knowledge of the terrain. They had no choice but to surrender.
Satellite imagery suggests that the majority of our surviving personnel were taken prisoner.
But not all. Get me that casualty count.
Contact the A.F.E. leadership. Inform them that we are prepared to discuss terms.

Terms, Mr. President? Can you be more specific? I want to be completely sure I understand before I--

Surrender, Herman. This was our last shot. We lost. It's time to move on.

Is this my fault, AJ? You've been with me from the start of all this.

I thought I was doing the right thing.

You're in *command*, sir. Everything you do is the right thing.

Even when it's not.

I'm so sorry to interrupt, Mr. President, but I thought you would want to take this call immediately.

Unless it's God himself, Elizabeth...

Sir...

...they've re-established contact with the *Clarke*.

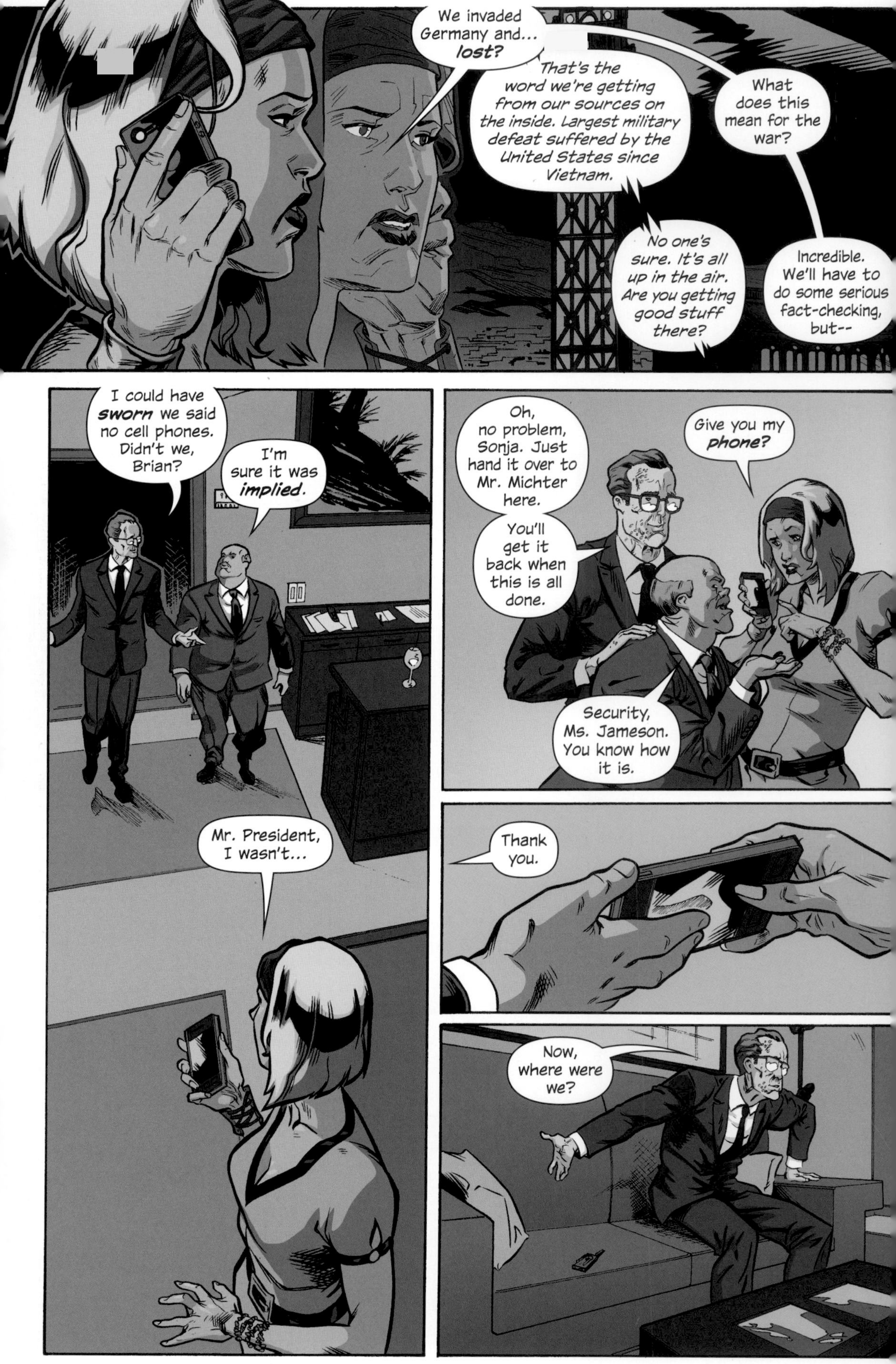

We invaded Germany and... lost?
That's the word we're getting from our sources on the inside. Largest military defeat suffered by the United States since Vietnam.
What does this mean for the war?
No one's sure. It's all up in the air. Are you getting good stuff there?
Incredible. We'll have to do some serious fact-checking, but--
I could have sworn we said no cell phones. Didn't we, Brian?
I'm sure it was implied.
Mr. President, I wasn't...
Oh, no problem, Sonja. Just hand it over to Mr. Michter here.
You'll get it back when this is all done.
Give you my phone?
Security, Ms. Jameson. You know how it is.
Thank you.
Now, where were we?

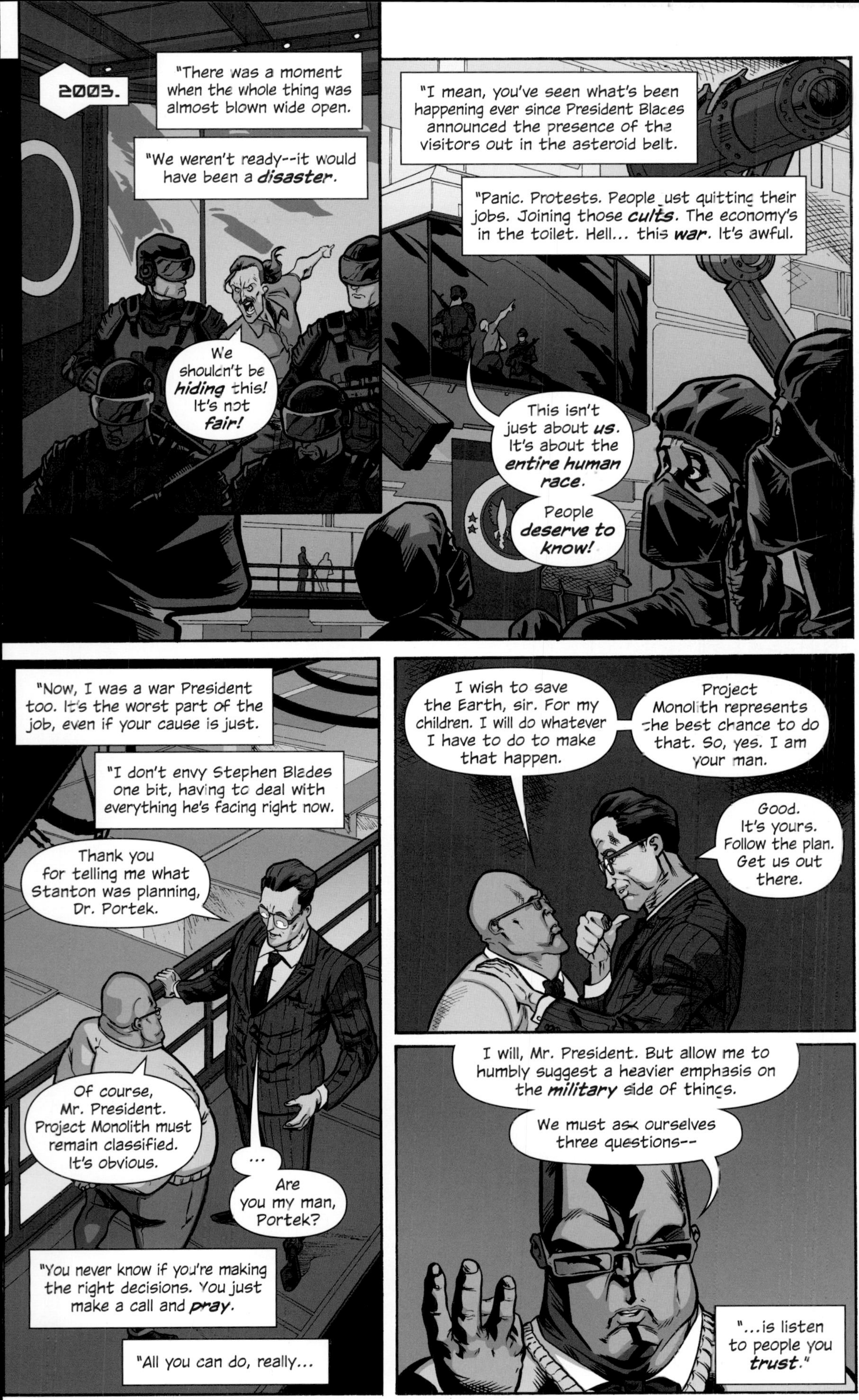
2003.
"There was a moment when the whole thing was almost blown wide open.
"We weren't ready--it would have been a *disaster*.
We shouldn't be *hiding* this! It's not *fair!*
"I mean, you've seen what's been happening ever since President Blades announced the presence of the visitors out in the asteroid belt.
"Panic. Protests. People just quitting their jobs. Joining those *cults*. The economy's in the toilet. Hell... this *war*. It's awful.
This isn't just about *us*. It's about the *entire human race*.
People *deserve to know!*
"Now, I was a war President too. It's the worst part of the job, even if your cause is just.
"I don't envy Stephen Blades one bit, having to deal with everything he's facing right now.
Thank you for telling me what Stanton was planning, Dr. Portek.
Of course, Mr. President. Project Monolith must remain classified. It's obvious.
...
Are you my man, Portek?
"You never know if you're making the right decisions. You just make a call and *pray*.
"All you can do, really...
I wish to save the Earth, sir. For my children. I will do whatever I have to do to make that happen.
Project Monolith represents the best chance to do that. So, yes. I am your man.
Good. It's yours. Follow the plan. Get us out there.
I will, Mr. President. But allow me to humbly suggest a heavier emphasis on the *military* side of things.
We must ask ourselves three questions--
"...is listen to people you *trust*."

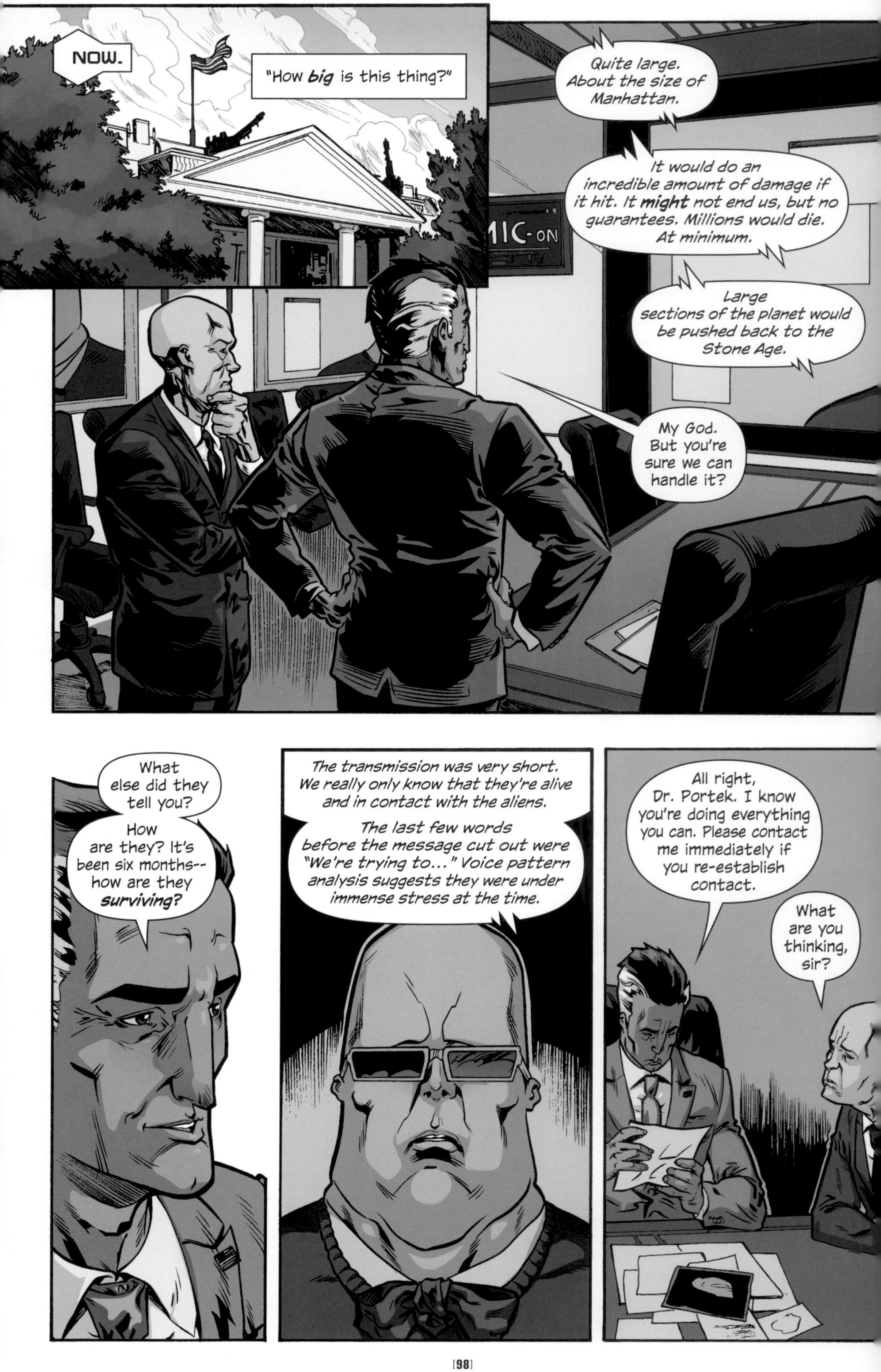
NOW.
"How big is this thing?"
Quite large. About the size of Manhattan.
It would do an incredible amount of damage if it hit. It might not end us, but no guarantees. Millions would die. At minimum.
Large sections of the planet would be pushed back to the Stone Age.
My God. But you're sure we can handle it?
What else did they tell you?
How are they? It's been six months-- how are they surviving?
The transmission was very short. We really only know that they're alive and in contact with the aliens.
The last few words before the message cut out were "We're trying to..." Voice pattern analysis suggests they were under immense stress at the time.
All right, Dr. Portek. I know you're doing everything you can. Please contact me immediately if you re-establish contact.
What are you thinking, sir?

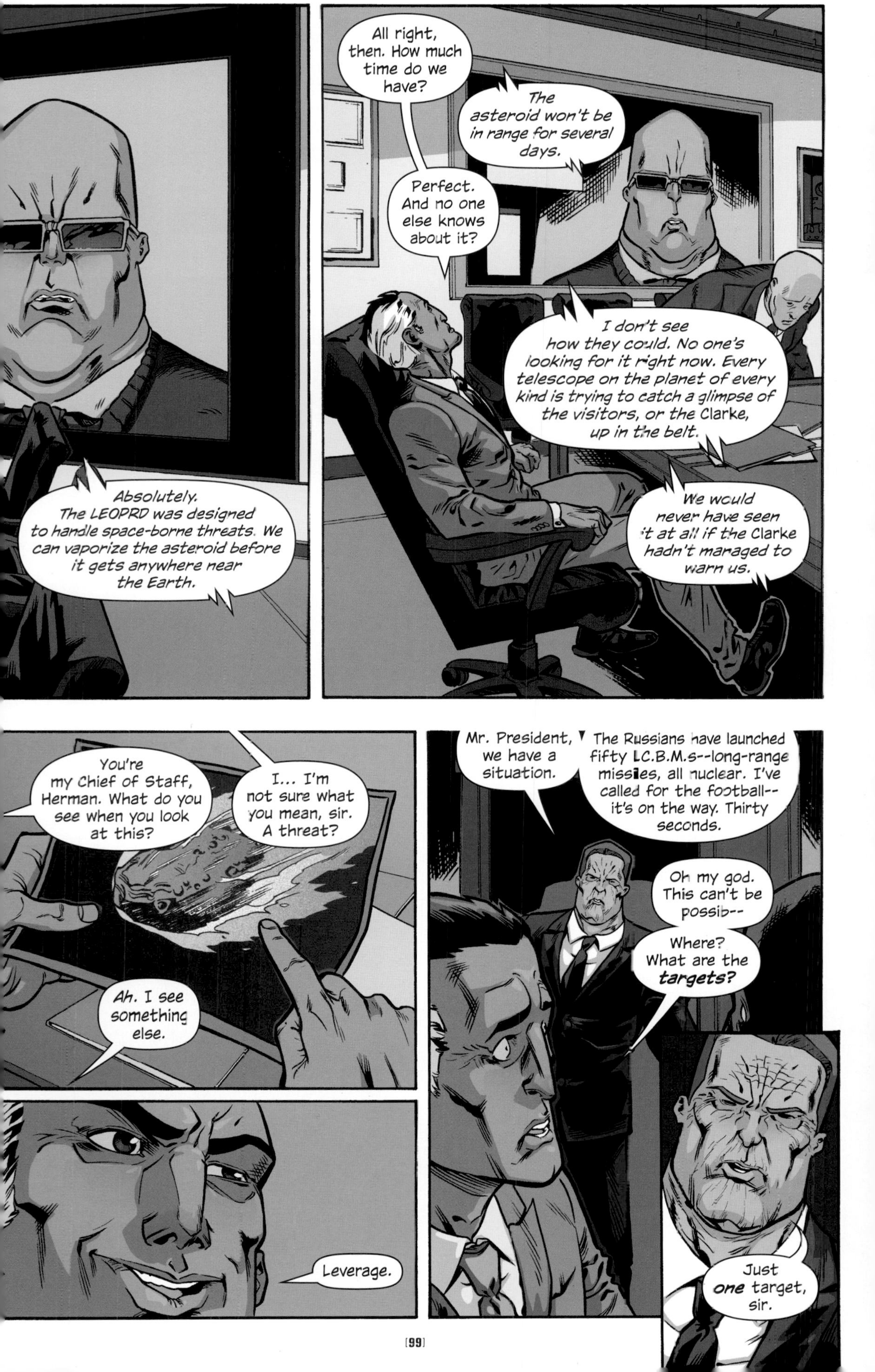
All right, then. How much time do we have?
The asteroid won't be in range for several days.
Perfect. And no one else knows about it?
I don't see how they could. No one's looking for it right now. Every telescope on the planet of every kind is trying to catch a glimpse of the visitors, or the Clarke, up in the belt.
We would never have seen it at all if the Clarke hadn't managed to warn us.
Absolutely. The LEOPRD was designed to handle space-borne threats. We can vaporize the asteroid before it gets anywhere near the Earth.
You're my Chief of Staff, Herman. What do you see when you look at this?
I... I'm not sure what you mean, sir. A threat?
Ah. I see something else.
Leverage.
Mr. President, we have a situation.
The Russians have launched fifty I.C.B.M.s--long-range missiles, all nuclear. I've called for the football--it's on the way. Thirty seconds.
Oh my god. This can't be possib--
Where? What are the ***targets?***
Just ***one*** target, sir.

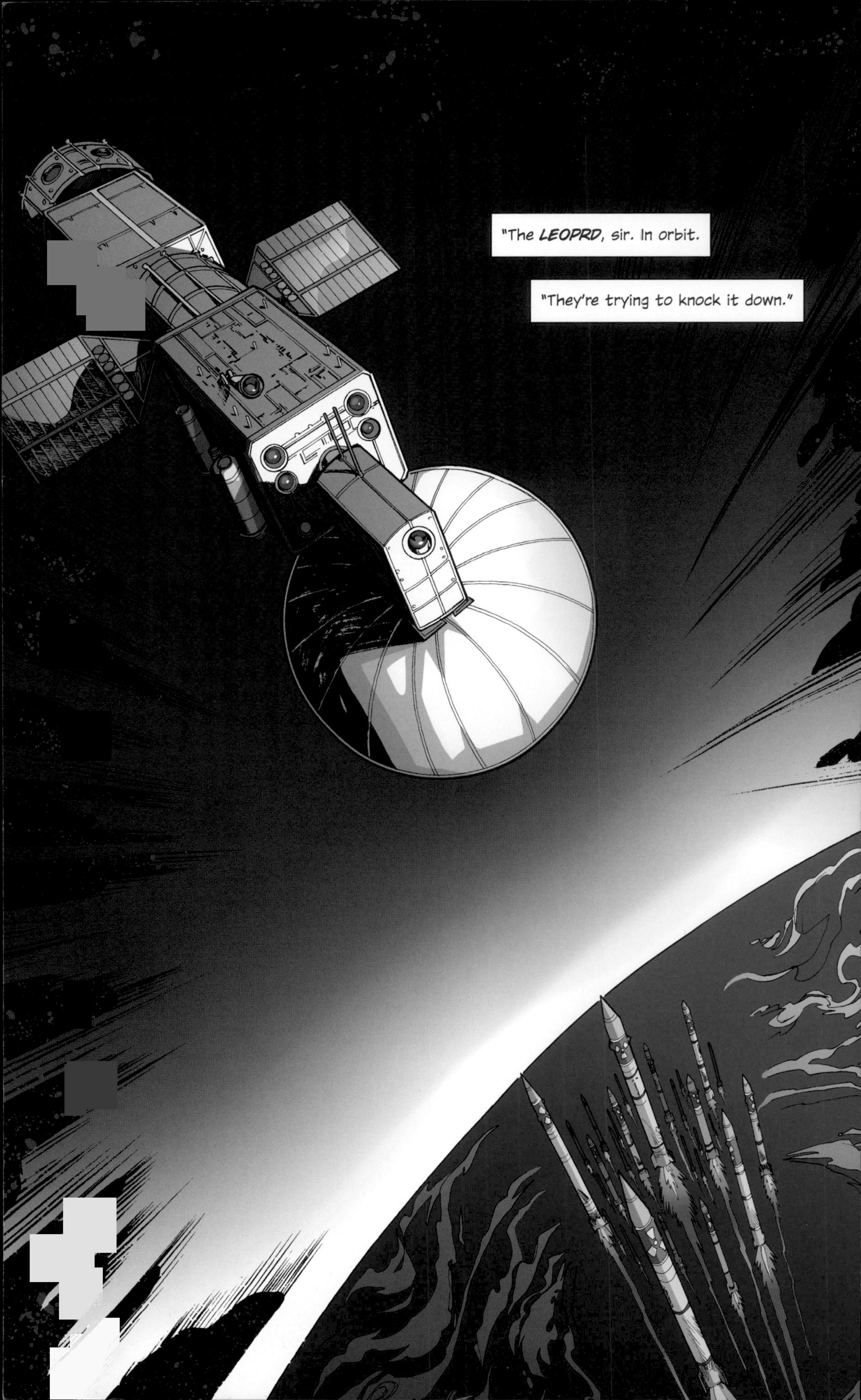
"The LEOPRD, sir. In orbit.
"They're trying to knock it down."

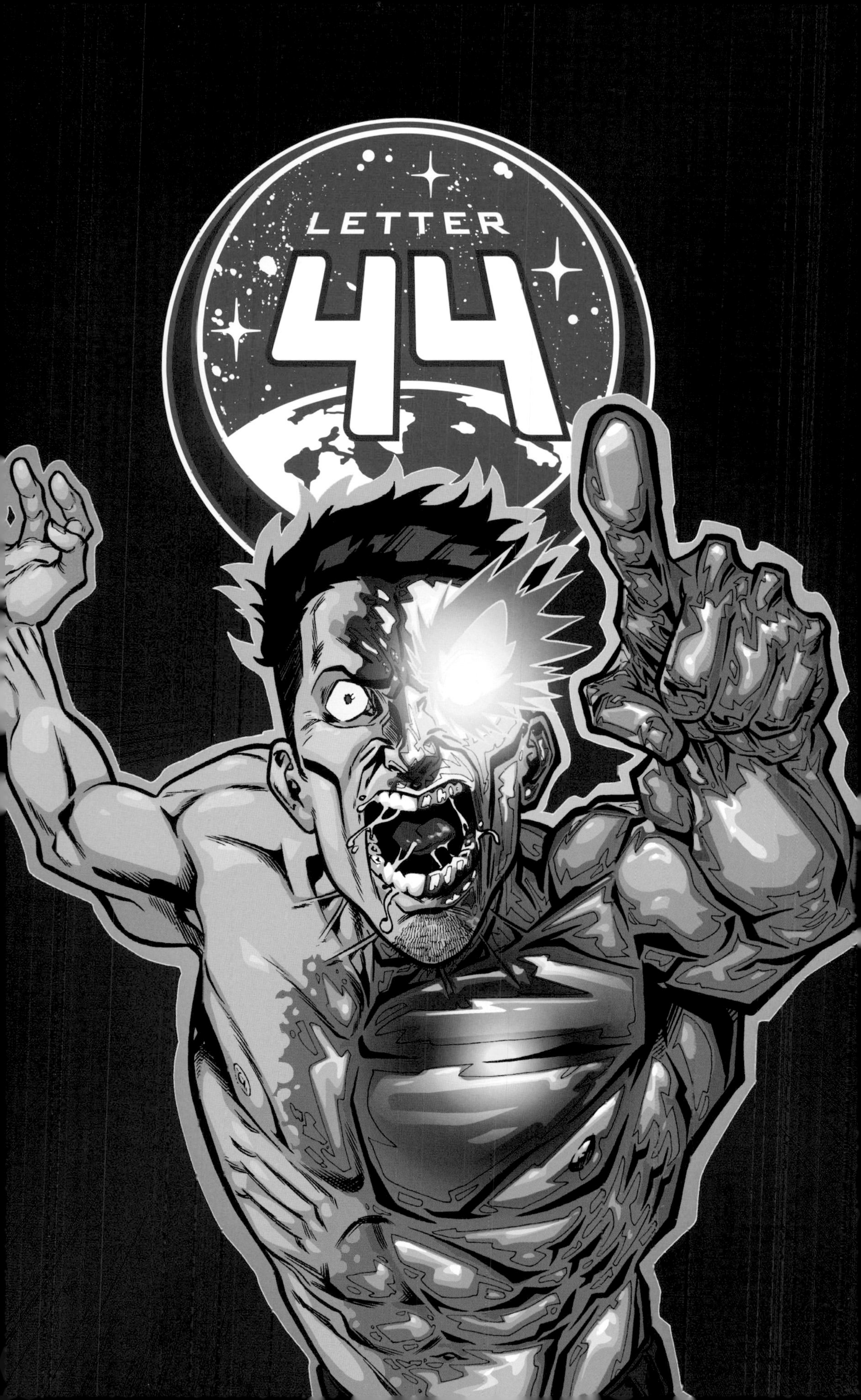
LETTER
44

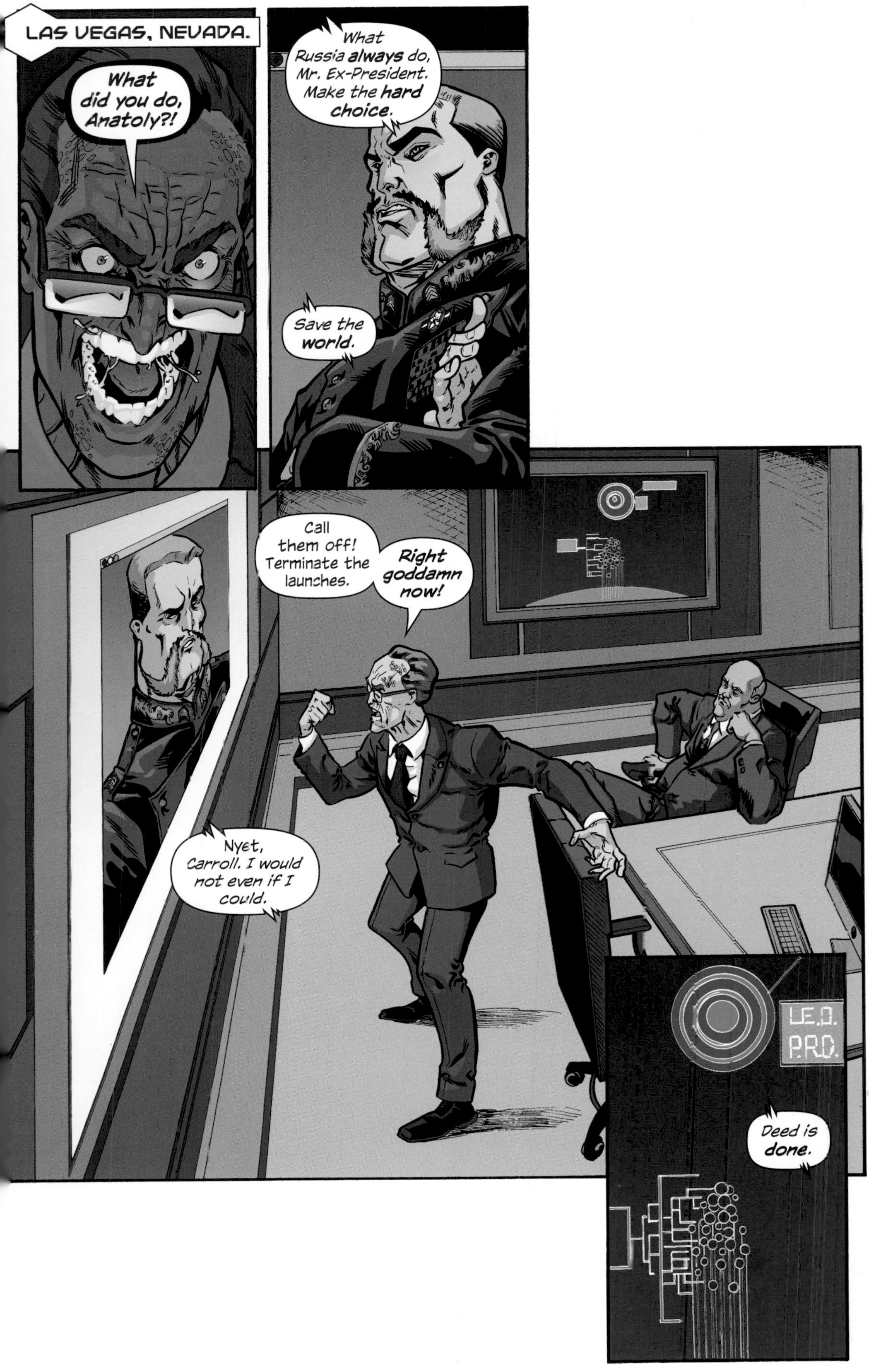
LAS VEGAS, NEVADA.
What did you do, Anatoly?!
What Russia always do, Mr. Ex-President. Make the hard choice.
Save the world.
Call them off! Terminate the launches.
Right goddamn now!
Nyet, Carroll. I would not even if I could.
LE.D. P.R.D.
Deed is done.

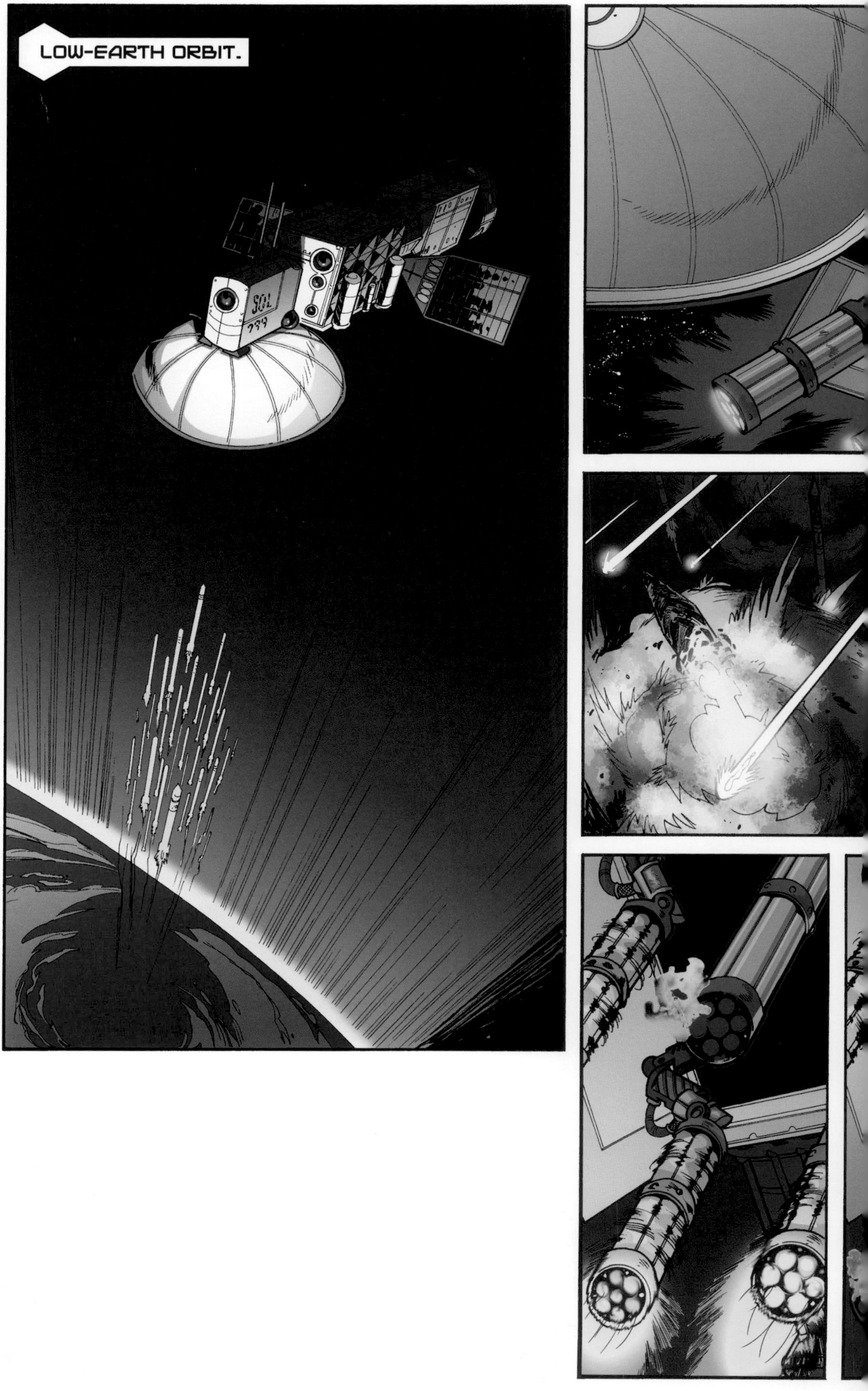
LOW-EARTH ORBIT.
SOL

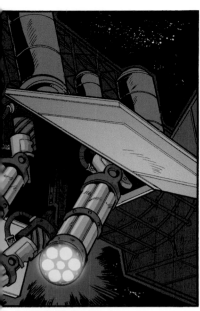

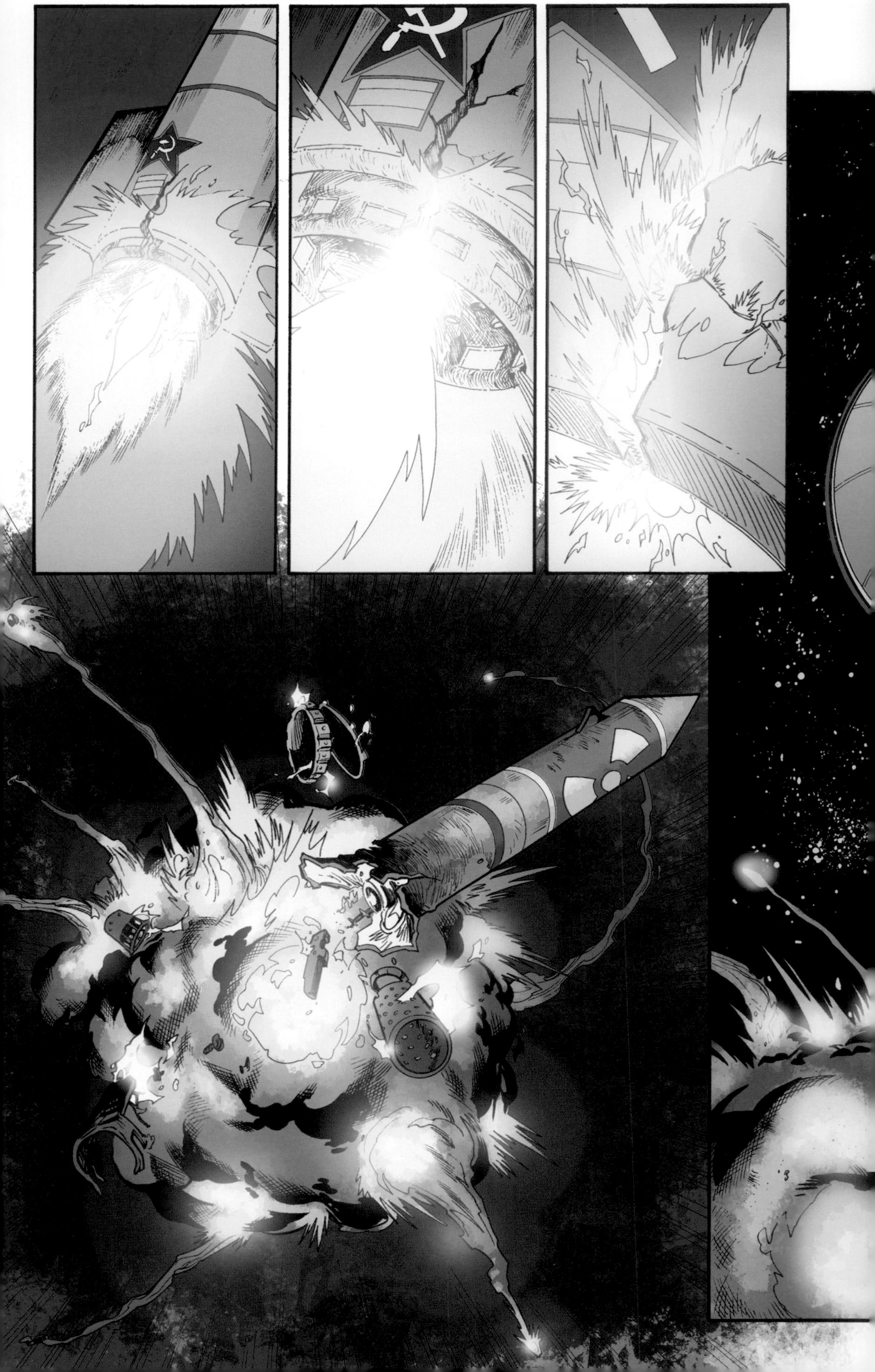

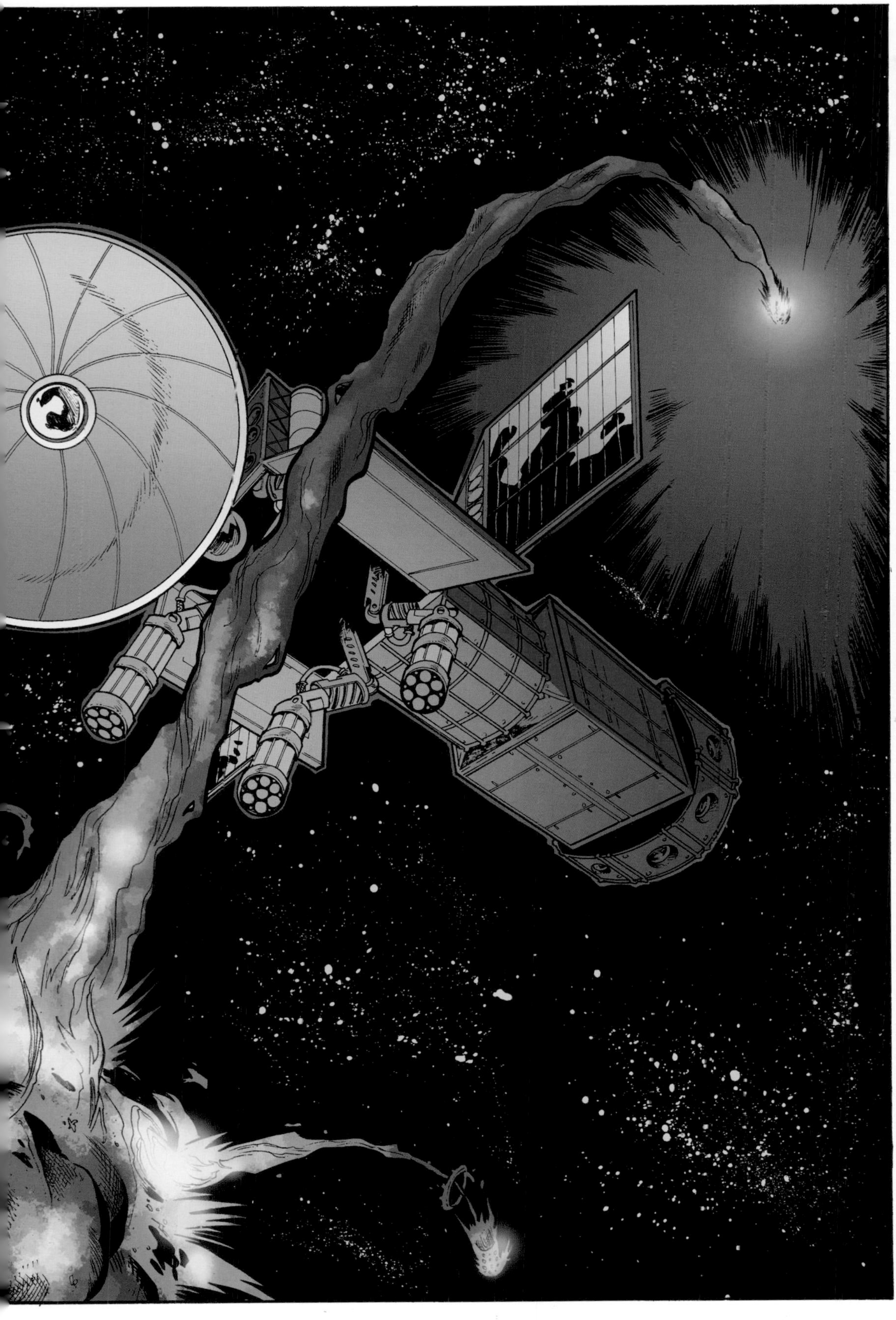

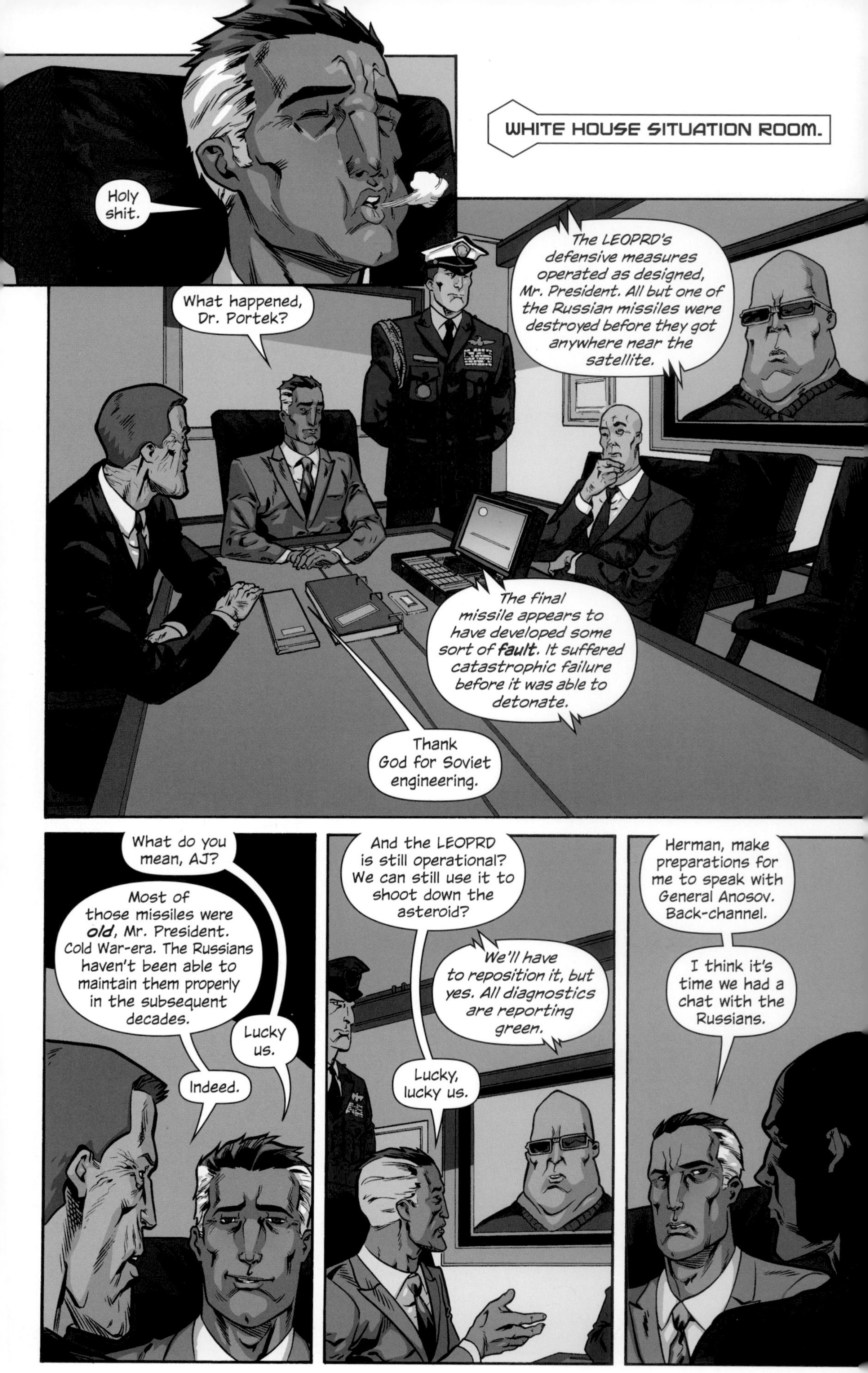
WHITE HOUSE SITUATION ROOM.
Holy shit.
What happened, Dr. Portek?
The LEOPRD's defensive measures operated as designed, Mr. President. All but one of the Russian missiles were destroyed before they got anywhere near the satellite.
The final missile appears to have developed some sort of **fault**. It suffered catastrophic failure before it was able to detonate.
Thank God for Soviet engineering.
What do you mean, AJ?
Most of those missiles were ***old***, Mr. President. Cold War-era. The Russians haven't been able to maintain them properly in the subsequent decades.
Lucky us.
Indeed.
And the LEOPRD is still operational? We can still use it to shoot down the asteroid?
We'll have to reposition it, but yes. All diagnostics are reporting green.
Lucky, lucky us.
Herman, make preparations for me to speak with General Anosov. Back-channel.
I think it's time we had a chat with the Russians.

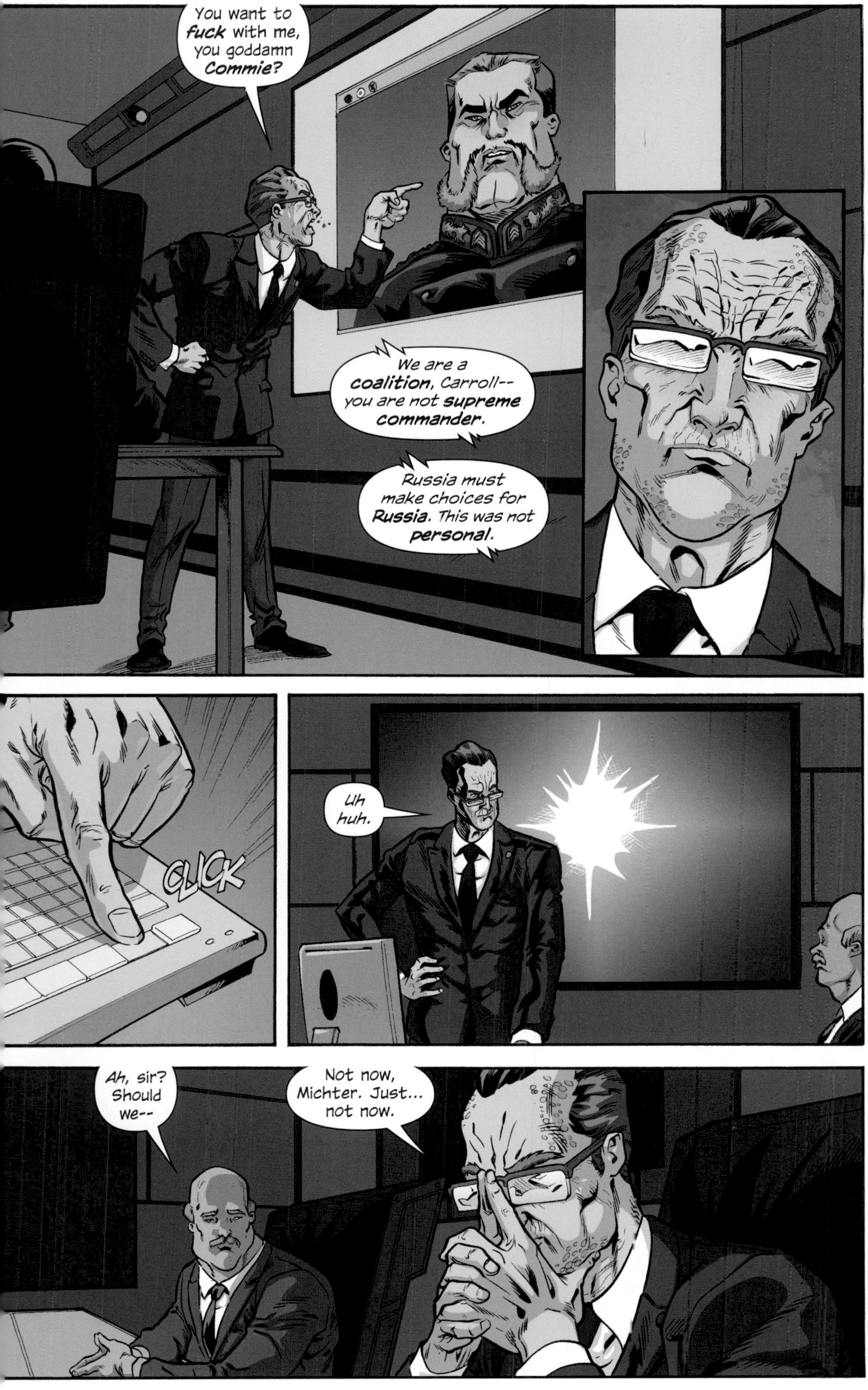
You want to fuck with me, you goddamn Commie?
We are a coalition, Carroll-- you are not supreme commander.
Russia must make choices for Russia. This was not personal.
CLICK
Uh huh.
Ah, sir? Should we--
Not now, Michter. Just... not now.

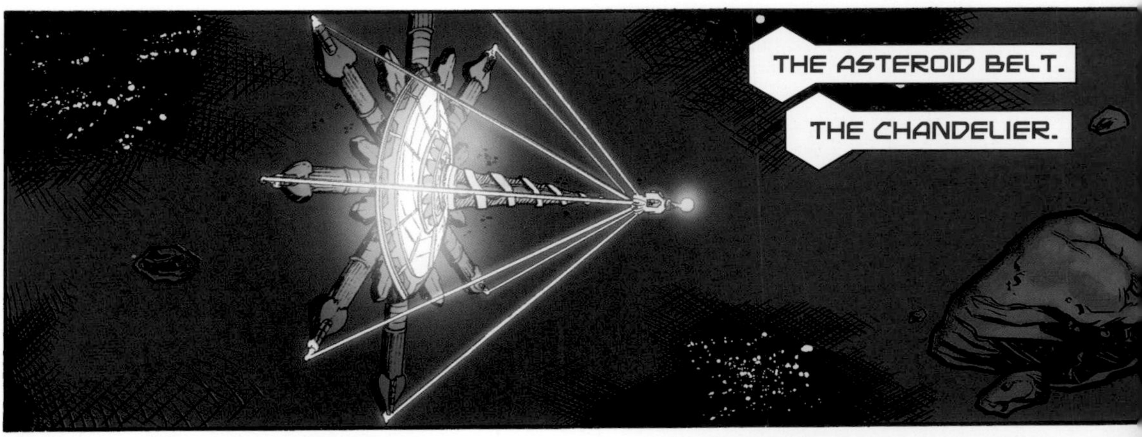
THE ASTEROID BELT.
THE CHANDELIER.

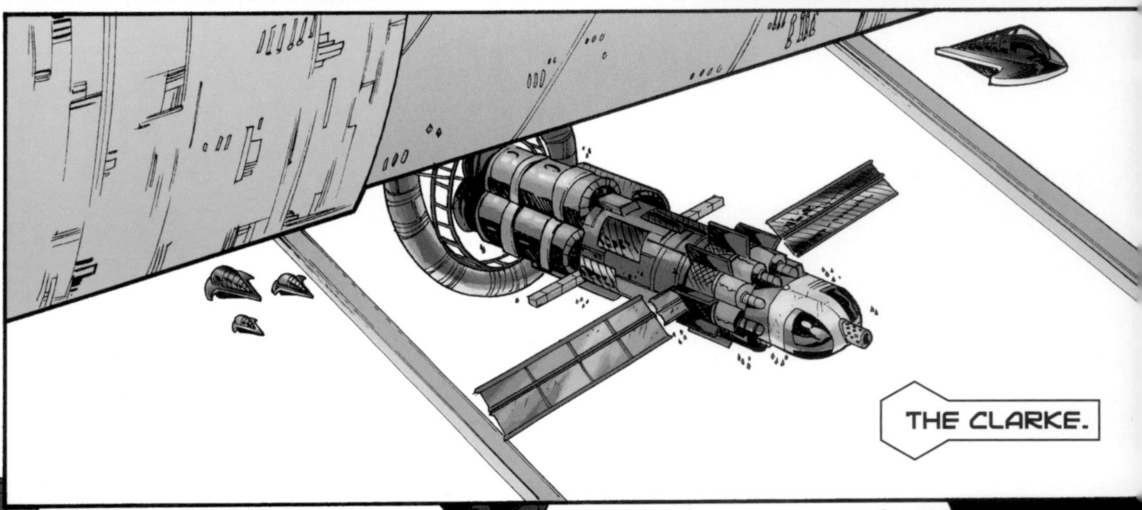
THE CLARKE.

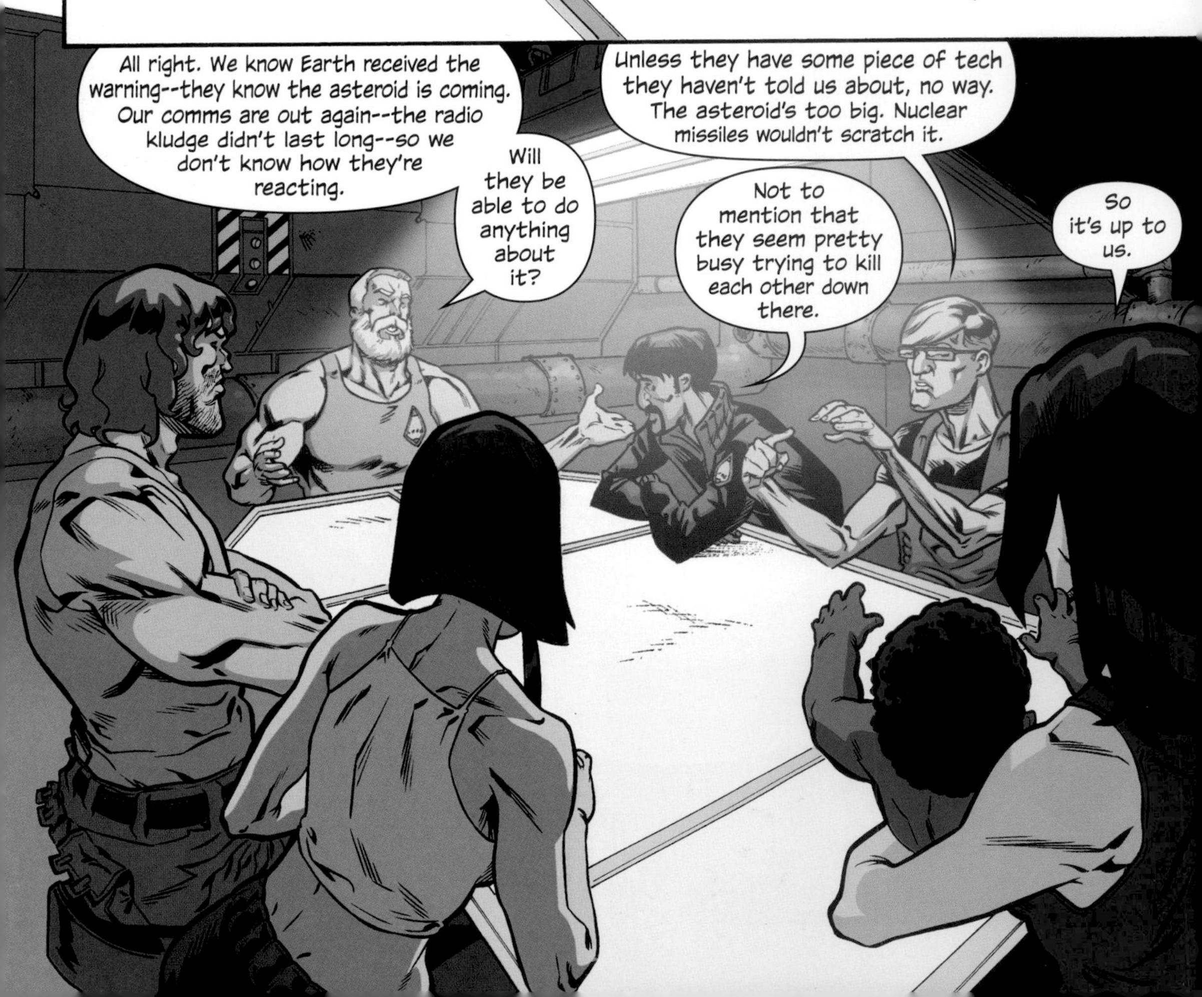
All right. We know Earth received the warning--they know the asteroid is coming. Our comms are out again--the radio kludge didn't last long--so we don't know how they're reacting.
Will they be able to do anything about it?
Unless they have some piece of tech they haven't told us about, no way. The asteroid's too big. Nuclear missiles wouldn't scratch it.
Not to mention that they seem pretty busy trying to kill each other down there.
So it's up to us.

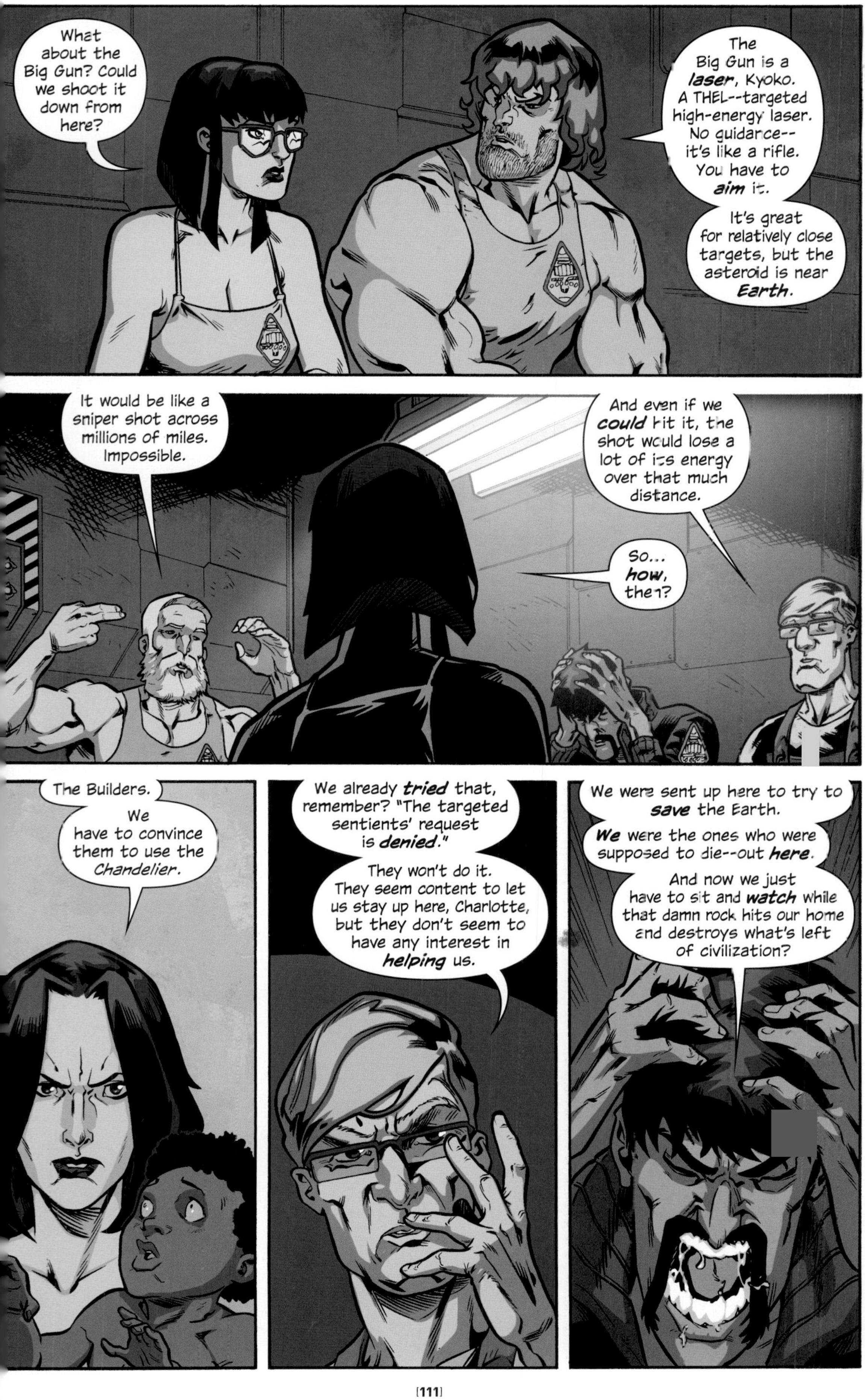

What about the Big Gun? Could we shoot it down from here?
The Big Gun is a *laser*, Kyoko. A THEL--targeted high-energy laser. No guidance--it's like a rifle. You have to *aim* it.
It's great for relatively close targets, but the asteroid is near *Earth*.
It would be like a sniper shot across millions of miles. Impossible.
And even if we *could* hit it, the shot would lose a lot of its energy over that much distance.
So... *how*, then?
The Builders.
We have to convince them to use the *Chandelier*.
We already *tried* that, remember? "The targeted sentients' request is *denied*."
They won't do it. They seem content to let us stay up here, Charlotte, but they don't seem to have any interest in *helping* us.
We were sent up here to try to *save* the Earth.
We were the ones who were supposed to die--out *here*.
And now we just have to sit and *watch* while that damn rock hits our home and destroys what's left of civilization?

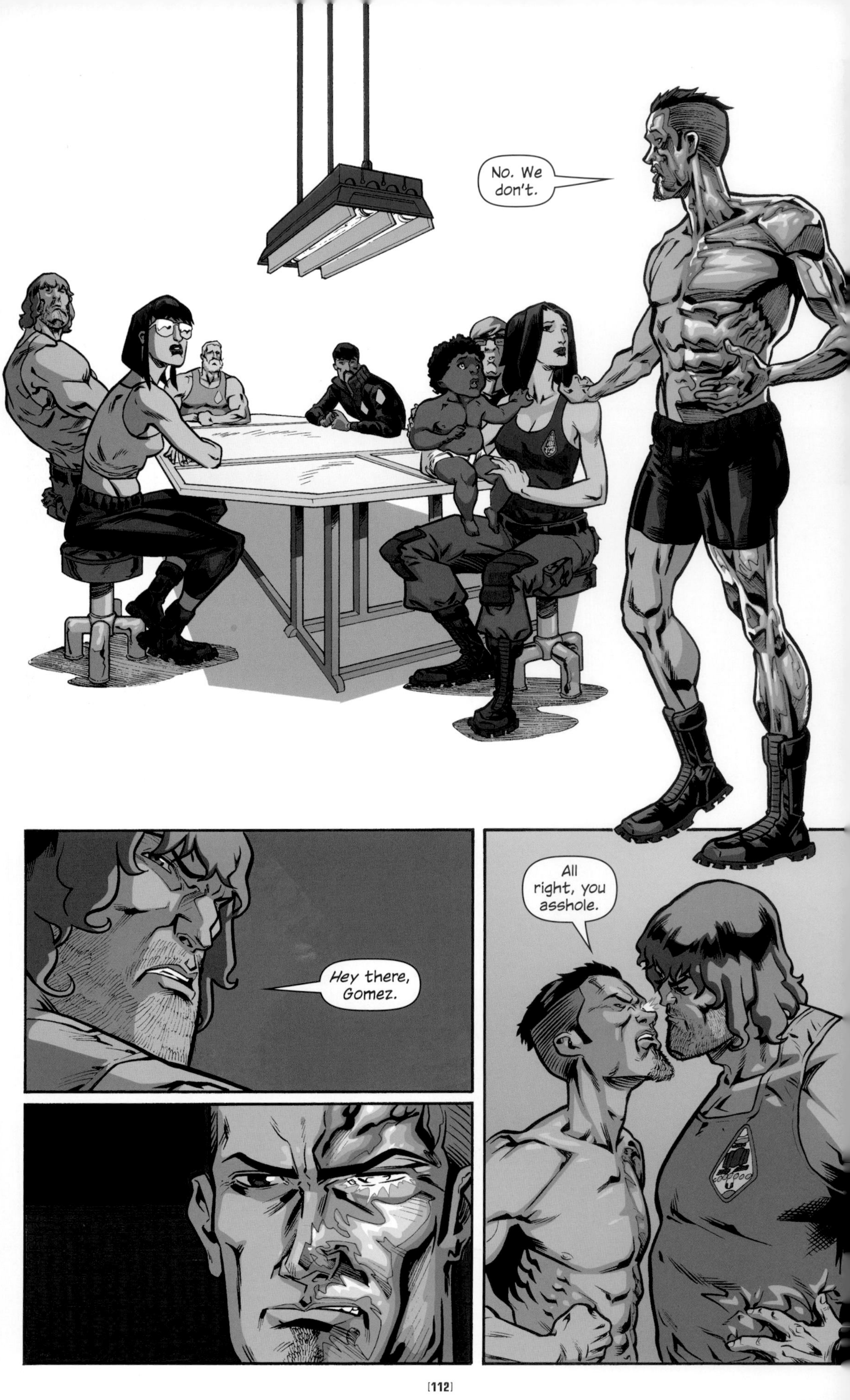
No. We don't.
Hey there, Gomez.
All right, you asshole.

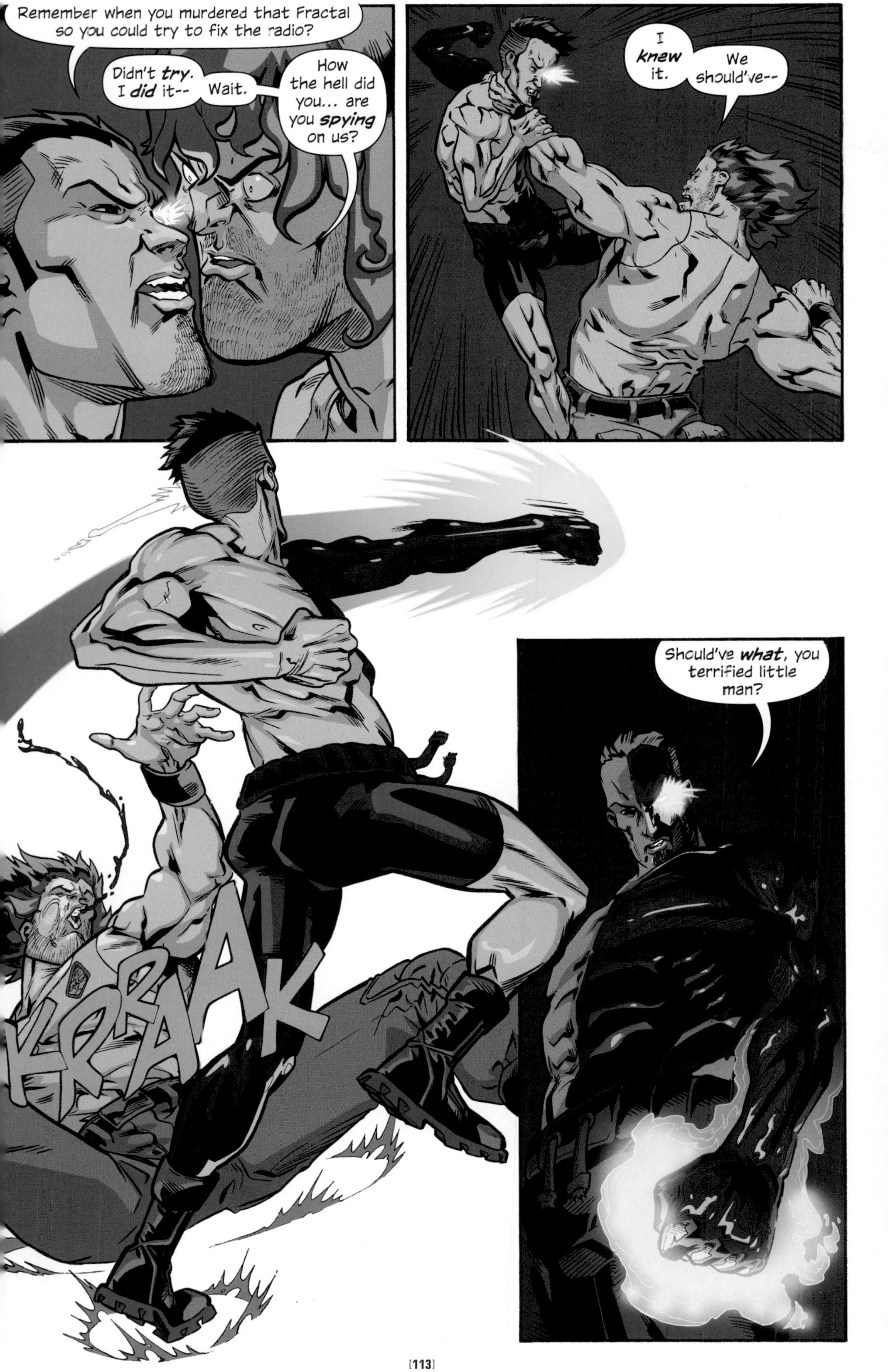
Remember when you murdered that Fractal so you could try to fix the radio?
Didn't try. I did it--
Wait.
How the hell did you... are you spying on us?
I knew it.
We should've--
KRAAK
Should've what, you terrified little man?

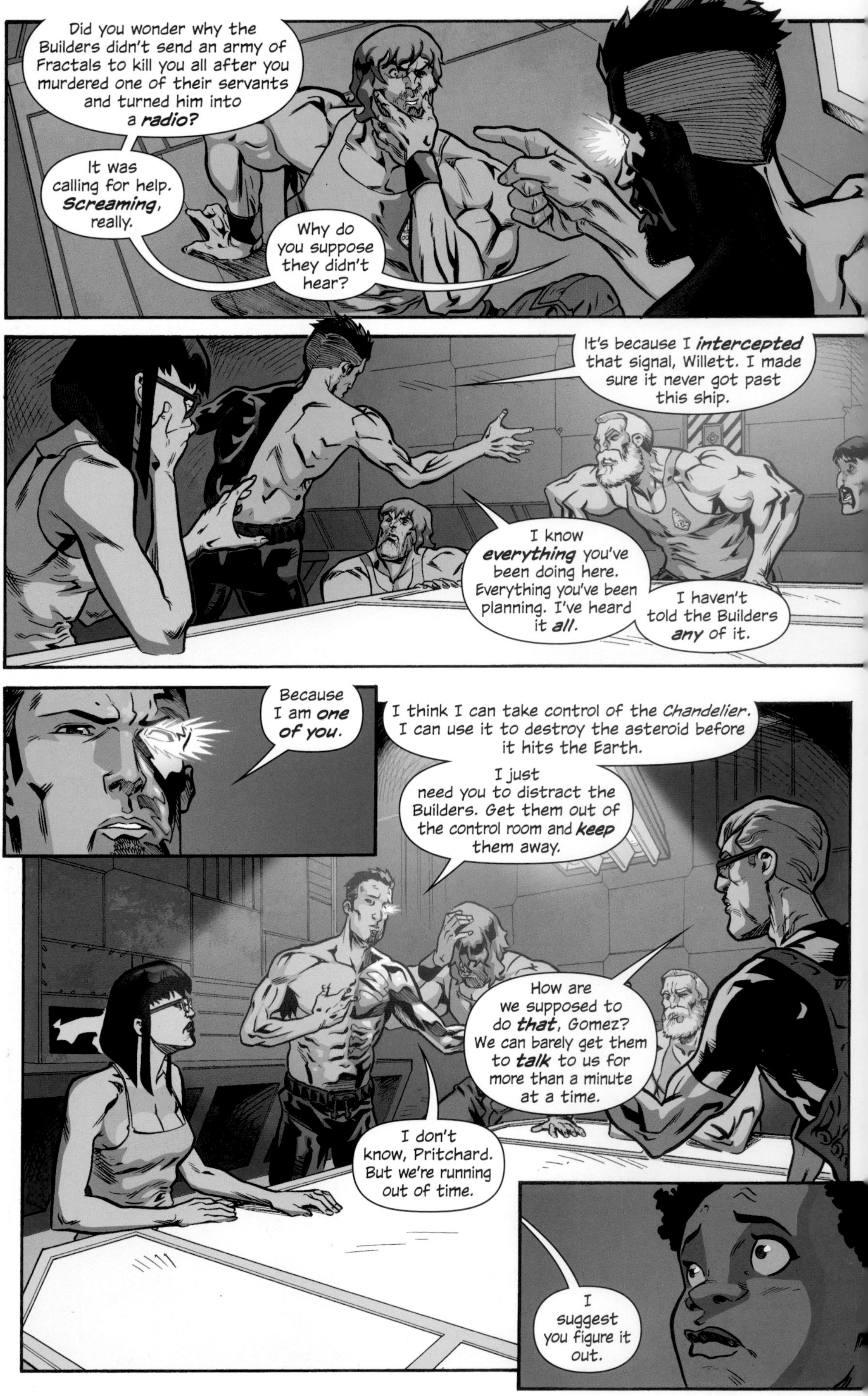

Did you wonder why the Builders didn't send an army of Fractals to kill you all after you murdered one of their servants and turned him into a *radio?*
It was calling for help. *Screaming*, really.
Why do you suppose they didn't hear?
It's because I *intercepted* that signal, Willett. I made sure it never got past this ship.
I know *everything* you've been doing here. Everything you've been planning. I've heard it *all*.
I haven't told the Builders *any* of it.
Because I am *one of you*.
I think I can take control of the *Chandelier*. I can use it to destroy the asteroid before it hits the Earth.
I just need you to distract the Builders. Get them out of the control room and *keep* them away.
How are we supposed to do *that*, Gomez? We can barely get them to *talk* to us for more than a minute at a time.
I don't know, Pritchard. But we're running out of time.
I suggest you figure it out.

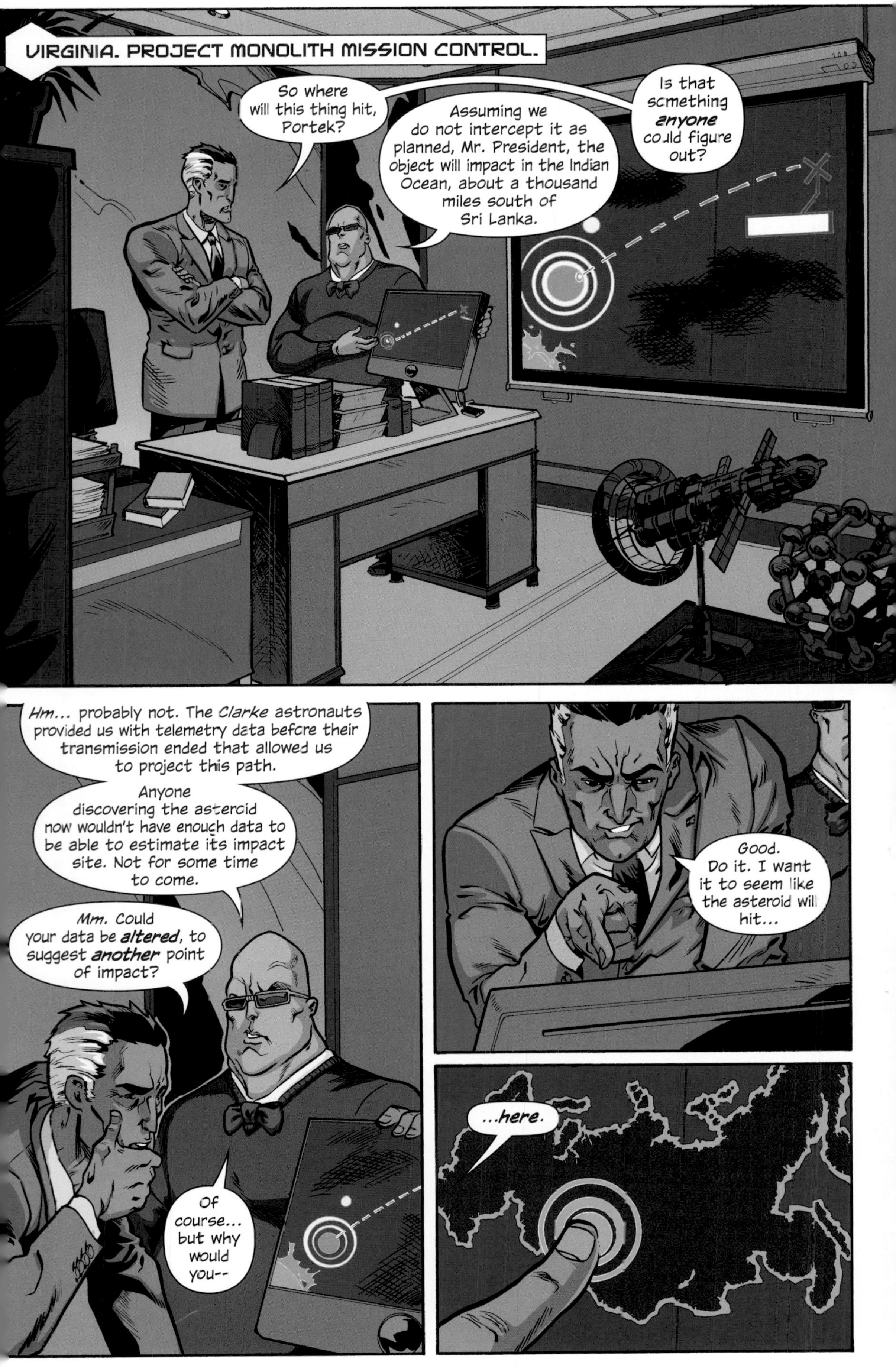
VIRGINIA. PROJECT MONOLITH MISSION CONTROL.
So where will this thing hit, Portek?
Assuming we do not intercept it as planned, Mr. President, the object will impact in the Indian Ocean, about a thousand miles south of Sri Lanka.
Is that something *anyone* could figure out?
Hm... probably not. The *Clarke* astronauts provided us with telemetry data before their transmission ended that allowed us to project this path.
Anyone discovering the asteroid now wouldn't have enough data to be able to estimate its impact site. Not for some time to come.
Mm. Could your data be ***altered***, to suggest ***another*** point of impact?
Of course... but why would you--
Good. Do it. I want it to seem like the asteroid will hit...
...*here*.

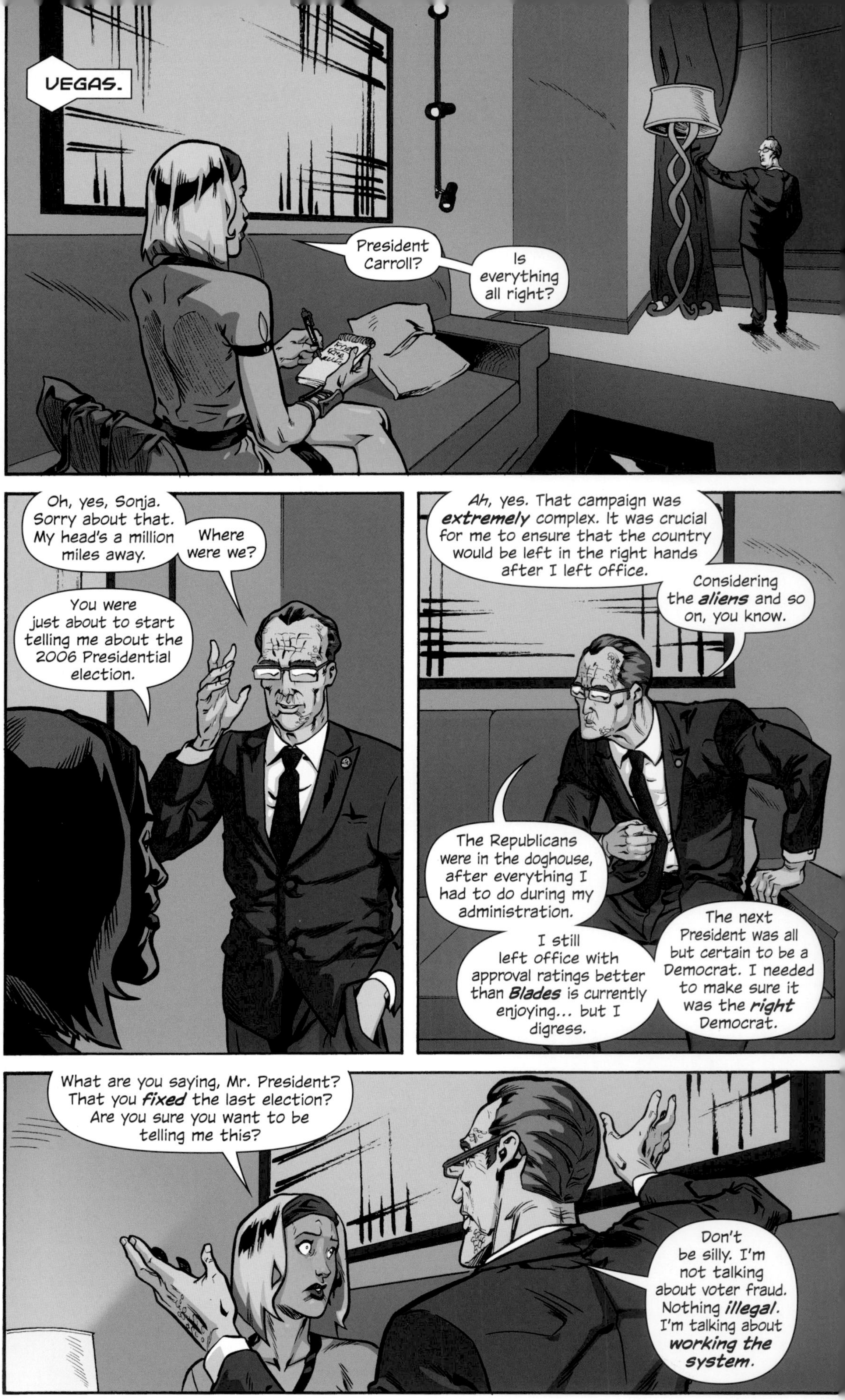
VEGAS.
President Carroll?
Is everything all right?
Oh, yes, Sonja. Sorry about that. My head's a million miles away.
Where were we?
You were just about to start telling me about the 2006 Presidential election.
Ah, yes. That campaign was extremely complex. It was crucial for me to ensure that the country would be left in the right hands after I left office.
Considering the aliens and so on, you know.
The Republicans were in the doghouse, after everything I had to do during my administration.
I still left office with approval ratings better than Blades is currently enjoying... but I digress.
The next President was all but certain to be a Democrat. I needed to make sure it was the right Democrat.
What are you saying, Mr. President? That you fixed the last election? Are you sure you want to be telling me this?
Don't be silly. I'm not talking about voter fraud. Nothing illegal. I'm talking about working the system.

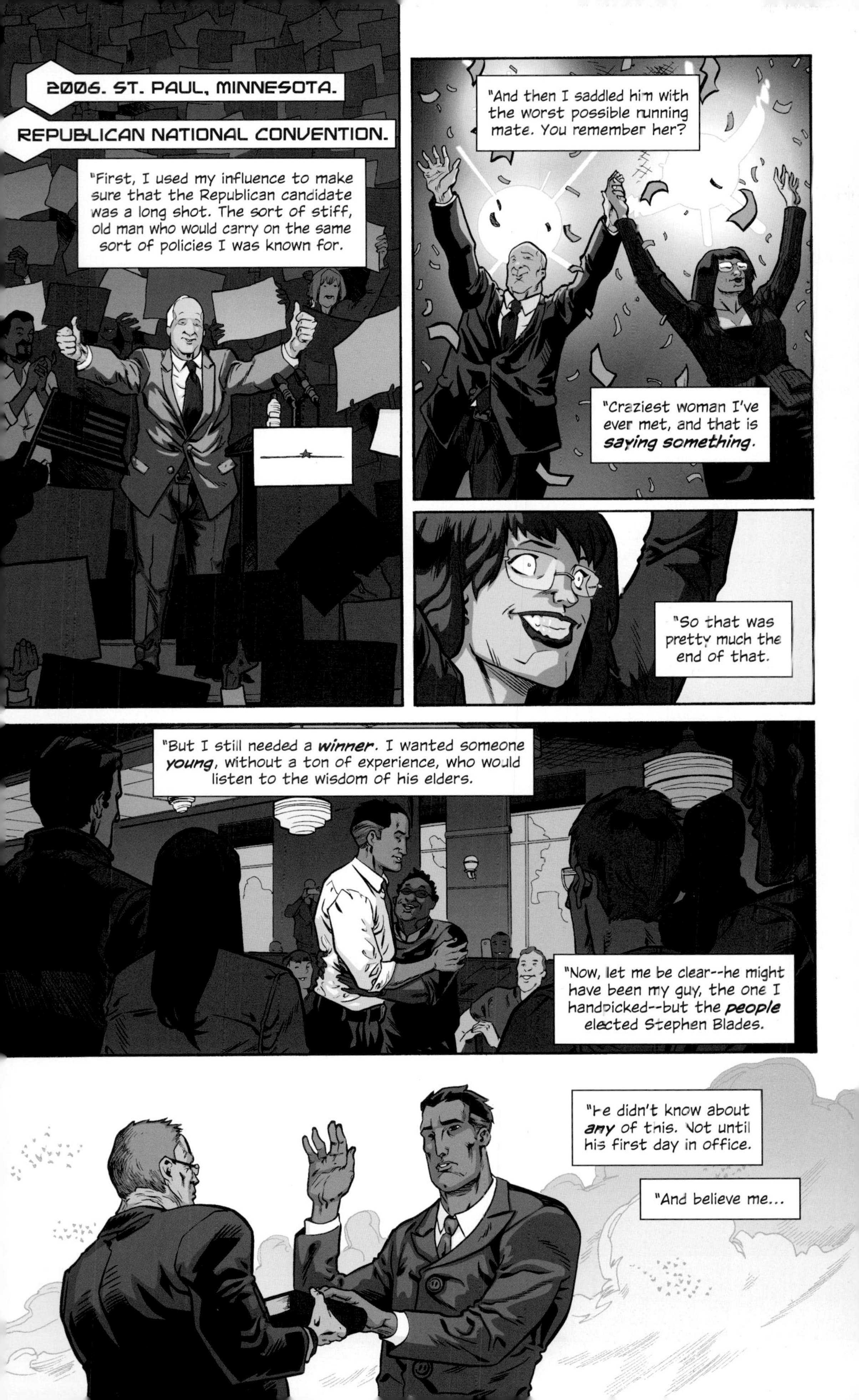
2006. ST. PAUL, MINNESOTA.
REPUBLICAN NATIONAL CONVENTION.
"First, I used my influence to make sure that the Republican candidate was a long shot. The sort of stiff, old man who would carry on the same sort of policies I was known for.
"And then I saddled him with the worst possible running mate. You remember her?
"Craziest woman I've ever met, and that is *saying something*.
"So that was pretty much the end of that.
"But I still needed a *winner*. I wanted someone *young*, without a ton of experience, who would listen to the wisdom of his elders.
"Now, let me be clear--he might have been my guy, the one I handpicked--but the *people* elected Stephen Blades.
"He didn't know about *any* of this. Not until his first day in office.
"And believe me...

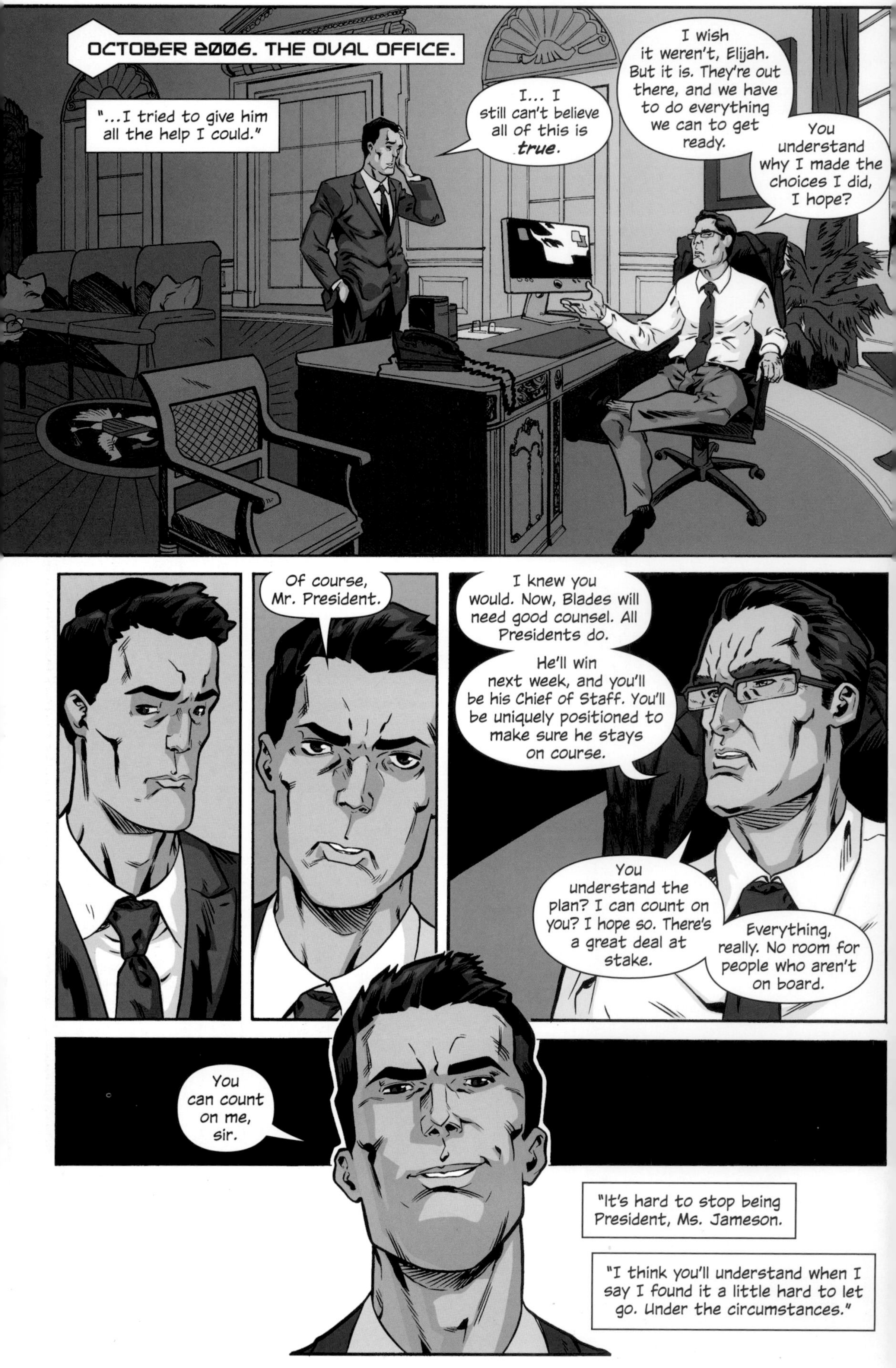
OCTOBER 2006. THE OVAL OFFICE.
"...I tried to give him all the help I could."
I... I still can't believe all of this is *true*.
I wish it weren't, Elijah. But it is. They're out there, and we have to do everything we can to get ready.
You understand why I made the choices I did, I hope?
Of course, Mr. President.
I knew you would. Now, Blades will need good counsel. All Presidents do.
He'll win next week, and you'll be his Chief of Staff. You'll be uniquely positioned to make sure he stays on course.
You understand the plan? I can count on you? I hope so. There's a great deal at stake.
Everything, really. No room for people who aren't on board.
You can count on me, sir.
"It's hard to stop being President, Ms. Jameson.
"I think you'll understand when I say I found it a little hard to let go. Under the circumstances."

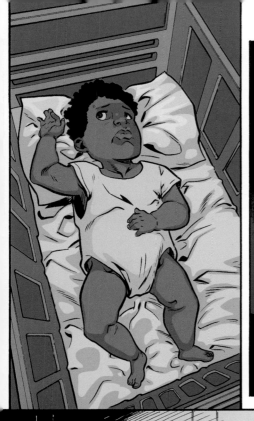

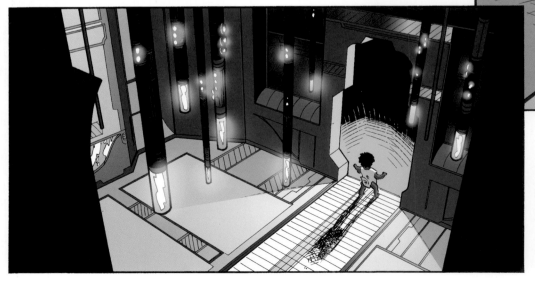

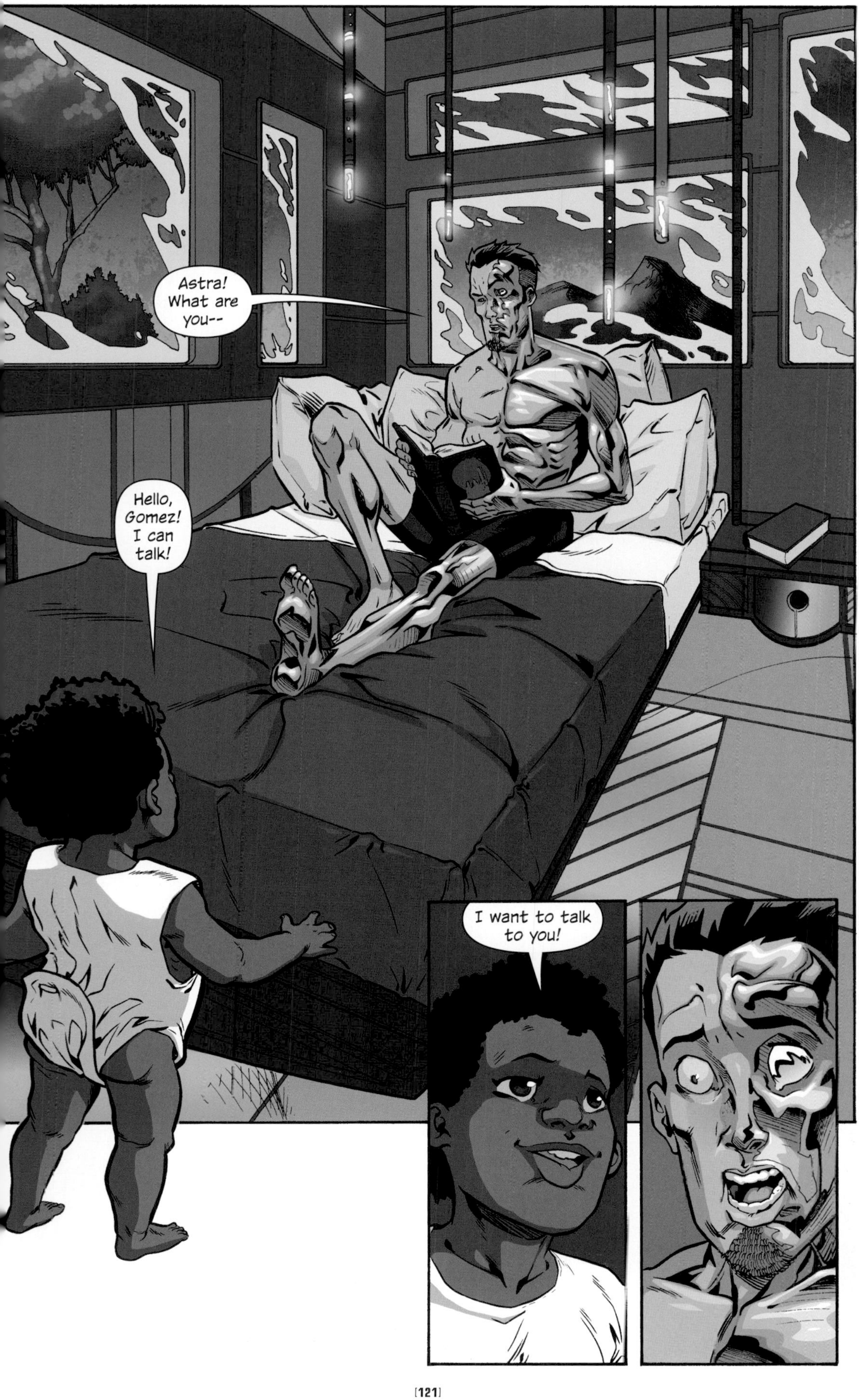
Astra! What are you--
Hello, Gomez! I can talk!
I want to talk to you!

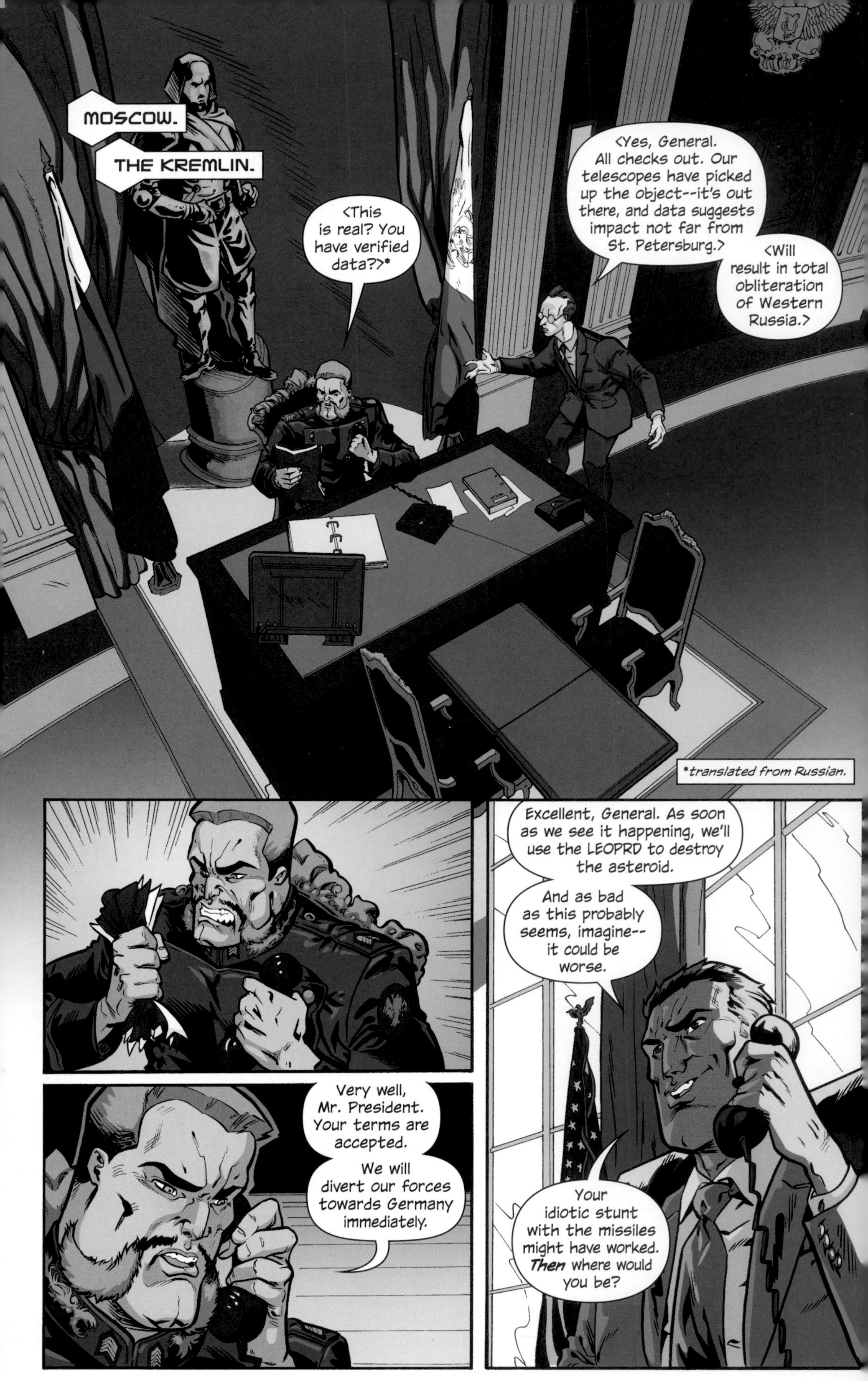

MOSCOW.
THE KREMLIN.
<This is real? You have verified data?>*
<Yes, General. All checks out. Our telescopes have picked up the object--it's out there, and data suggests impact not far from St. Petersburg.>
<Will result in total obliteration of Western Russia.>
*translated from Russian.
Excellent, General. As soon as we see it happening, we'll use the LEOPRD to destroy the asteroid.
And as bad as this probably seems, imagine-- it could be worse.
Very well, Mr. President. Your terms are accepted.
We will divert our forces towards Germany immediately.
Your idiotic stunt with the missiles might have worked. *Then* where would you be?

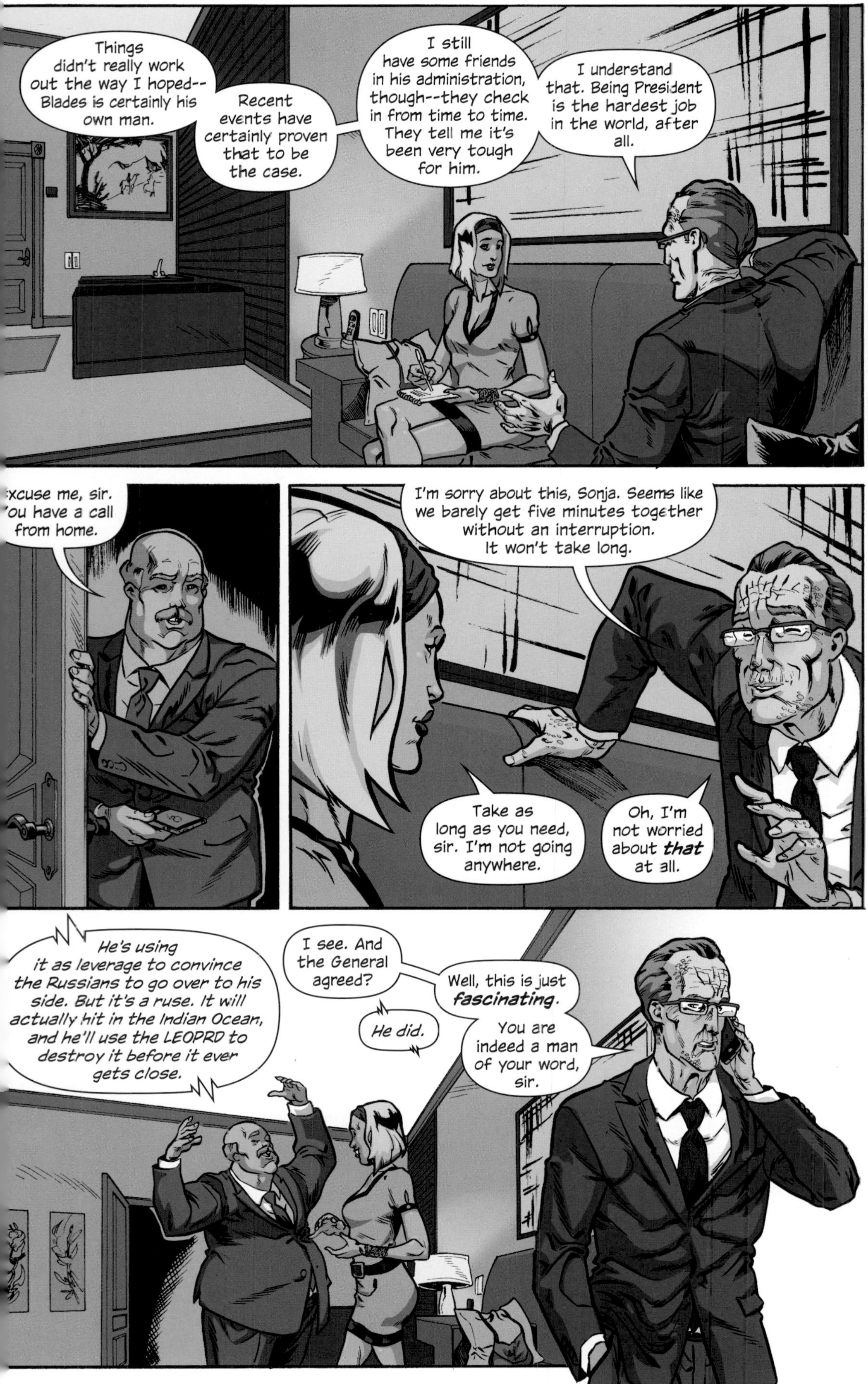

Things didn't really work out the way I hoped--Blades is certainly his own man.
Recent events have certainly proven that to be the case.
I still have some friends in his administration, though--they check in from time to time. They tell me it's been very tough for him.
I understand that. Being President is the hardest job in the world, after all.
xcuse me, sir. 'ou have a call from home.
I'm sorry about this, Sonja. Seems like we barely get five minutes together without an interruption. It won't take long.
Take as long as you need, sir. I'm not going anywhere.
Oh, I'm not worried about *that* at all.
He's using it as leverage to convince the Russians to go over to his side. But it's a ruse. It will actually hit in the Indian Ocean, and he'll use the LEOPRD to destroy it before it ever gets close.
I see. And the General agreed?
He did.
Well, this is just ***fascinating***.
You are indeed a man of your word, sir.

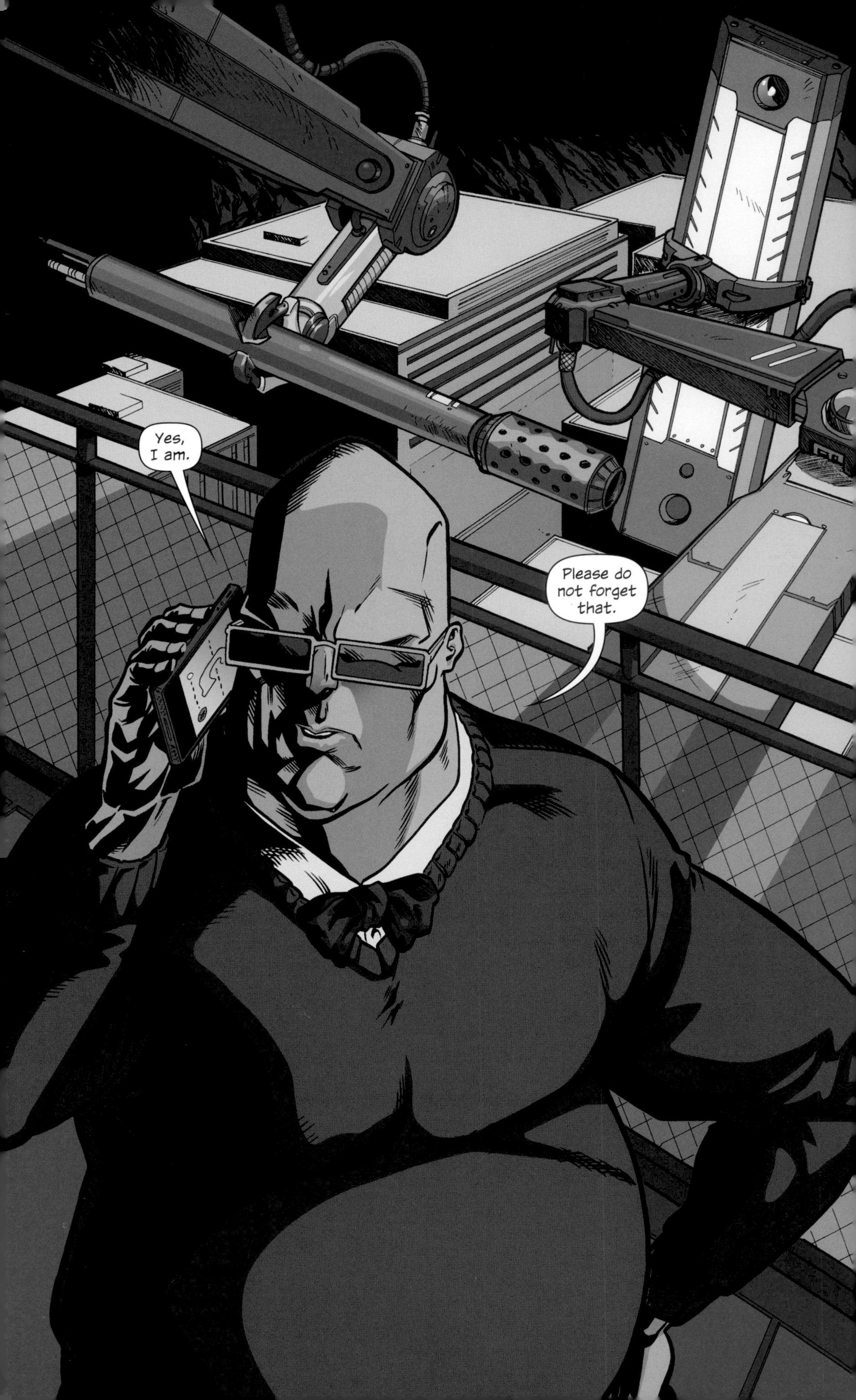
Yes, I am.
Please do not forget that.

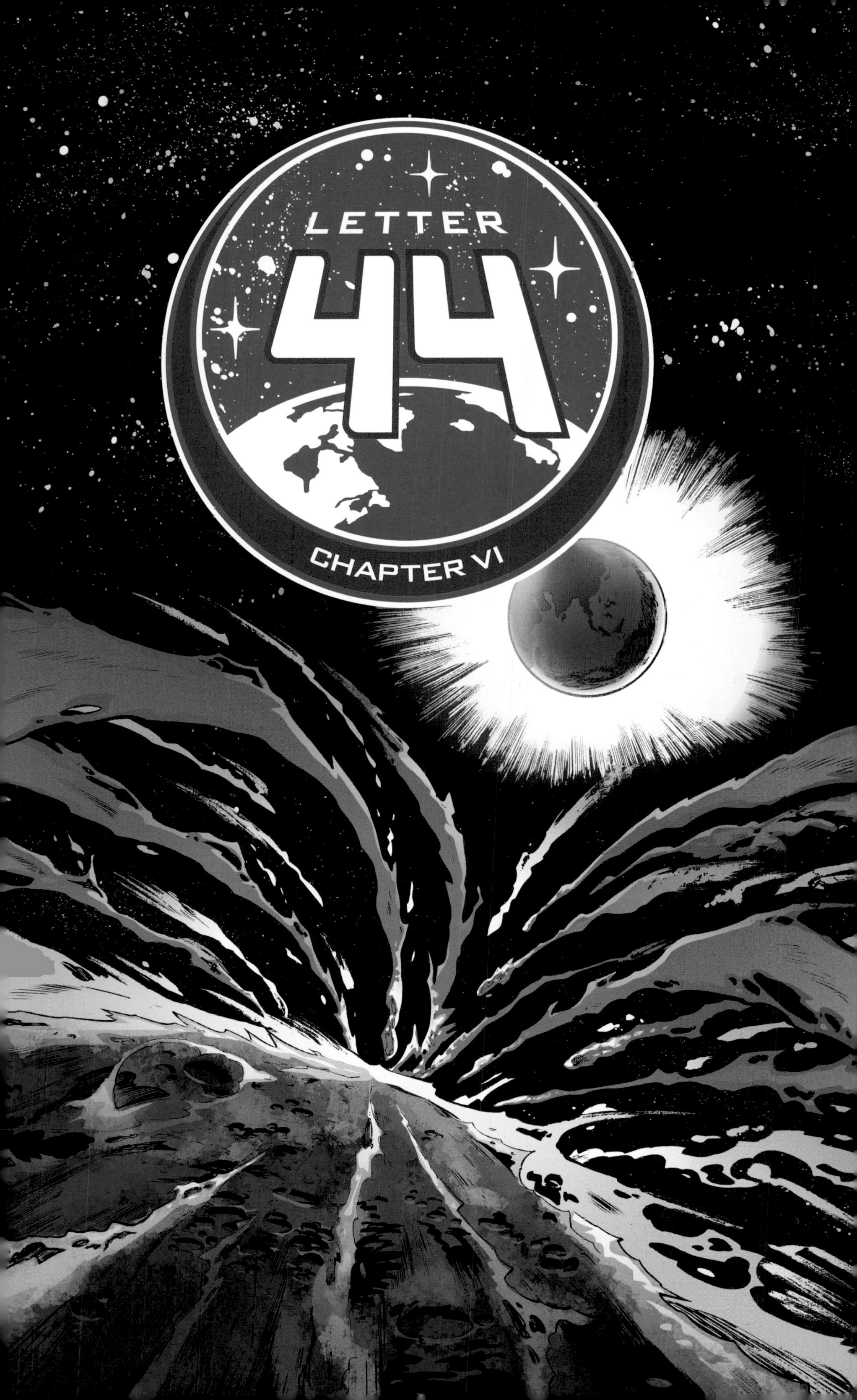
LETTER
44
CHAPTER VI

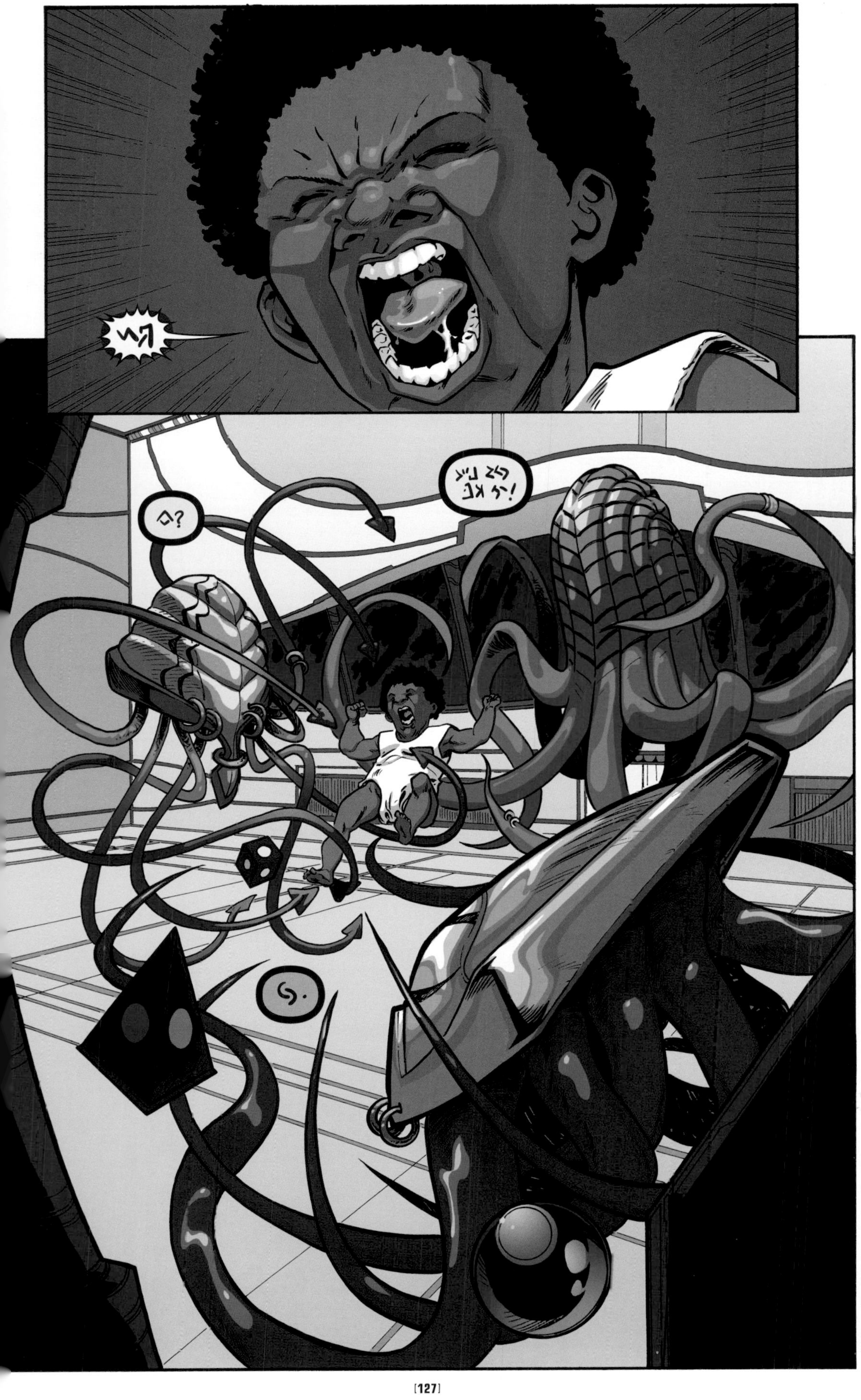

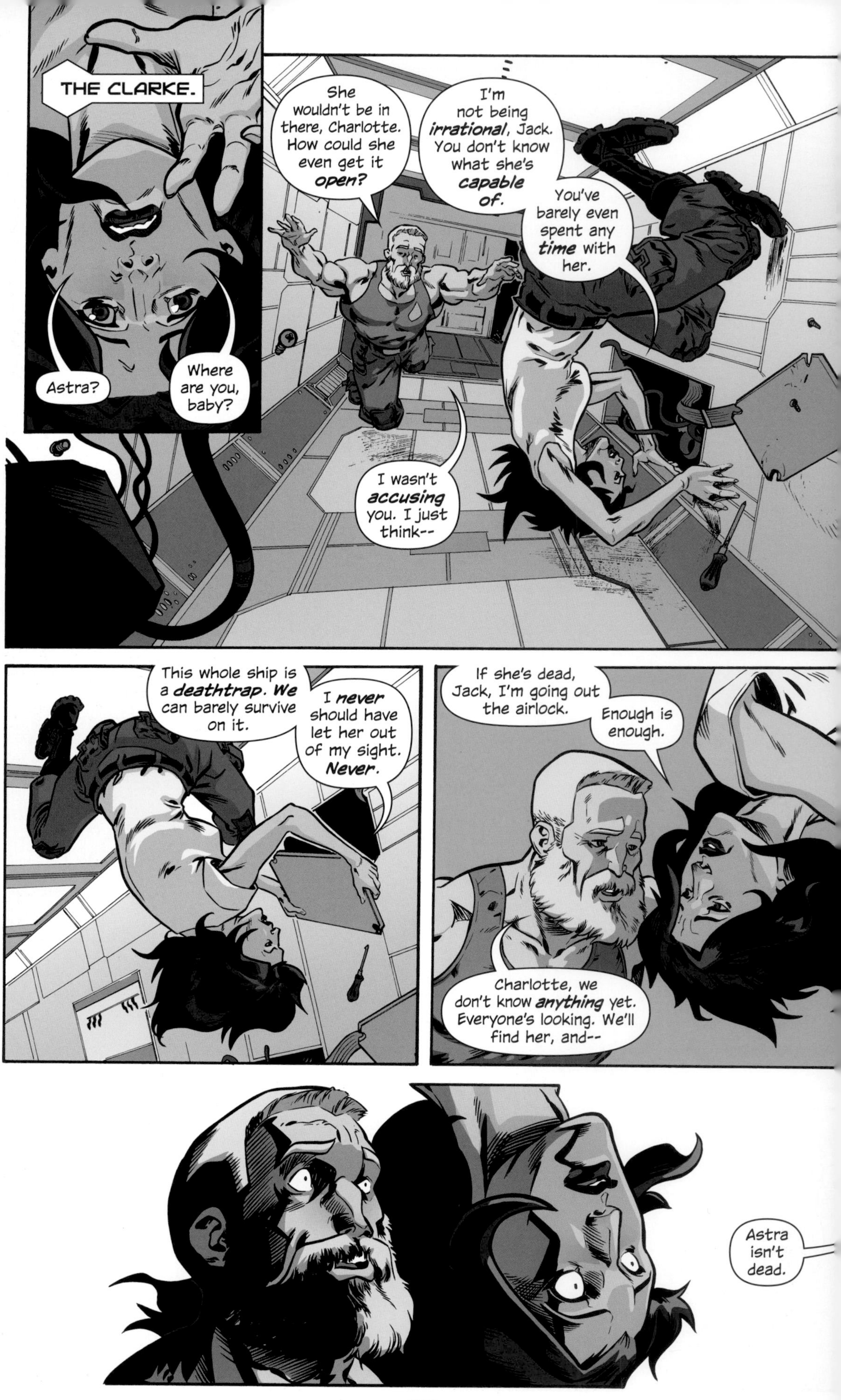
THE CLARKE.
Astra?
Where are you, baby?
She wouldn't be in there, Charlotte. How could she even get it open?
I'm not being irrational, Jack. You don't know what she's capable of.
You've barely even spent any time with her.
I wasn't accusing you. I just think--
This whole ship is a deathtrap. We can barely survive on it.
I never should have let her out of my sight. Never.
If she's dead, Jack, I'm going out the airlock.
Enough is enough.
Charlotte, we don't know anything yet. Everyone's looking. We'll find her, and--
Astra isn't dead.

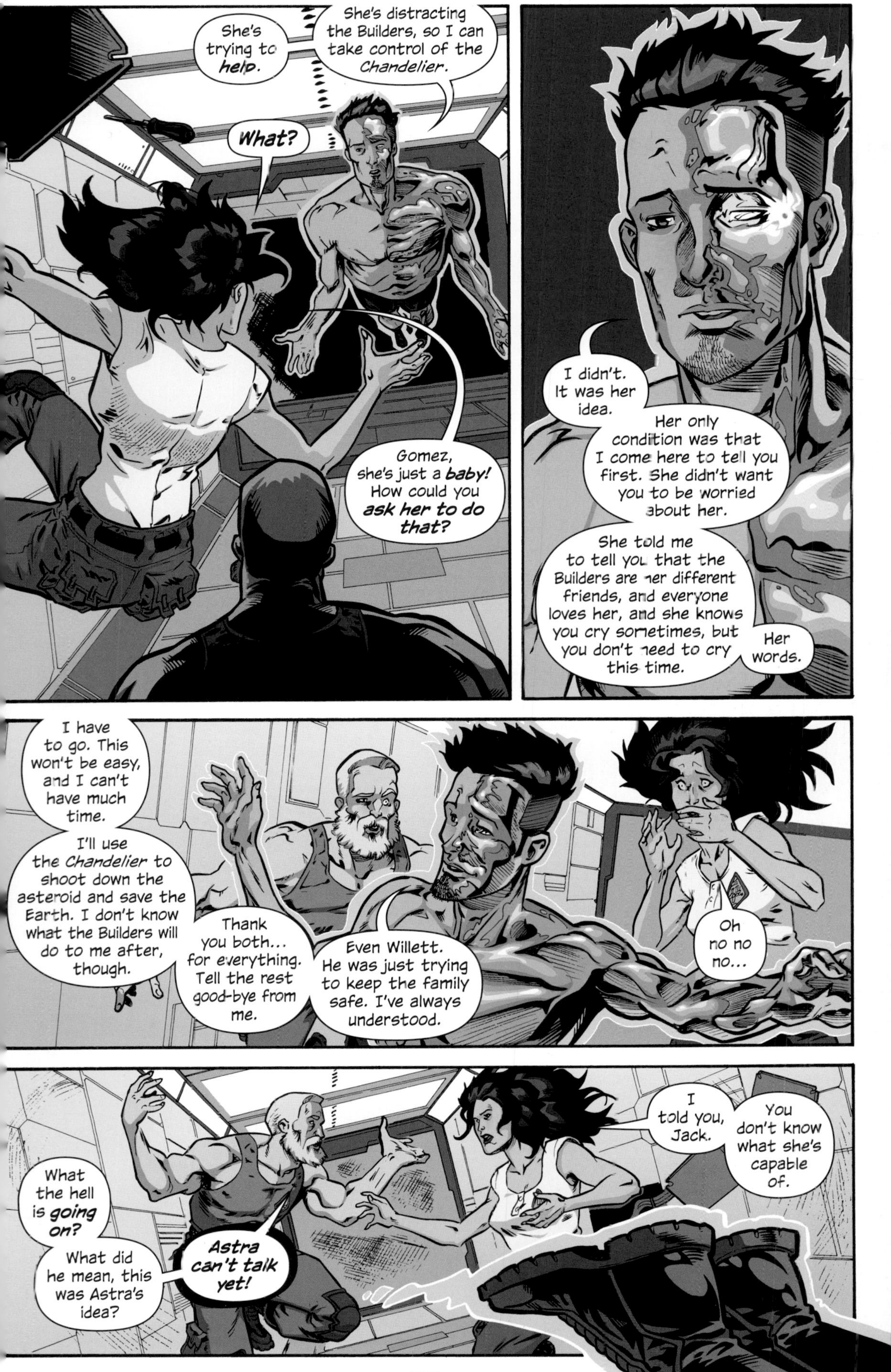
She's trying to *help*.
She's distracting the Builders, so I can take control of the *Chandelier*.
What?
Gomez, she's just a *baby!* How could you *ask her to do that?*
I didn't. It was her idea.
Her only condition was that I come here to tell you first. She didn't want you to be worried about her.
She told me to tell you that the Builders are her different friends, and everyone loves her, and she knows you cry sometimes, but you don't need to cry this time.
Her words.
I have to go. This won't be easy, and I can't have much time.
I'll use the *Chandelier* to shoot down the asteroid and save the Earth. I don't know what the Builders will do to me after, though.
Thank you both... for everything. Tell the rest good-bye from me.
Even Willett. He was just trying to keep the family safe. I've always understood.
Oh no no no...
What the hell is *going on?*
What did he mean, this was Astra's idea?
Astra can't talk yet!
I told you, Jack.
You don't know what she's capable of.

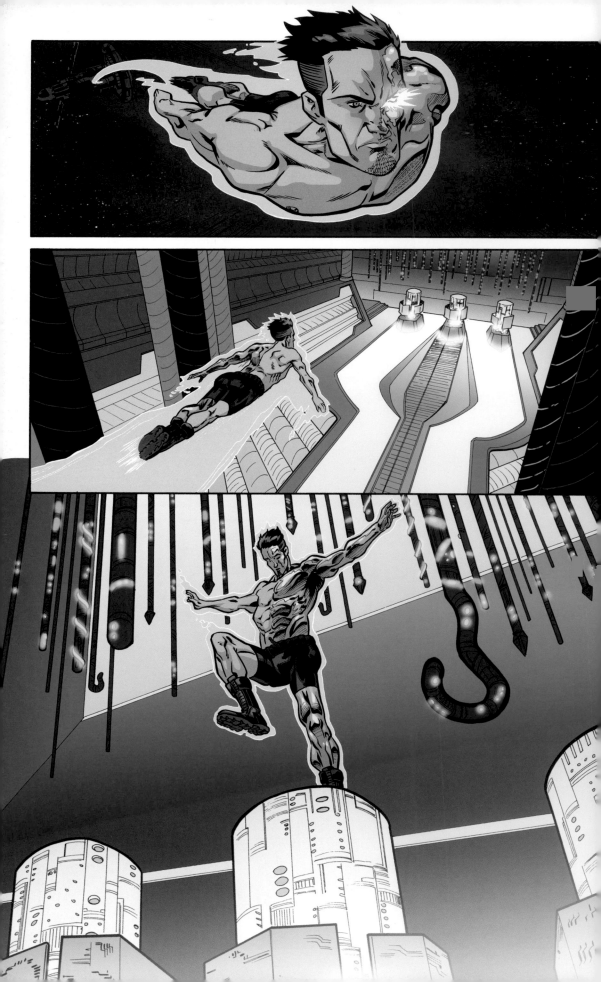

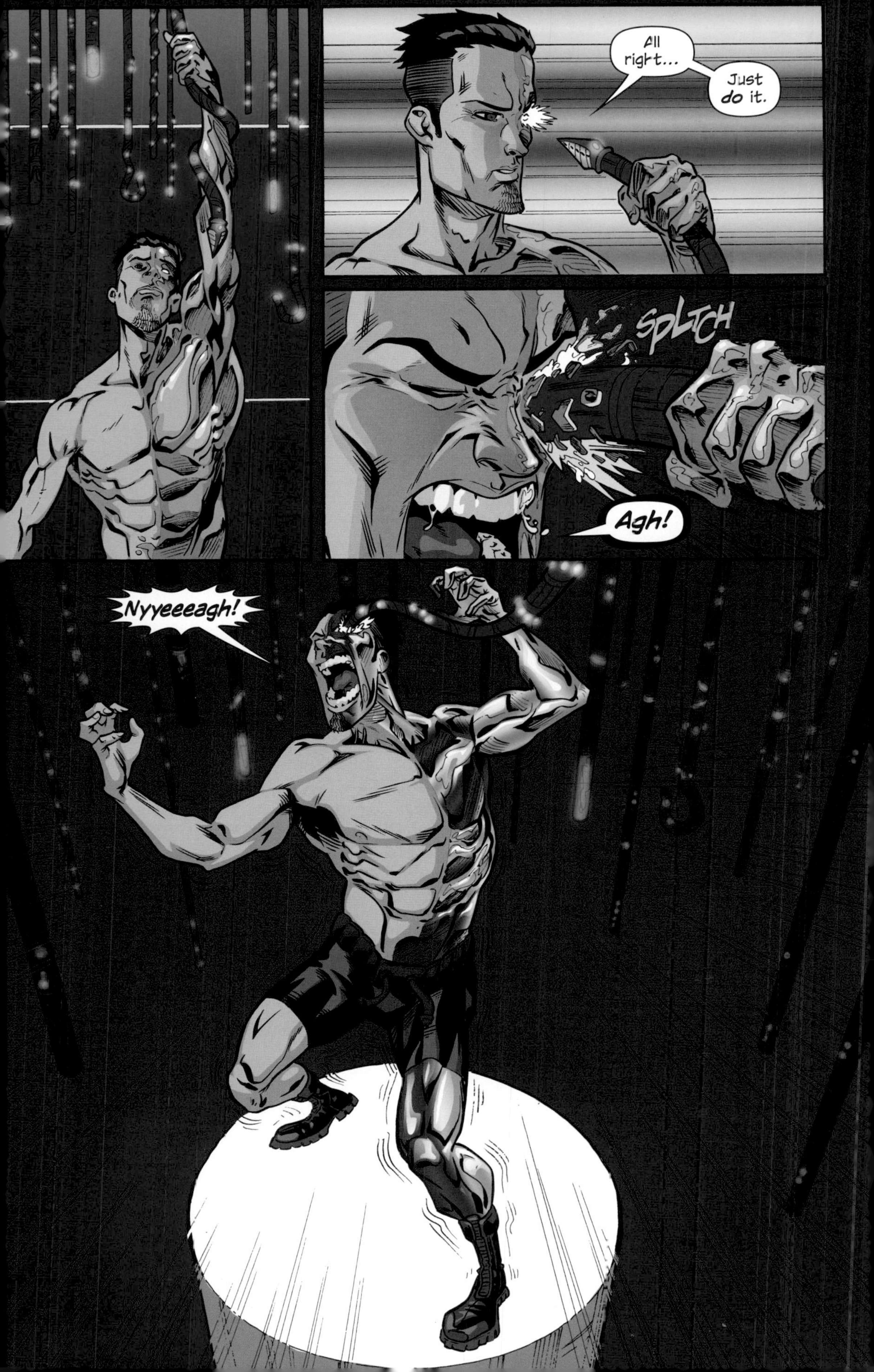
All right...
Just do it.
SPLTCH
Agh!
Nyyeeeagh!

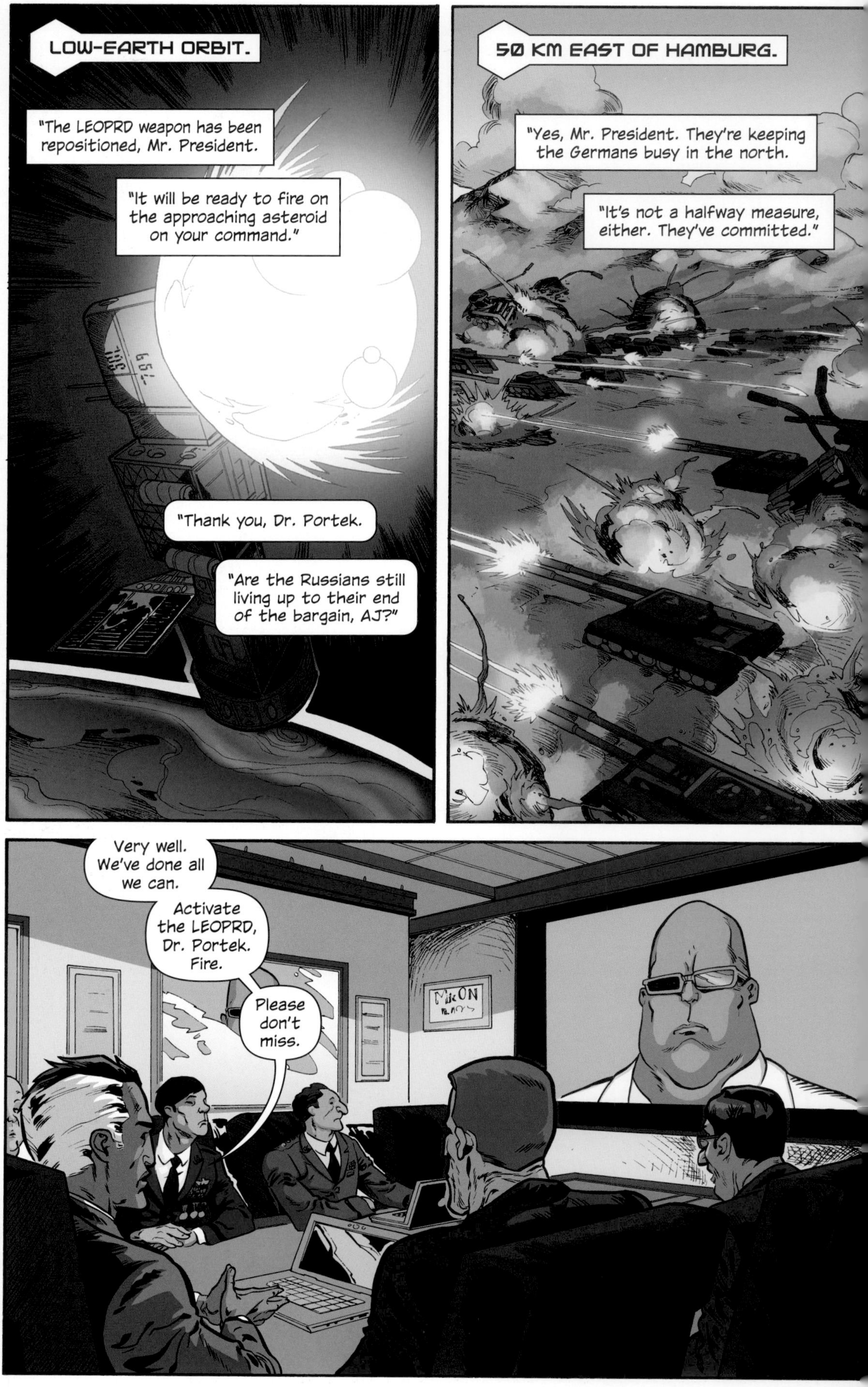
LOW-EARTH ORBIT.
"The LEOPRD weapon has been repositioned, Mr. President.
"It will be ready to fire on the approaching asteroid on your command."
"Thank you, Dr. Portek.
"Are the Russians still living up to their end of the bargain, AJ?"
50 KM EAST OF HAMBURG.
"Yes, Mr. President. They're keeping the Germans busy in the north.
"It's not a halfway measure, either. They've committed."
Very well. We've done all we can.
Activate the LEOPRD, Dr. Portek. Fire.
Please don't miss.

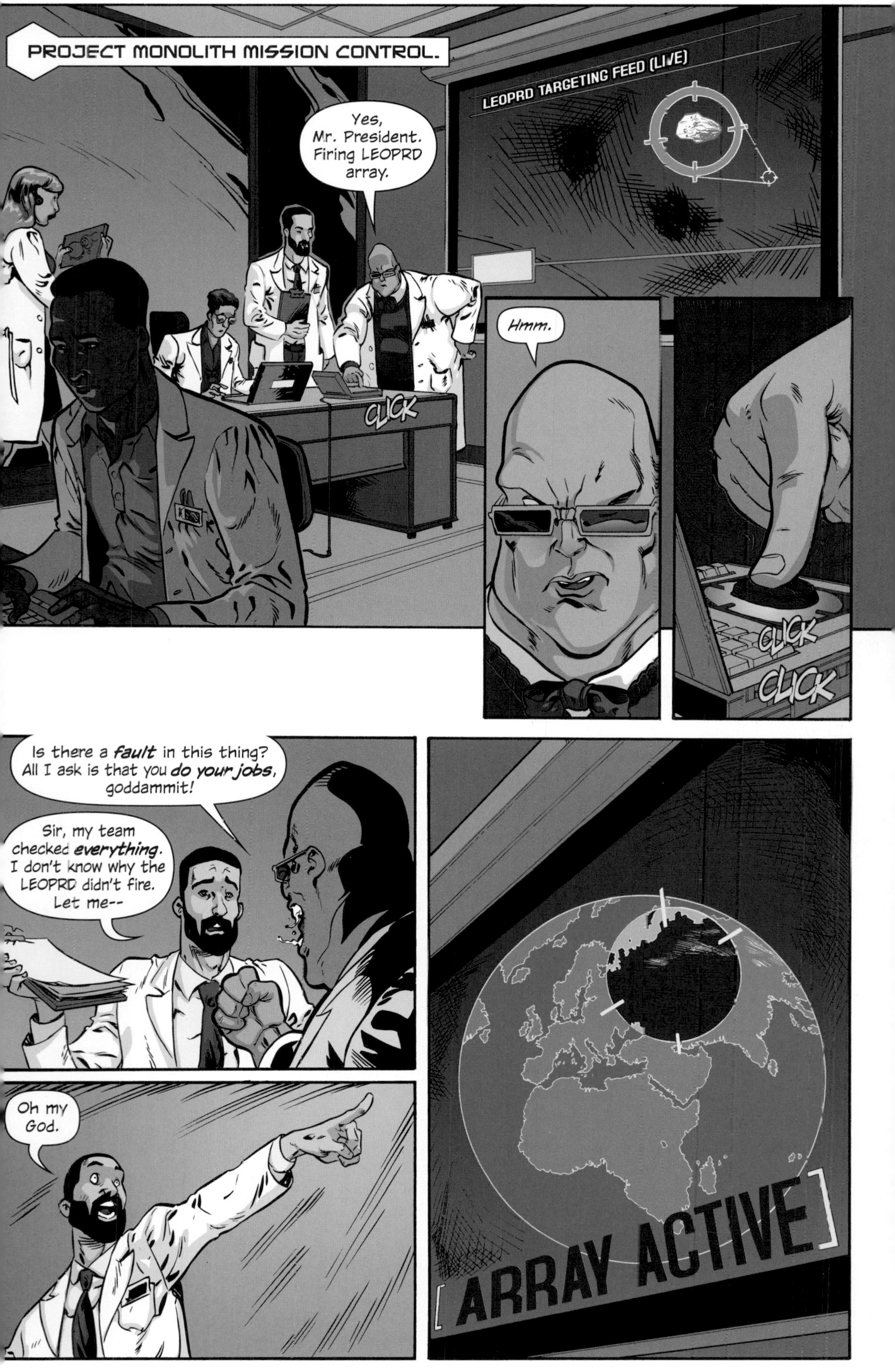
PROJECT MONOLITH MISSION CONTROL.
LEOPRD TARGETING FEED (LIVE)
Yes, Mr. President. Firing LEOPRD array.
CLICK
Hmm.
CLICK
CLICK
Is there a *fault* in this thing? All I ask is that you ***do your jobs***, goddammit!
Sir, my team checked ***everything***. I don't know why the LEOPRD didn't fire. Let me--
Oh my God.
[ARRAY ACTIVE]

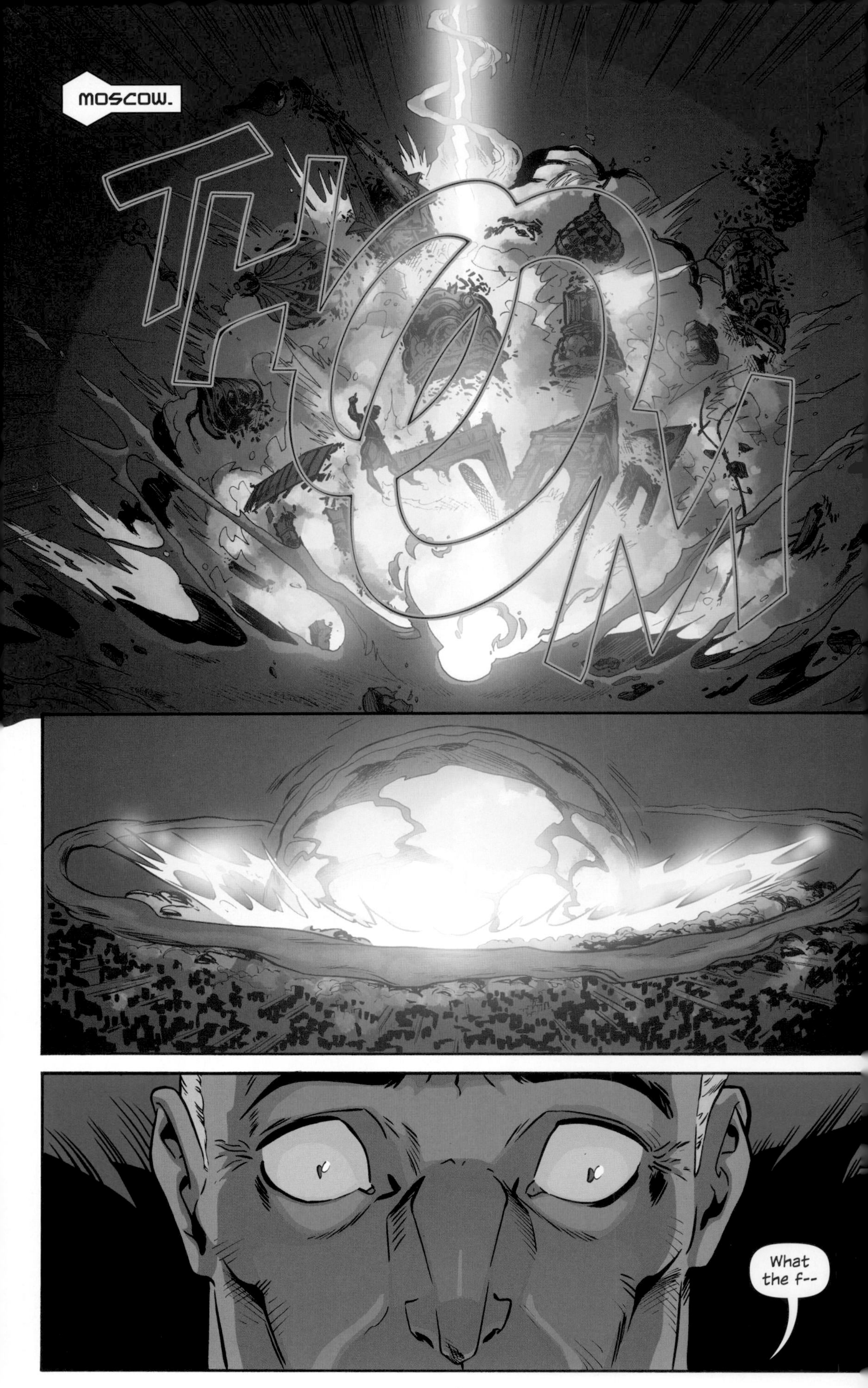
MOSCOW.
THOOM
What the f--

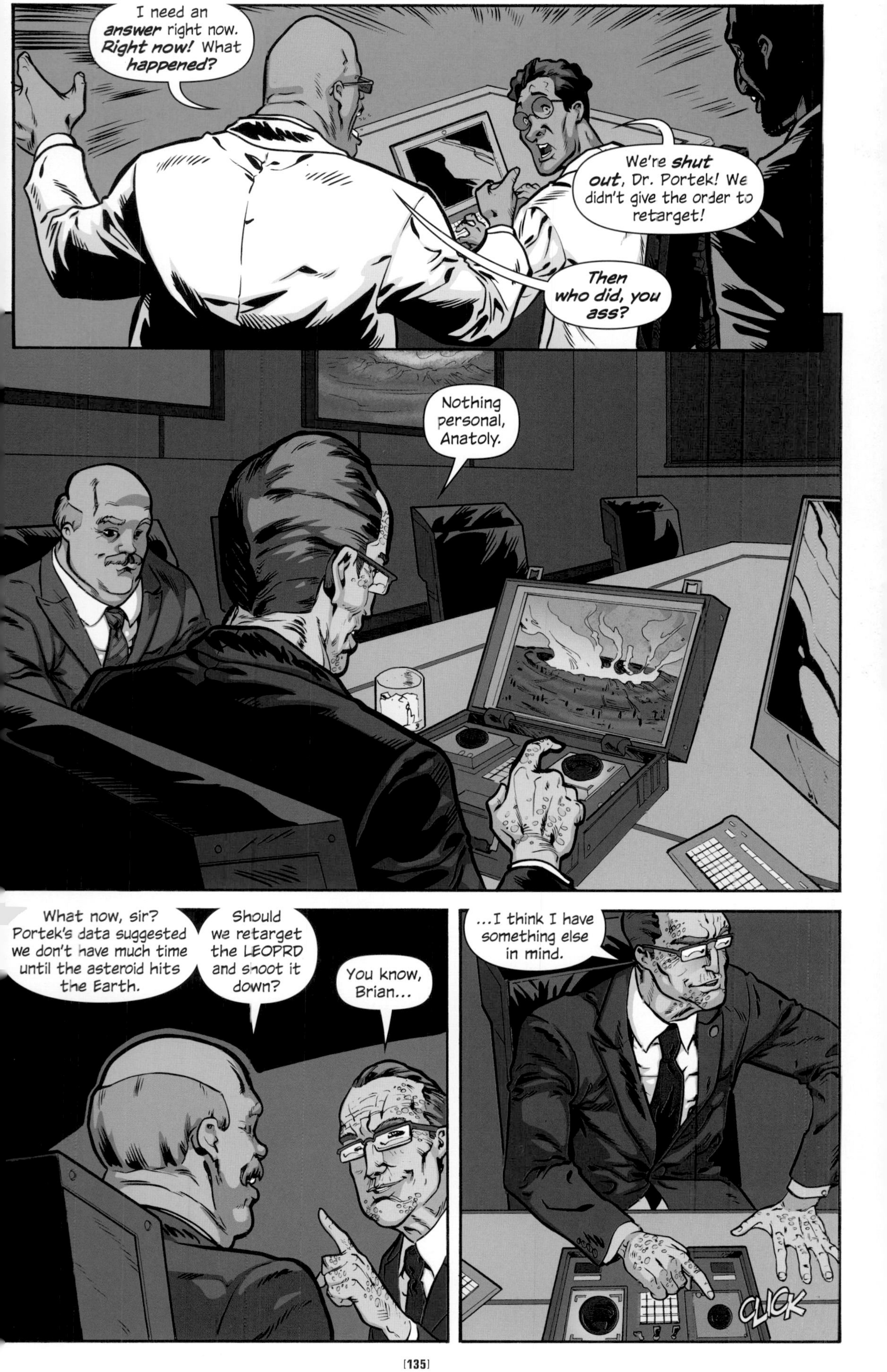
I need an answer right now. Right now! What happened?
We're shut out, Dr. Portek! We didn't give the order to retarget!
Then who did, you ass?
Nothing personal, Anatoly.
What now, sir? Portek's data suggested we don't have much time until the asteroid hits the Earth.
Should we retarget the LEOPRD and shoot it down?
You know, Brian...
...I think I have something else in mind.
CLICK

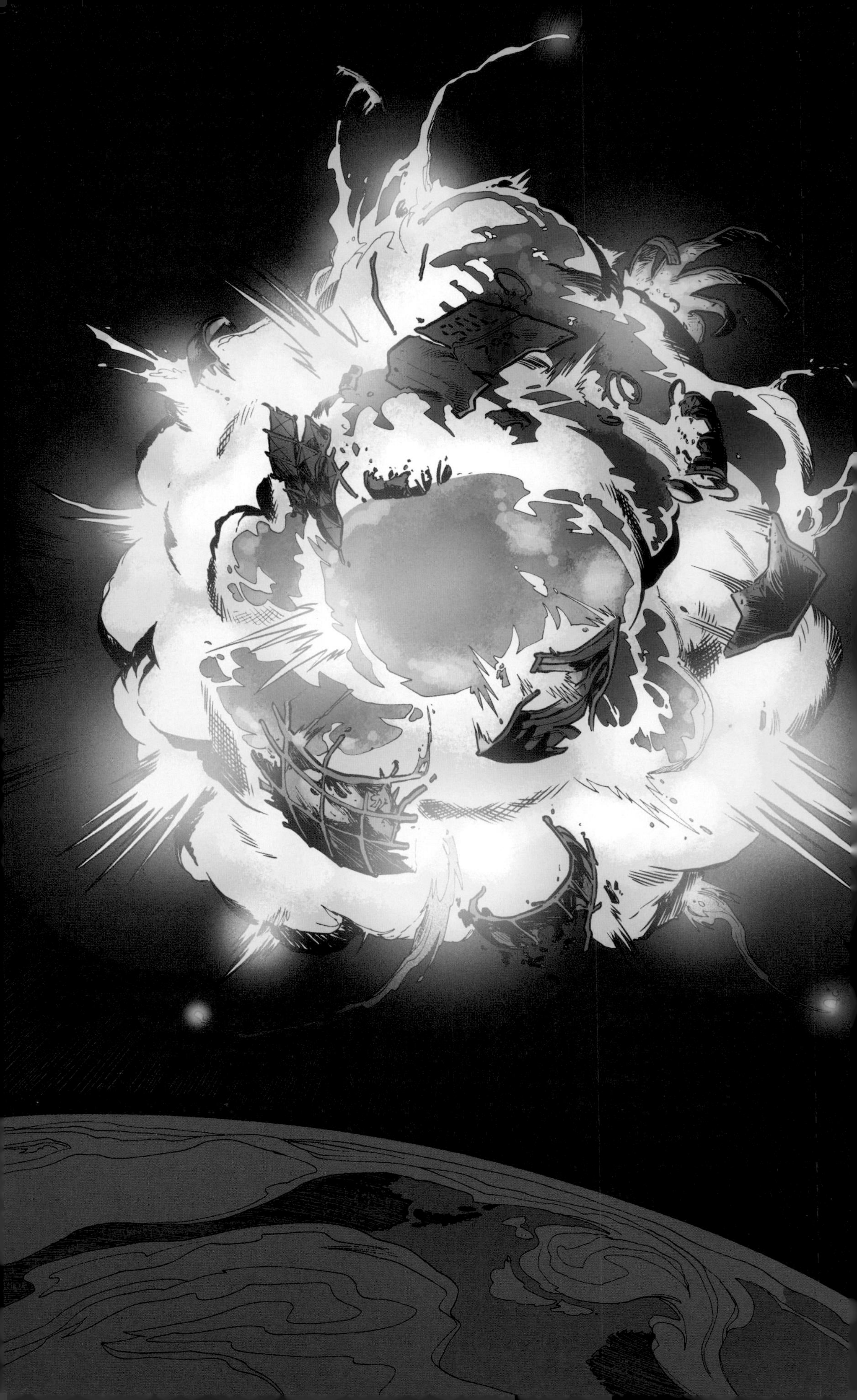

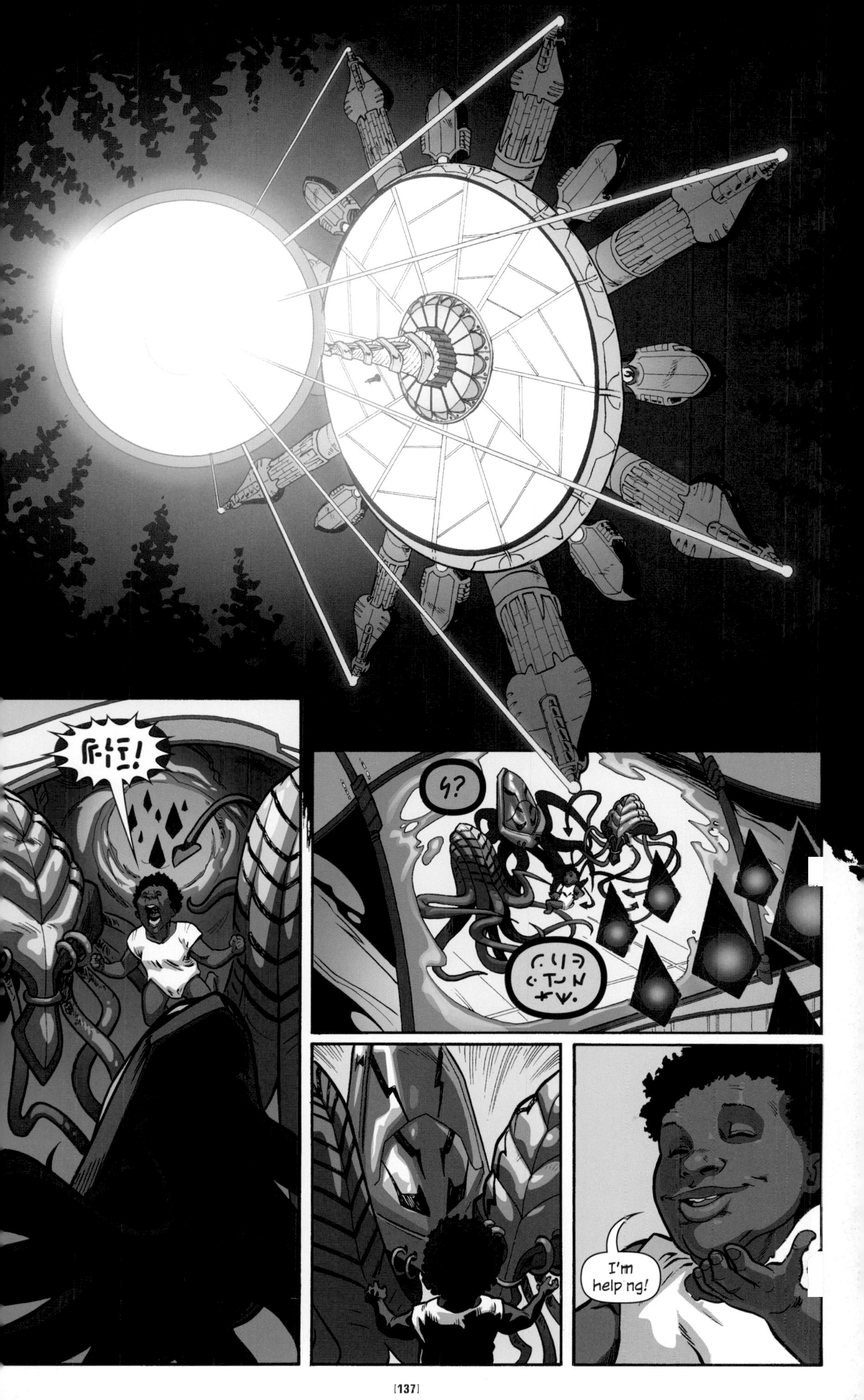
I'm help ng!

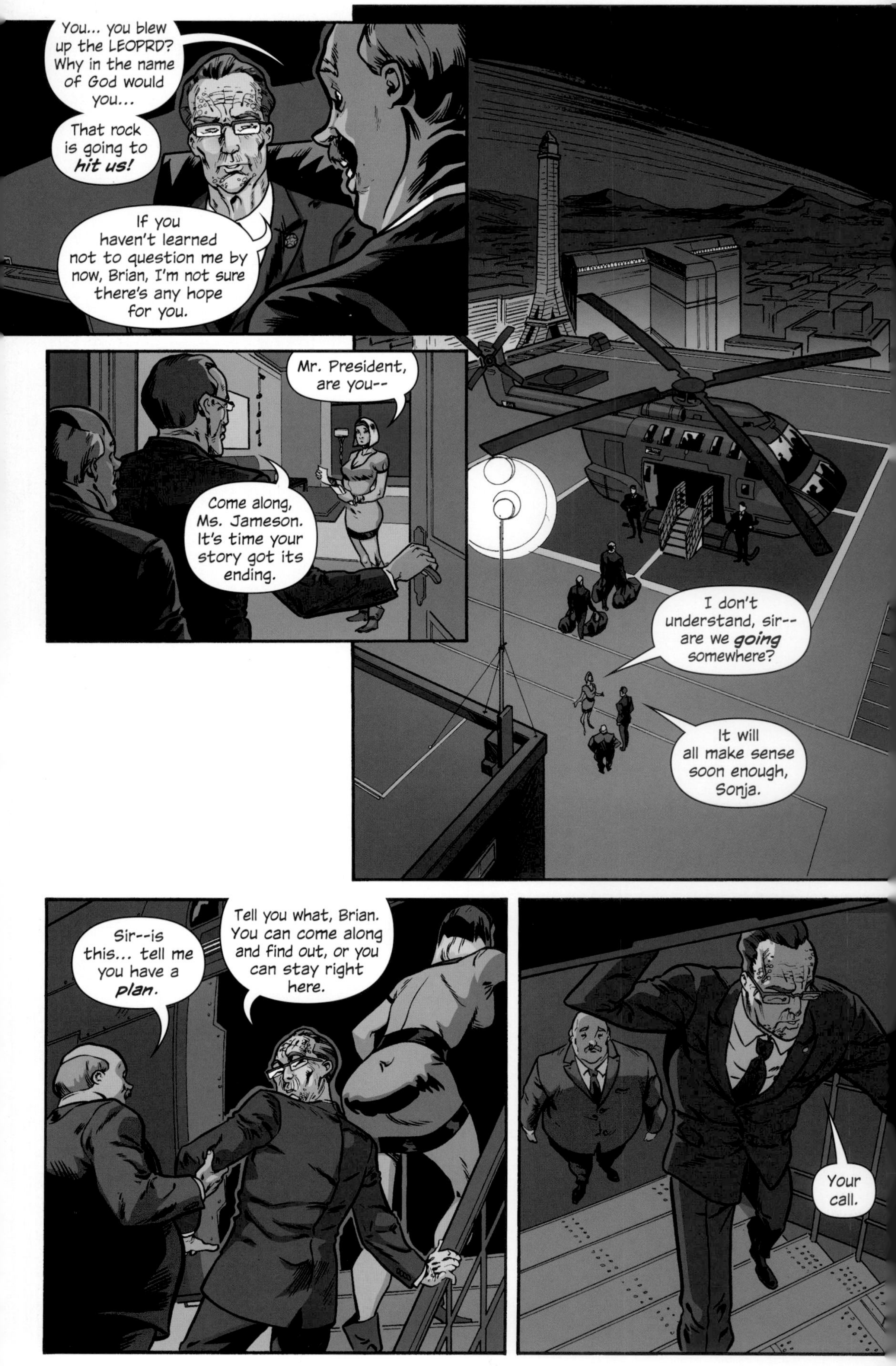
You... you blew up the LEOPRD? Why in the name of God would you...
That rock is going to ***hit us!***
If you haven't learned not to question me by now, Brian, I'm not sure there's any hope for you.
Mr. President, are you--
Come along, Ms. Jameson. It's time your story got its ending.
I don't understand, sir--are we ***going*** somewhere?
It will all make sense soon enough, Sonja.
Sir--is this... tell me you have a ***plan***.
Tell you what, Brian. You can come along and find out, or you can stay right here.
Your call.

"Where are we going, Mr. President?"

"Oh, I wouldn't want to ruin the surprise, Sonja. I know, I know, it's bizarre, but I'm old-fashioned that way."

"..."

"Well, would you mind if we continued the interview, while we're on the way to... wherever we're going?"

Certainly. Ask away.

I'm wondering... how did you *tell* President Blades about all of this? How did he *react?*

"You know, Ms. Jameson...

"...that's old news.

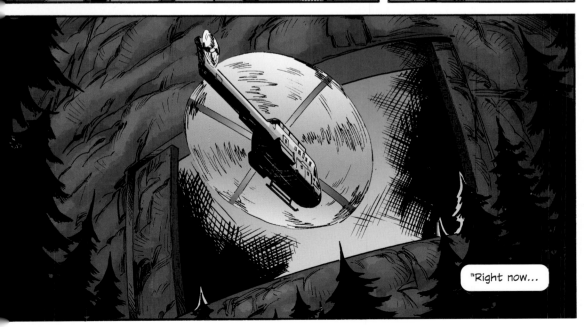

"Right now...

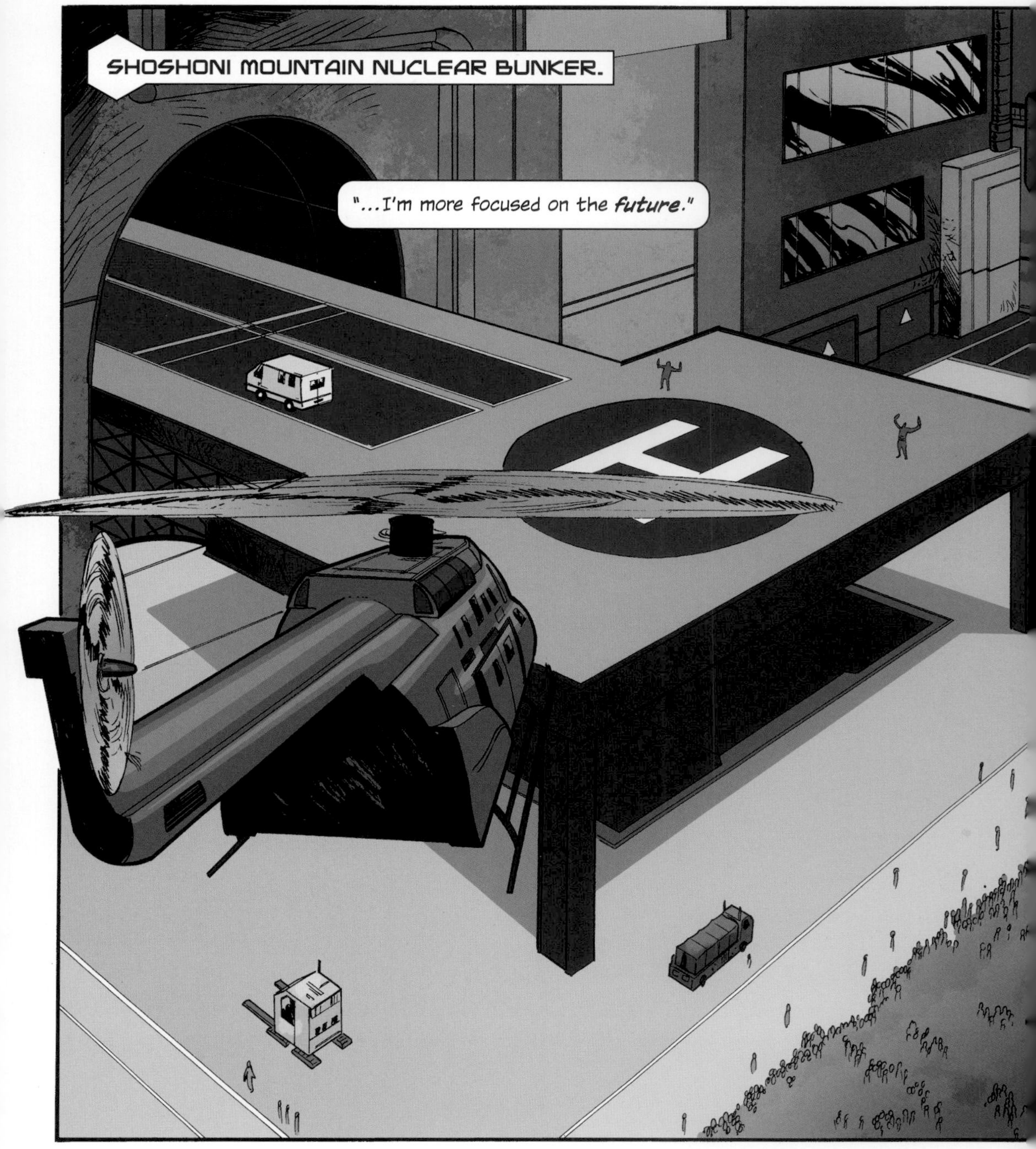
SHOSHONI MOUNTAIN NUCLEAR BUNKER.
"...I'm more focused on the *future*."

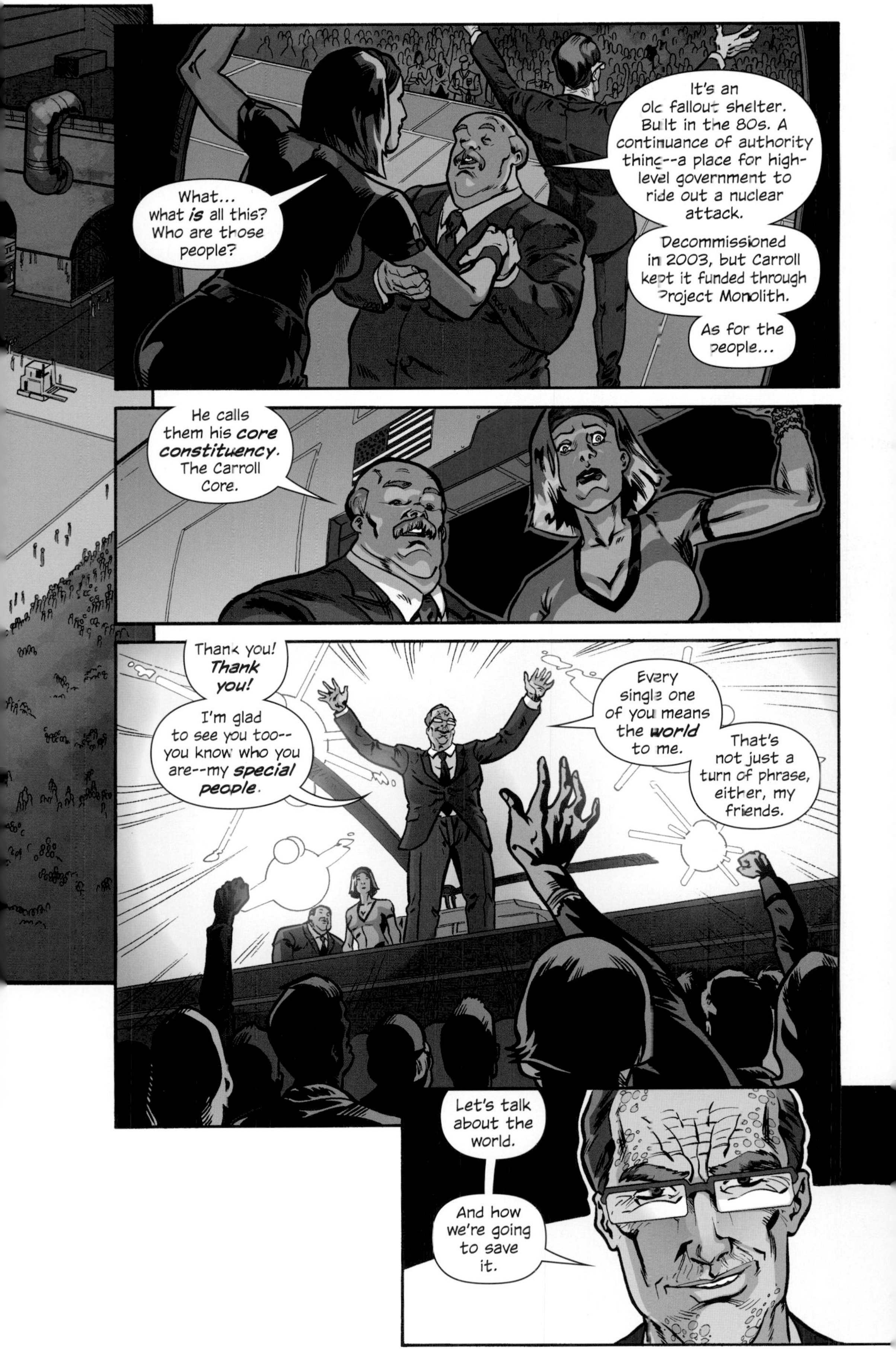
What... what *is* all this? Who are those people?
It's an old fallout shelter. Built in the 80s. A continuance of authority thing--a place for high-level government to ride out a nuclear attack.
Decommissioned in 2003, but Carroll kept it funded through Project Monolith.
As for the people...
He calls them his **core constituency**. The Carroll Core.
Thank you! ***Thank you!***
I'm glad to see you too--you know who you are--my ***special people***.
Every single one of you means the ***world*** to me.
That's not just a turn of phrase, either, my friends.
Let's talk about the world.
And how we're going to save it.

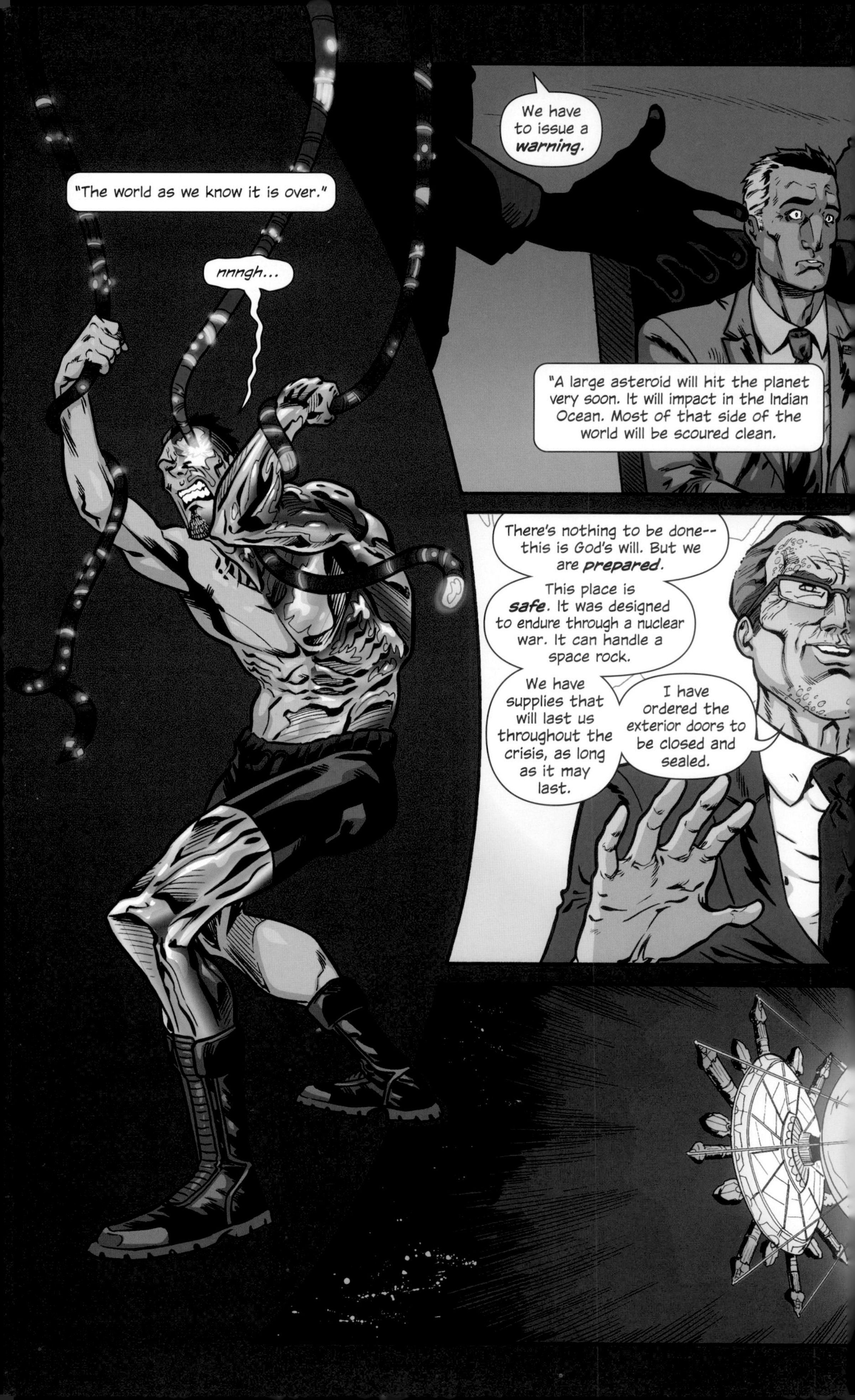
"The world as we know it is over."
nnngh...
We have to issue a *warning*.
"A large asteroid will hit the planet very soon. It will impact in the Indian Ocean. Most of that side of the world will be scoured clean.
There's nothing to be done-- this is God's will. But we are *prepared*.
This place is *safe*. It was designed to endure through a nuclear war. It can handle a space rock.
We have supplies that will last us throughout the crisis, as long as it may last.
I have ordered the exterior doors to be closed and sealed.

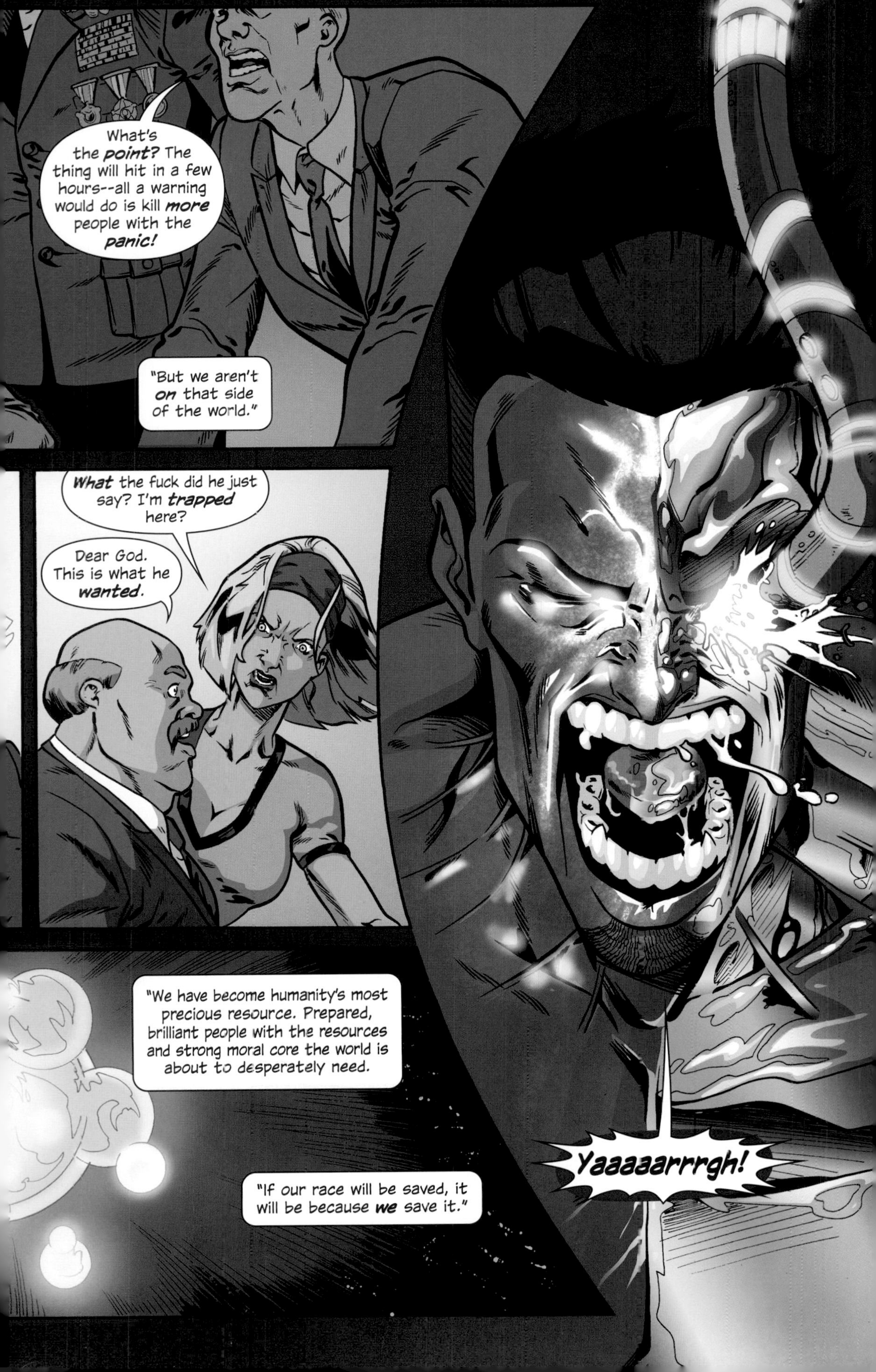
What's the *point?* The thing will hit in a few hours--all a warning would do is kill *more* people with the *panic!*
"But we aren't *on* that side of the world."
What the fuck did he just say? I'm *trapped* here?
Dear God. This is what he *wanted*.
"We have become humanity's most precious resource. Prepared, brilliant people with the resources and strong moral core the world is about to desperately need.
Yaaaaarrrgh!
"If our race will be saved, it will be because *we* save it."

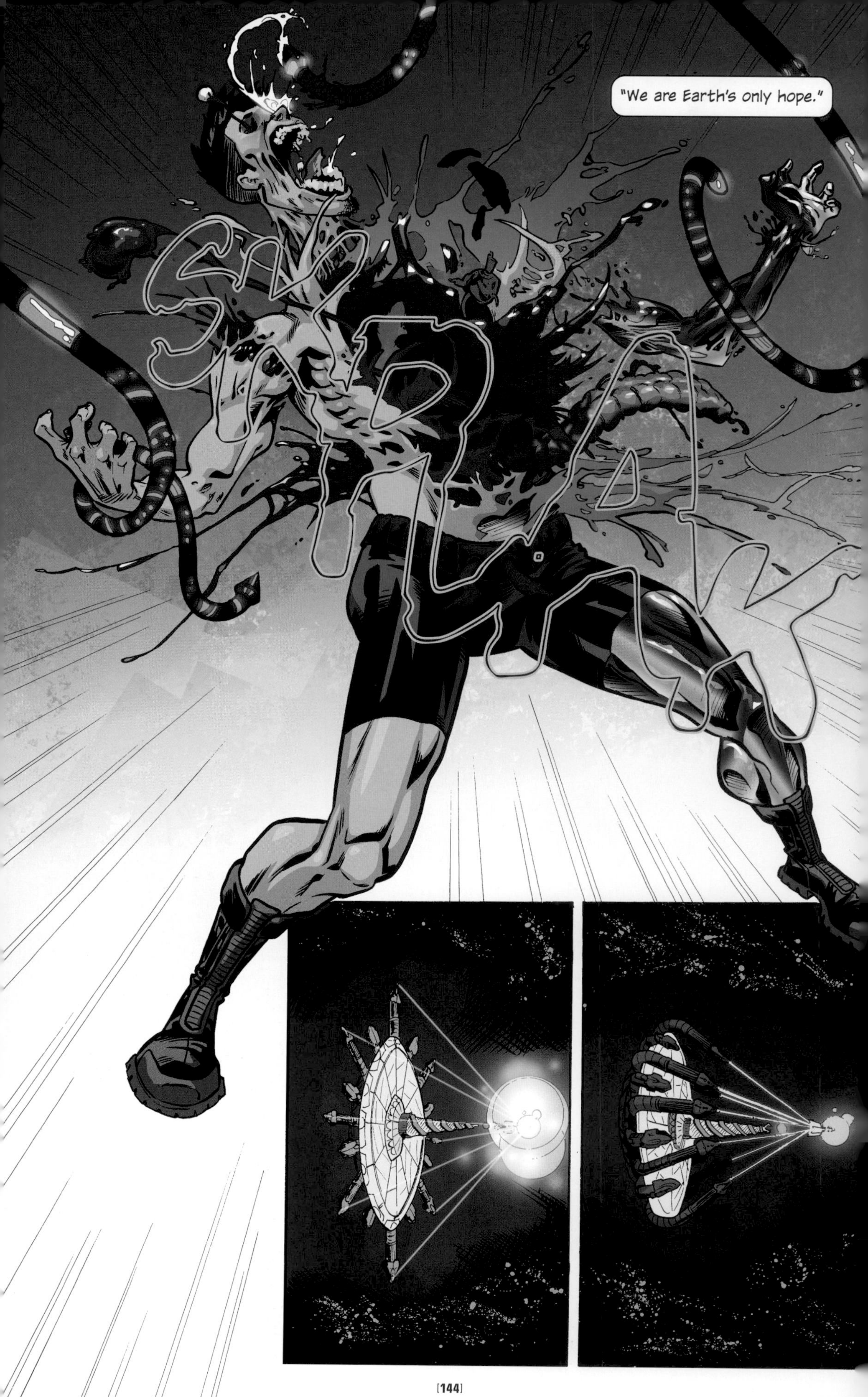
"We are Earth's only hope."

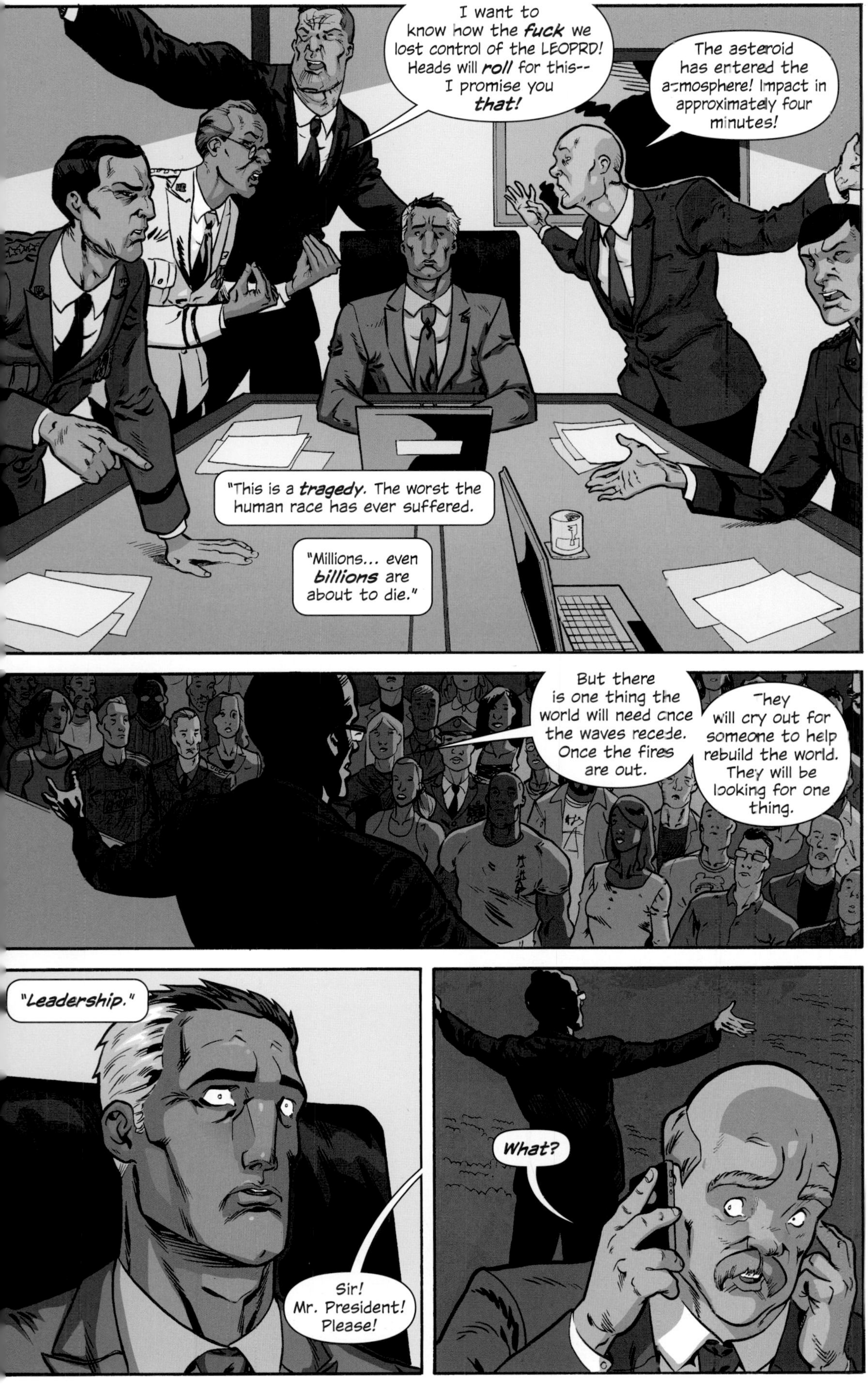

I want to know how the *fuck* we lost control of the LEOPRD! Heads will *roll* for this-- I promise you *that!*
The asteroid has entered the atmosphere! Impact in approximately four minutes!
"This is a *tragedy.* The worst the human race has ever suffered.
"Millions... even *billions* are about to die."
But there is one thing the world will need once the waves recede. Once the fires are out.
They will cry out for someone to help rebuild the world. They will be looking for one thing.
"*Leadership.*"
Sir! Mr. President! Please!
What?

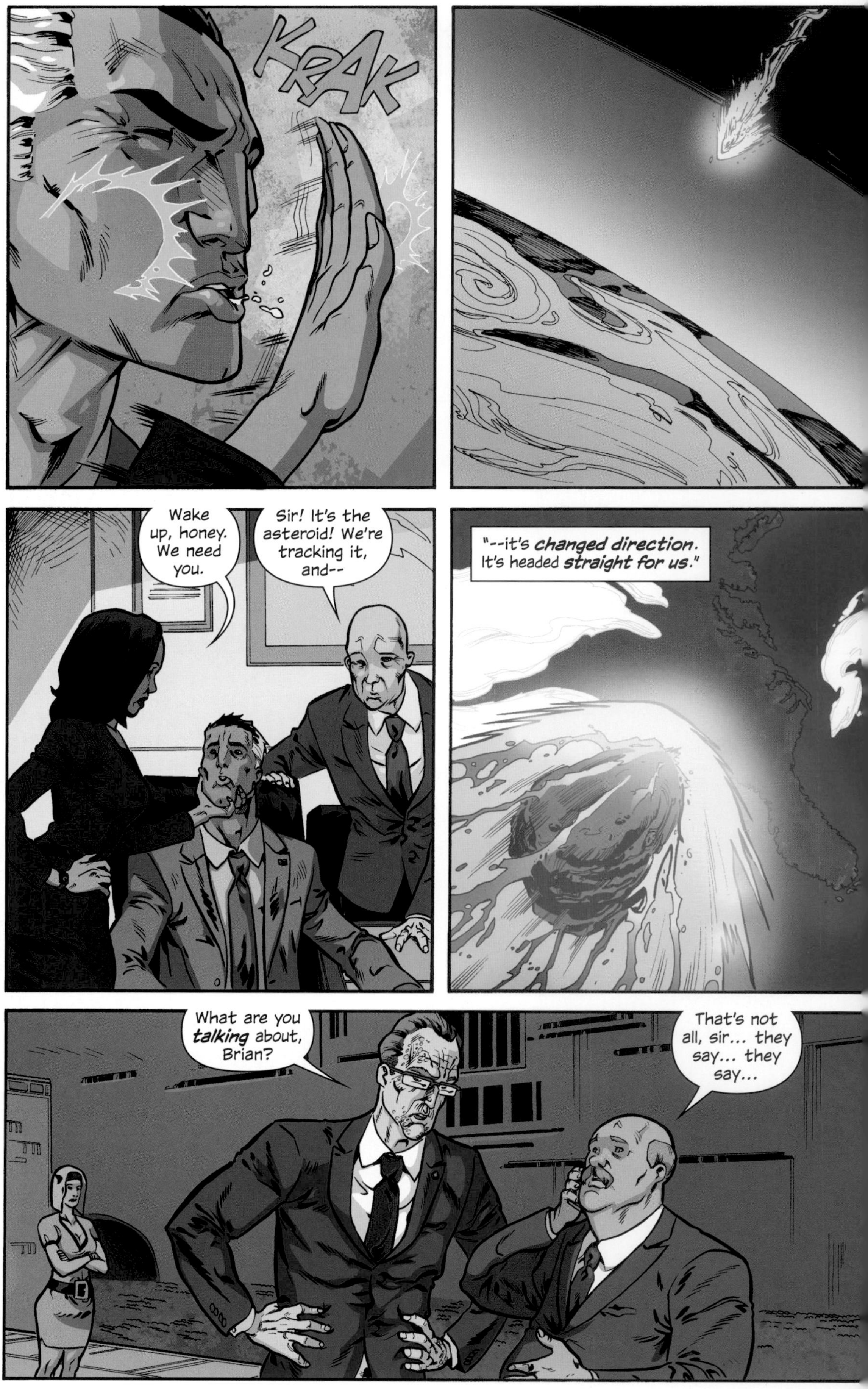
KRAK
Wake up, honey. We need you.
Sir! It's the asteroid! We're tracking it, and--
"--it's changed direction. It's headed straight for us."
What are you talking about, Brian?
That's not all, sir... they say... they say...

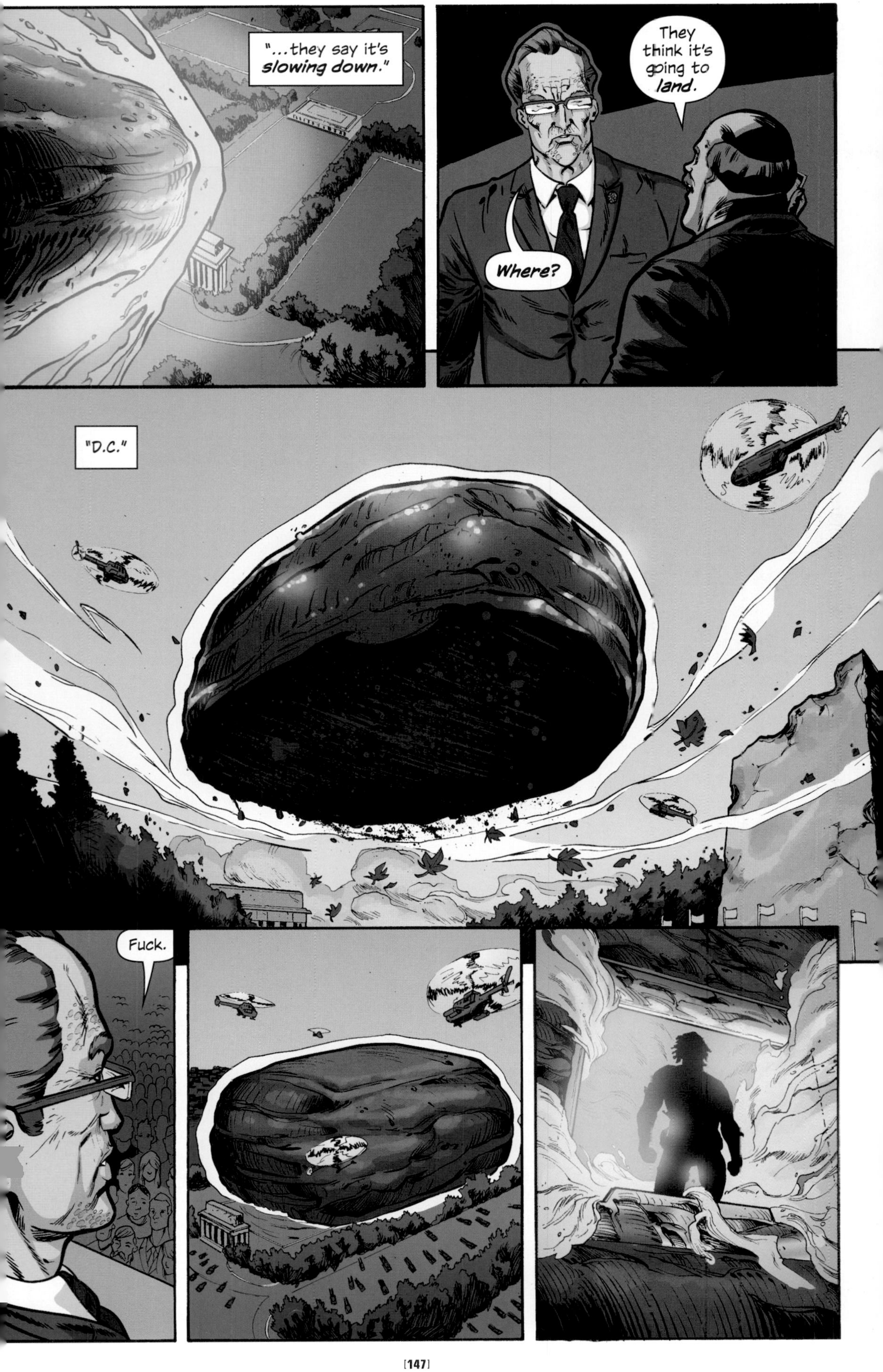
"...they say it's *slowing down*."
They think it's going to *land*.
Where?
"D.C."
Fuck.

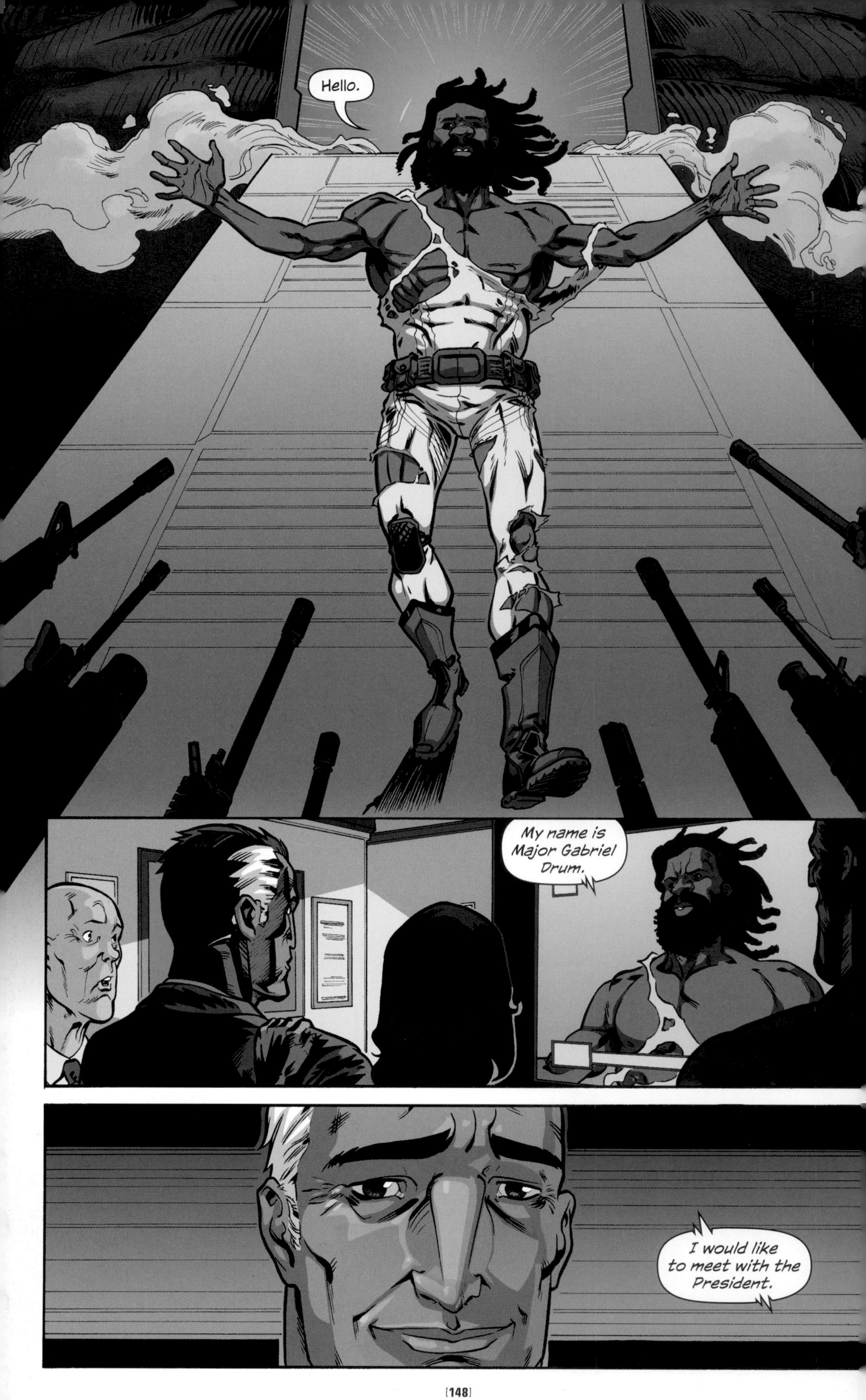
Hello.
My name is Major Gabriel Drum.
I would like to meet with the President.

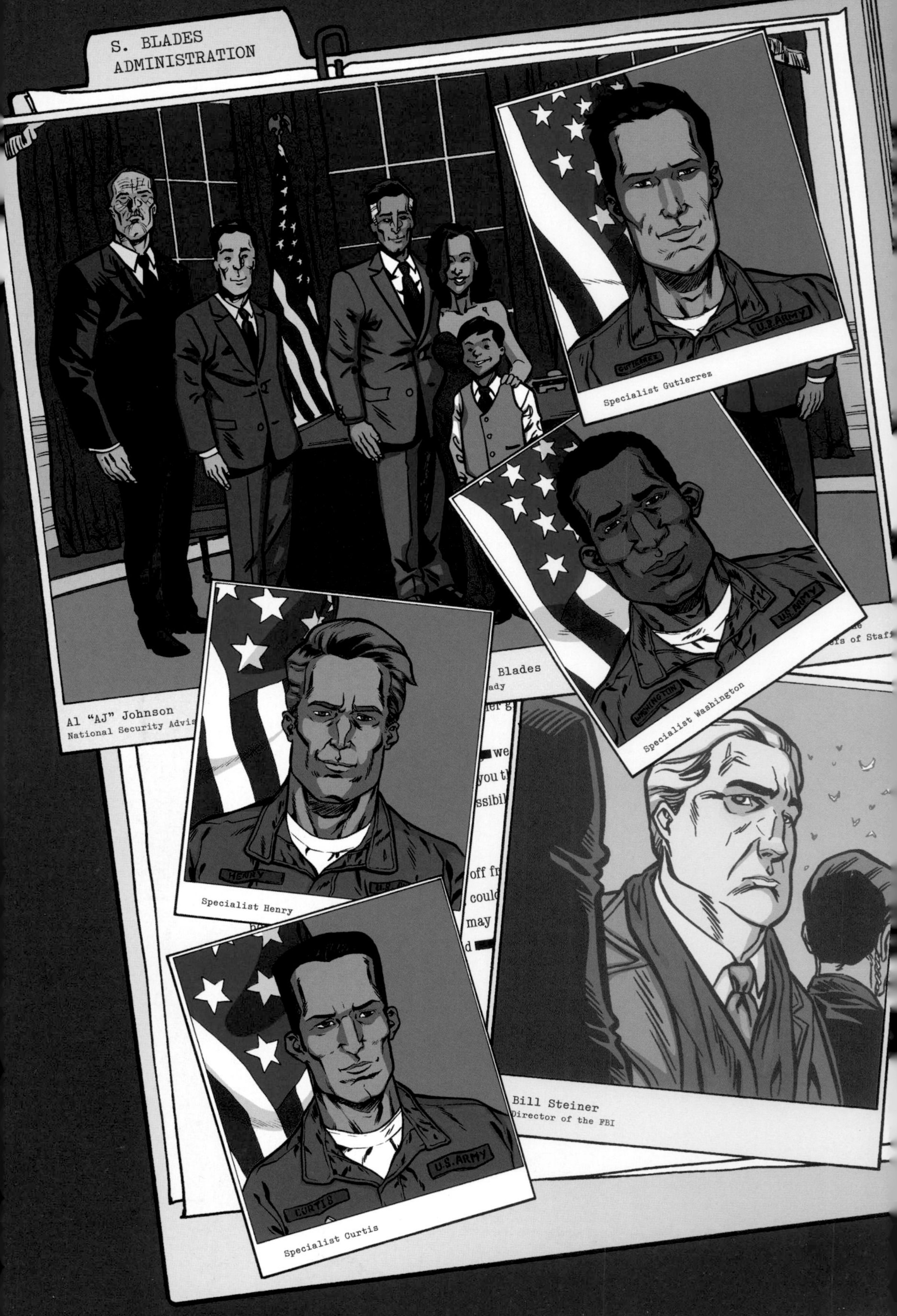
S. BLADES
ADMINISTRATION
Specialist Gutierrez
Specialist Washington
Al "AJ" Johnson
National Security Advis
Blades
Specialist Henry
Specialist Curtis
Bill Steiner
Director of the FBI

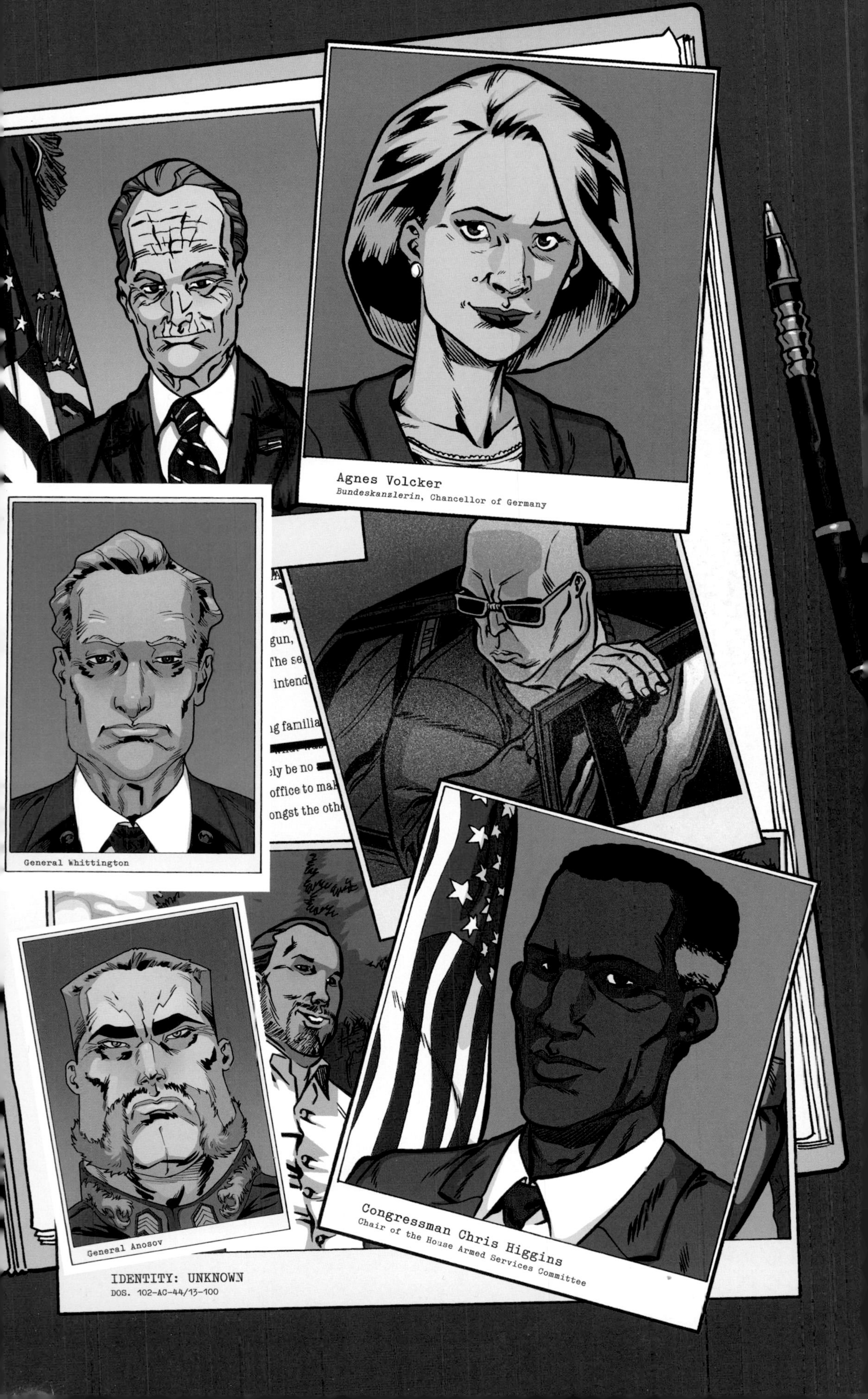
Agnes Volcker
Bundeskanzlerin, Chancellor of Germany
General Whittington
General Anosov
Congressman Chris Higgins
Chair of the House Armed Services Committee
IDENTITY: UNKNOWN
DOS. 102-AC-44/13-100

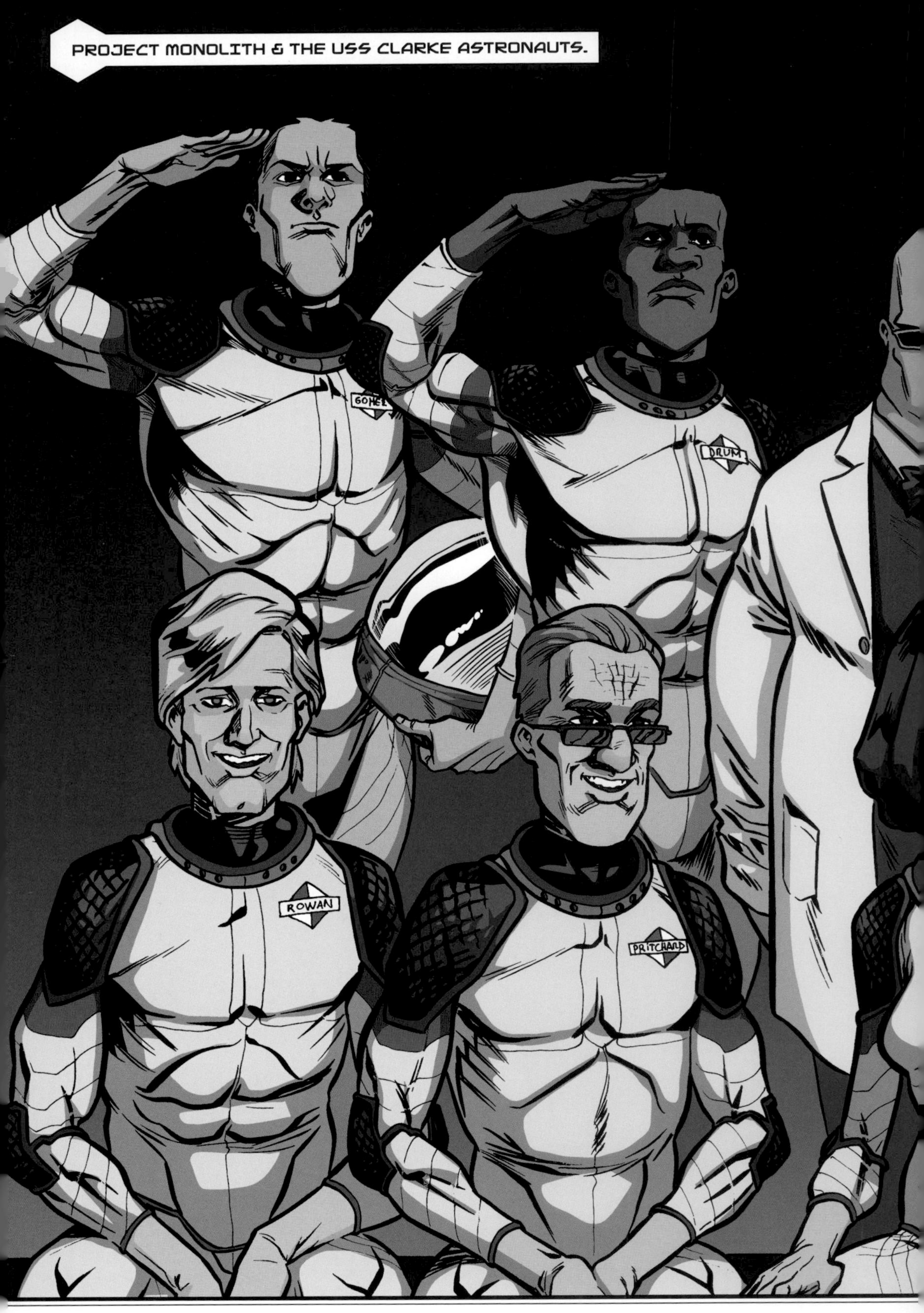
PROJECT MONOLITH & THE USS CLARKE ASTRONAUTS.
DRUM
ROWAN
PRITCHARD

TOP ROW [FROM LEFT TO RIGHT]:

LIEUTENANT ALBERTO GOMEZ, MAJOR GABRIEL DRUM, DR. PORTEK [HEAD OF PROJECT MONOLITH], **COLONEL JACK OVERHOLT, SERGEANT JOHN WILLET**

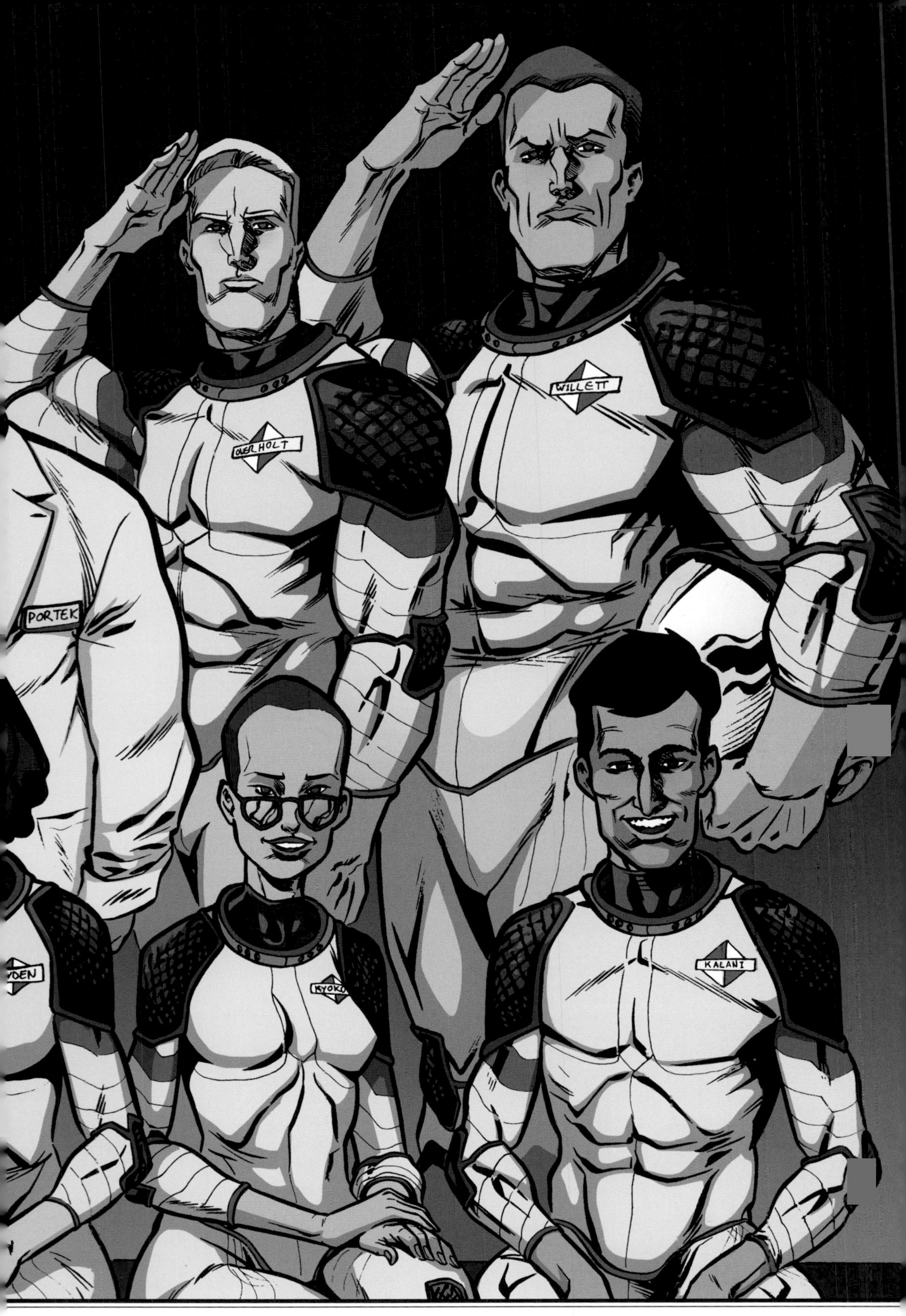
OVERHOLT
WILLETT
PORTEK
KYOKO
KALANI

BOTTOM ROW [FROM LEFT TO RIGHT]:

CARY ROWAN [GEOLOGIST], **DONALD PRITCHARD** [CHIEF ASTRONOMER], **CHARLOTTE HAYDEN** [SENIOR MISSION COMMANDER], **KYOKO TAKAHASHI** [DOCTOR], **MANESH KALANI** [LINGUIST AND COMPUTER SPECIALIST]

Cindy Reed (NSA), Brian Michter (Secretary of Defense), Francis Carroll (P.O.T.U.S.), Bridget Carroll (First Lady), George Cohen (Chief of Staff), Chairman of the Joint Chiefs

Non-terrestrial construction project discovered in the asteroid belt by astronomer Andy Howlett.

US President Francis T. Carroll authorizes Project Monolith, with stated mission goal to investigate alien anomaly, under Director Edward Stanton.

The first members of the *Clarke* crew— Charlotte Hayden and Cary Rowan, both members of the vessel's scientific team —are recruited into Project Monolith.

Sergeant John Willett recruited to join *Clarke* crew, conditional on agreement of Overholt to lead military team.

Edward Stanton replaced as head of Project Monolith by Dr. Radislav Portek. Portek urges Carroll to take a more militaristic approach to the alien anomaly.

1999   **2000**   **2001**   **2002**   **2003**

The United States invades Iraq.

The United States invades Afghanistan.

Colonel Jack Overholt enters into discussions to lead the *Clarke*'s military team.

NOVEMBER— President Carroll wins re-election to a second term.

Clarke orbital assembly launches commence.

CLASSIFIED.

DECEMBER 17— The *Clarke* departs Earth orbit. (REFER TO MISSION DATALOGS 23-26 FOR ADDITIONAL INFORMATION.)

Edward Stanton

Senator Stephen H. Blades announces that he will attempt to secure the nomination as the Democratic candidate for President in the 2006 election.

OCTOBER—President Carroll recruits Elijah Green into Project Monolith.

JANUARY 6—Blades receives a letter from his predecessor informing him of the existence of an alien presence in our solar system and the measures that have been taken to deal with it: Project Monolith.

2004 ▶ 2005 ▶ 2006 ▶ 2007

NOVEMBER—Stephen Blades is elected President with 54% of the popular vote.

Charles Soule
Writer-In-Chief

Alberto J. Alburquerque
Executive Artist

Dan Jackson
Exeeutive Colorist

Crank!
Chief of Letters

THE
WHITE HOUSE
1600 PENNSYLVANIA AVE NW, WASHINGTON, DC 20500

FROM THE DESK OF THE 44TH PRESIDENT, STEPHEN HENRY BLADES

NAME:

Charles Soule

LOCATION:

Brooklyn, NY, United States of America

BIO:

Charles Soule was born in the Midwest but often
wishes he had been born in space. He lives in
Brooklyn, and has written a wide variety of titles for
a variety of publishers, including others' characters
(*Swamp Thing*, *Superman/Wonder Woman*, *Red
Lanterns* (DC); *Death of Wolverine*, *She-Hulk*, *Inhuman*
(Marvel)); and his own: *27* (Image); *Strongman* (SLG)
and *Strange Attractors* (Archaia). When not writing
–which is rare–he runs a law practice and works,
writes and performs as a musician.

One of his biggest regrets is never personally
witnessing a Space Shuttle launch.

Charles Soule
Writer-In-Chief

Alberto J. Alburquerque
Executive Artist

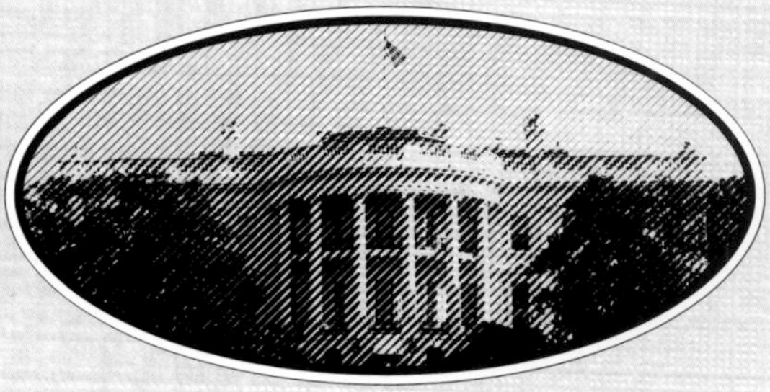

Dan Jackson
Executive Colorist

Crank!
Chief of Letters

THE WHITE HOUSE

1600 PENNSYLVANIA AVE NW, WASHINGTON, DC 20500

FROM THE DESK OF THE 44TH PRESIDENT, STEPHEN HENRY BLADES

NAME:

Alberto Jiménez Alburquerque

LOCATION:

Madrid, Spain

BIO:

Alberto Jiménez Alburquerque (AJA) is an artist born, raised and currently living in Madrid, Spain. He has put lines in French comic-books (BD's) for almost a decade now, working for Paquet Ed. and Soleil Ed. Some of his titles are: *Fugitifs de l'Ombre* (Paquet), *Le Dieu des Cendres* (Soleil), and *Elle* (Soleil). He has also drawn some short stories for the American comics *Skull Kickers* (Image) and *Pathfinder's Goblins* (Dynamite), and *Robert E. Howard's Savage Sword* (Dark Horse). He's currently the regular artist in the new series *Letter 44* (Oni Press) with writer Charles Soule and is starting a new project for the French market with Glènat Ed.

CLASSIFIED
AUTH. JMB*JS

Charles Soule
Writer-In-Chief

Alberto J. Alburquerque
Executive Artist

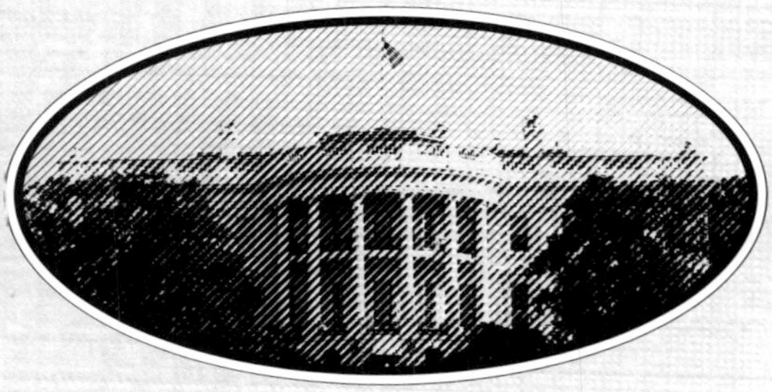

Dan Jackson
Executive Colorist

Crank!
Chief of Letters

THE WHITE HOUSE

1600 PENNSYLVANIA AVE NW, WASHINGTON, DC 20500

FROM THE DESK OF THE 44TH PRESIDENT, STEPHEN HENRY BLADES

NAME:

Dan Jackson

LOCATION:

Portland, Oregon, United States of America

BIO:

What is the most unfair thing you can think of? Got it in your head? Okay, forget that because there's a worse one: There's this guy who gets paid money for coloring comic books. Right. Dan Jackson has been gainfully employed to one degree or another with the coloring of comic books for the better part of 17 years. He's done other Great Big Projects with the fine folks at Oni Press, and he's done a bunch of covers and short projects with them as well. He's a pretty versatile guy. Even writes his own bios.

[CLASSIFIED]

Mr. Jackson lives in the beautiful Pacific Northwest with his scorching hot wife (see? UN-FAIR!), and two hilarious kids.

MORE BOOKS FROM ONI PRESS

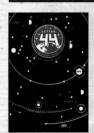

LETTER 44: VOLUME 1 ESCAPE VELOCITY

CHARLES SOULE, ALBERTO JIMÉNEZ ALBURQUERQUE, GUY MAJOR, AND DAN JACKSON

160 PAGES /// SOFTCOVER /// COLOR INTERIORS

ISBN 978-1-62010-133-9

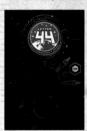

LETTER 44: VOLUME 2 REDSHIFT

CHARLES SOULE, ALBERTO JIMÉNEZ ALBURQUERQUE, AND DAN JACKSON

160 PAGES /// SOFTCOVER /// COLOR INTERIORS

ISBN 978-1-62010-206-0

THE
BUNKER

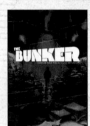

THE BUNKER: VOLUME 1

BY JOSHUA HALE FIALKOV AND JOE INFURNARI

136 PAGES /// SOFTCOVER /// COLOR INTERIORS

ISBN 978-1-62010-164-3

THE SIXTH GUN
BUNN
HURTT

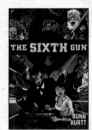

THE SIXTH GUN: VOLUME 1 COLD DEAD FINGERS

BY CULLEN BUNN, BRIAN HURTT, AND BILL CRABTREE

176 PAGES /// SOFTCOVER /// COLOR INTERIORS

ISBN 978-1-934964-60-6

WASTELAND
BOOK 01

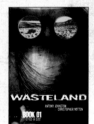

WASTELAND: VOLUME 1

BY ANTONY JOHNSTON AND CHRISTOPHER MITTEN

160 PAGES /// SOFTCOVER /// B&W INTERIORS

ISBN 978-1-932664-59-1

STUMPTOWN

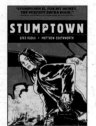

STUMPTOWN: VOLUME 1

BY GREG RUCKA AND MATTHEW SOUTHWORTH

160 PAGES /// HARDCOVER /// COLOR INTERIORS

ISBN 978-1-934964-37-8

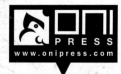

ONI PRESS
www.onipress.com

FOR MORE INFORMATION ON THESE AND OTHER FINE ONI PRESS COMIC BOOKS AND GRAPHIC NOVELS, VISIT WWW.ONIPRESS.COM. TO FIND A COMIC SPECIALTY STORE IN YOUR AREA, CALL 1-888-COMICBOOK OR VISIT WWW.COMICSHOPS.US.